Media Narratives

Studies in Critical Social Sciences Book Series

Haymarket Books is proud to be working with Brill Academic Publishers (www.brill.nl) to republish the *Studies in Critical Social Sciences* book series in paperback editions. This peer-reviewed book series offers insights into our current reality by exploring the content and consequences of power relationships under capitalism, and by considering the spaces of opposition and resistance to these changes that have been defining our new age. Our full catalog of *SCSS* volumes can be viewed at https://www.haymarketbooks.org/series_collections/4-studies-in-critical-social-sciences.

Media Narratives

Productions and Representations of Contemporary Mythologies

Edited by

Christiana Constantopoulou

Haymarket Books
Chicago, IL

First published in 2023 by Brill Academic Publishers, The Netherlands

Published in paperback in 2024 by
Haymarket Books
P.O. Box 180165
Chicago, IL 60618
773-583-7884
www.haymarketbooks.org

ISBN: 979-8-88890-222-6

Distributed to the trade in the US through Consortium Book Sales and Distribution (www.cbsd.com) and internationally through Ingram Publisher Services International (www.ingramcontent.com).

This book was published with the generous support of Lannan Foundation, Wallace Action Fund, and the Marguerite Casey Foundation.

Cover design by Jamie Kerry and Ragina Johnson.

Printed in the United States.

Library of Congress Cataloging-in-Publication data is available.

Contents

Acknowledgement

We would like to thank Professor *David Fasenfest*, Editor of the Brill Series *Studies in Critical Social Sciences* who has accepted this collective work and whose kind advice helped us to complete our project.

Figures and Tables

Figures

Tables

Notes on Contributors

Lucía Acuña-Pedro
studied Political Sciences in the Complutense University of Madrid, specialized in Spanish contemporary protests. During the degree, she spent one year in the Helsinki University, where she studied different contexts of social vulnerability, such as women in post-conflict regions or cultural cleavages in the former Yugoslavia. After that, she studied a Master of advanced studies in political communication, focusing in genre studies. Lately, she collaborated with a research group of the Complutense University, studying the concept of vulnerability in social sciences.

Graziela Ares
is a Ph.D. candidate in Sociology at the Center for Social Studies/CES at the University of Coimbra/UC (Portugal). B.A. in Economics and M.A. in Science and Technology Policy at the State University of Campinas/UNICAMP (Brazil). M.A. in Business at the University of Applied Sciences in Vorarlberg/FHV (Austria). Member of the organizing committee of the XII edition of the Gender Workshop, hosted by CES and the Ph.D. program in Feminist Studies at the University of Coimbra. Pier reviewer of the Interdisciplinary Social Sciences Journal Collection. Current research interests include disinformation, memory and heritage studies, and far-right politics. (https://orcid.org/0000-0002-5512-580X).

Eduardo Barbabela
is a Political Theory, and Political Communication researcher at the Universidade do Estado do Rio de Janeiro. He holds a Bachelor, a Masters and a Ph.D. in Political Science. He has been researching the area of Political Communication and Elections since 2010. He is one of the senior researchers of Manchetometro's project, a political research project that has studied the daily political coverage and the election coverage in Brazilian's media since 2014. He has also researched Democratic Theory, Freedom of Speech and Media Regulation since 2016.

Mercedes Calzado
is an adjunct researcher of the National Scientific and Technical Research Council of Argentina (CONICET) at Gino Germani Institute (School of Social Sciences, Buenos Aires University). Ph.D. in Social Sciences, master's degree in Social Sciences Research, and a bachelor's degree in Social Communication

(Buenos Aires University). Professor in Communication Sciences Program (Social Sciences Faculty, Buenos Aires University). Fulbright postdoctoral scholarship (2017) and visiting researcher at the Center for Latin American Studies at Georgetown University (2017/2018) and Universidade Federal de Rio de Janeiro (2021–2022). Director of the Group on Communication, Politics, and Security at Buenos Aires University. She researches the problem of urban security in Argentina and its connection with communication media, the political arena, and the emergence of insecurity victims' movements.

Omar Cerrillo Garnica
is a Mexican researcher and professor of Instituto Tecnológico y de Estudios Superiores de Monterrey; in 2019, he became Director of School of Humanities and Education in Tec de Monterrey at Cuernavaca. As researcher, he is specialized in social analysis of art, music and culture, in subjects as rock culture in Mexico City; Mexico's Bicentenary through artistic expressions and their impact in national identity; also in digital culture phenomena and social media protests. He has publications in four different languages about art, music, digital culture and other sociocultural matters.

Miranda Claudio Cornejo
started her studies in Modern Languages, Culture and Communication in 2012, at the Autonoma University of Madrid. There, she focused on language functioning and language learning, studying English, French and Spanish. Later, she studied Classical Languages and Culture at the Complutense University of Madrid. She specialized in Greek and Roman mythology. Her work focuses on how this popular knowledge is transmitted through language and literature to the present.

Christiana Constantopoulou
is Professor of Sociology of Communication (has been Assistant Professor at the University of Rouen –France, and Professor at the University of Macedonia –Thessaloniki, Greece) and actually teaches at Panteion University and is Visiting Professor at the National and Kapodistrian University of Athens. Author of many scientific articles and monographic works (mostly in Greek, French and English but also translated in Portuguese & Bulgarian) focusing essentially on the *communicational structures of contemporary societies*. Active member of the "Association Internationale des Sociologues de Langue Française", and elected member of the executive board (1996–2000, 2000–2004 & 2008–2012, 2012–2016); President of RC 14 "Sociology of Communication, Knowledge and Culture" of the International Sociological Association (2006–2010,

2010–2014, 2014–2018, 2018–2022, www.rc14-isa.com); member of the board of RC13 "Sociology of Leisure" 2010–2014; member of organizational and scientific committees of many conferences in Cyprus, Greece, France and Italy. Editor/ or member of the Scientific Committee of scientific journals (such as Sociétés, Socio-Anthropologie, Sociologies, OJSS etc.). Chevalier since 2012 (and Officer since 2021) of the Academic Palms (French Ministry of Education). Head of the Center of Studies of the Contemporary Communication in Europe (EURCECOM-eurcecom.webs.com), 2018–2021.

Mariana Fernández
has a degree in Communication Sciences and a Ph.D. in Social Sciences from the Faculty of Social Sciences of the University of Buenos Aires. Postdoctoral fellow of the National Council for Scientific and Technical Research (CONICET/ IIGG) and professor at the National University of La Matanza. He is also part of the Political Communication and Security Observatory directed by M. Calzado and is a member of the editorial committee of the Political Communication and Security Magazine and the Group of Studies on Communication, Politics and Security of the Gino Germani Research Institute.

Humberto Fernandes
is a Ph.D. candidate in Sociology at Rio de Janeiro State University. M.Sc. in Sociology and B.A. in International Relations. His research interests are public opinion, alienation, collectivities theory, social representations, democracy, community-building, and human-ature relations. Researcher at Nucleus for Studies in Social Theory and Latin America (NETSAL-IESP-UERJ), at ISA RC-14 (Sociology of Communication, Knowledge, and Culture), and ISA RC-36 (Alienation Theory and Research). He is the organizer of Talking Alienation permanent seminar and acts as Teaching Intern for Scientific English Writing and for University Internationalization at Northern Rio de Janeiro State University (UENF).

Jaqueline García Cordero
has a Bachelor's degree in Communication with a specialization in Corporate Communication from Universidad Nacional Autónoma de México. Winner of the State Award of Academic Trajectory 2021, Estado de México, and Bernardo Quintana Arrioja's medal for Patriotism 2016–2017. Her research interests are organizational psychology, communication, corporate communication, and social projects. Jaqueline has also studied markets and organizations at King's College London, England and will do a research assistantship at Universidad Complutense de Madrid, Spain.

Enrique García Romero

has a Ph.D. degree in Social Communication from the San Pablo-CEU University (Madrid, Spain), a Master's degree in Corporate and Political Communication from the Carlos III University of Madrid, and a Bachelor of Information Sciences from the Complutense University of Madrid. He is a professor and academic researcher at the Faculty of Communication of the University of Piura (Peru). Previously, he worked as a professor at the San Pablo-CEU University and the Council on International Educational Exchange, both based in Madrid; as a journalist in two Spanish media, and as a consultant in two PR agencies.

Leda Maria Caira Gitahy

is Associate professor of the Science and Technology Policy Program at the Institute of Geosciences of the State University of Campinas/UNICAMP (Brazil) and collaborating professor of the Society, Nature and Development Ph.D. Program at the Federal University of Western Pará/UFOPA (Brazil). B.A. (1979) and M.A. (1980) degrees in Social Sciences and a Ph.D. in Sociology (2000) from Uppsala University (Sweden). Founding member of the Laboratory of Technology and Social Transformations/LabTTS and member of the Research on Disinformation in Social Networks/EDReS group and Infovid Network.

Yamila Gómez

has a master's degree in Social Sciences Research and a bachelor's degree in Social Communication (Buenos Aires University). She is a Professor in Research Methodology for Social Sciences and in Public Opinion (Buenos Aires University, San Martin's National University and Del Salvador University). She is a researcher at School of Social Sciences (Buenos Aires University) and at Del Salvador University. She has teached, done research and published articles in several areas, including research methodology, news, audiences, and public opinion and social media.

Vanesa Lio

is a researcher of the National Scientific and Technical Research Council of Argentina (CONICET) at the Research Institute in Humanities and Social Sciences (School of Humanities and Educational Sciences, National University of La Plata). She got a bachelor's degree in Social Communication at Buenos Aires University (Argentina) and a master's degree in Public and Political Communication at Pisa University (Italy). She held funded doctoral and post-doctoral fellowships, earning her Ph.D. at Buenos Aires University. She has done research and published articles in several areas, including security policies, video surveillance, political communication, campaigns, qualitative research methods, new media, and television news. She also participates in several research projects, taking part of the Research Group on Communication, Politics and Security at the University of Buenos Aires and of the Nucleus of Security Studies in the Province of Buenos Aires (NESBA) at the National University of La Plata.

Melina Meimaridis

is a post-doctoral researcher with a fellowship by *Fundação Carlos Chagas Filho de Amparo à Pesquisa do Estado do Rio de Janeiro* (Faperj) at the Postgraduate Program in Communication at *Universidade Federal Fluminense* (UFF) in Brazil. Her interests include media industries, Comfort Series, and internet-distributed television in national and regional markets. Currently, she is developing two research projects: 1) the study of how television's serialized fiction constructs knowledge about social institutions and how these constructions circulate through international TV flows; 2) the study of Netflix's transnational expansion and its impact on countries belonging to the global periphery.

José A. Ruiz San Román

is professor at the Department of *Sociología Aplicada* (Applied Sociology), Universidad Complutense de Madrid (Spain). Author of "*Introducción a la tradición clásica de la opinión pública*" (Introduction to the Classical Tradition of Public Opinion) (1997) and co-author of "Sociología de la Comunicación" (*Sociology of* Communication) (1999) and "Investigar en Comunicación" (Research in Communication) (2005). His research interests include Public Opinion, Media Effects, Social Campaigns and Social Communities. Director of the Complutense Research Group on Responsible Communication and Vulnerable Audiences. Vice-Dean for International Relations, School of Communication, Universidad Complutense Madrid.

Pedro Paulo Martins Serra

holds a Ph.D. in Sociology (University of São Paulo/École des Hautes Études en Sciences Sociales) and a Master's degree in Latin American Studies (Sorbonne Nouvelle). Was a member of the editorial board of Revista Plural and is currently member of the Center for Sociology of Culture (Núcleo de Sociologia da Cultura), both at University of São Paulo. Has experience in the fields of International Relatons and Sociology, with emphasis on comparative research, culture, journalism and television.

Hara Stratoudaki
is senior researcher at National Centre for Social Research (EKKE). Studied Sociology at Panteion University and Social Work at the Higher School of Social Work and received her Ph.D. from Panteion University. Her thesis was focusing on Aspects of National Identity. Has participated in several research projects. Her current research has a focus in the fields of nationalism and national identity, Sociology of Institutions, values, and stereotypes, as well as immigration, xenophobia and racism. Her recent publications include papers and chapters on National Identity and National Pride in contemporary Greece.

Leandro R. Tessler
is Associated Professor at "Gleb Wataghin" Phisics Institute, Unicamp. BsC (UFRGS, 1982), MSc (Unicamp, 1985), Ph.D. (Tel Aviv University, 1989). Visiting researcher at Ecole Polytechnique, Palaiseau and University of Wisconsin-Madison. Author of more than 50 research papers, 4 book chapters and many articles in newspapers and magazines. Former Director of International Relations (2009–2012) at Unicamp. Founding member of Research on Disinformation in Social Networks/EDReS group. Current research interests include the use of machine learning and big data to map disinformation in social networks and understanding disinformation in the context of COVID-19.

Gabriela Villen
is International Communication Officer at the State University of Campinas/UNICAMP (Brazil). Ph.D. candidate in Science and Technology Policy Program at the State University of Campinas/UNICAMP (Brazil). M.Sc. in Communication Sciences at the University of São Paulo/USP (Brazil). B.A. in Social Communication with an emphasis in journalism and a young researcher scholarship in History at the Pontifical Catholic University of São Paulo/PUC-SP (Brazil). Member of Research on Disinformation in Social Networks/EDReS group. Current research interests include disinformation in higher education and public health and far-right expansion in the 21st century.

CHAPTER 1

Introduction

Media Narratives of Contemporary Mythologies

Christiana Constantopoulou

For a sociological approach of the contemporary societies, media constitute a privileged field of analysis; not only because communication is in the center of any society but also because the communicational structures of a community reveal it's "spirit".[1] As it is often illustrated by researchers the media (mass or social) represent the "extensions of man" (as expressed by Mac Luhan),[2] in the sense that it seems impossible nowadays to avoid the use and interference with the media activities (the "mediascapes"[3] characterizing the contemporary everyday life).

In accordance to the above theory, the media contents interfere dynamically with the current (popular) myths (such as popular ideas for life, love, justice etc.) of the "globalized" world. In this sense, even if television does not represent any more the "basic media" (as it was during past decades), it still provides current narratives in constant interaction with internet. Although internet becomes more and more important, television remains an "official" channel of politically correct information and entertainment. Thus, the ongoing stories seem to be the same either in television ("public" or "private" channels) or in the web (first because there is a big part of feedback between them-by journalists being active on both media, by "public journalism" and by performers and artists who always desire to be visible in any media). This is why, although in this volume most analyses refer to televisual productions,

1 In Edgar Morin's sense (1962): *L'esprit du temps*, Grasset, Paris: In this book E. Morin reveals the profound cultural revolution of the 20th century in practices and social representations. It is a revolution in ethics which brought common practices, new ways to get interested on one's self together with the praise of leisure; it was accompanied by communication modes (press, television and cinema) which diffuse in a very new way the ideas of well-being and of individual happiness. This analysis (first done for the mass media) also helps to understand behaviors in the frame of the (so called) social media.

2 Marshal Mac Luhan (1964), *Understanding Media, the Extensions of Man,* Mc Graw Hill, N.Y. 1964. Of course much literature –even polemic literature-has been written about this thesis.

3 A. Appadurai (1996) *Modernity at Large: Cultural Dimensions of Globalization*, MN: University of Minnesota Press, Minneapolis.

they can also be considered as a representative sample of some essential more or less global symbolizations (in other words global myths) of the contemporary everyday life.

Some extra facts further support the above premise (even if a large number of citizens around the world express disdain for televisual programs, preferring internet solutions for their information and entertainment), the following:

1) A good number of the social media topics do not differ at all from televisual standards, as television remains a dominant popular medium. If in all this we add the "effects of globalization" (in any direction: economic or cultural), we can state that there is a "global context" (to which local expressions stay conform) and which "shows" the "spirit" of the contemporary world: its realities but also its myths (narrating, explaining and justifying current options and values).
2) The proclaimed freedom of expression in the frame of social media, may be real but in fact limited for many reasons (most people pay attention only to dominant expressions, the diverse voices expressed are currently "lost" in the chaos of millions of opinions and ideas none of which seems more "important" than the others, etc.). When "information" is concerned the audiences pay more attention to the most current ideas (in order to avoid marginalization). Thus, the contemporary media narratives (some of which are analyzed in this volume) are in close relation to the dominant current ideas and fears. They are an excellent field for the research, because they reveal the *"anthropological dimensions"* of the dominant discourses (the role of the imaginary, the existence of various complexes relied to human materiality etc.) which seem "persisting" even if apparently "incompatible" with the modern rationality.

1 The Anthropological Aspects of Media Narratives

When media discourses are analyzed, some essential dimensions (which are important but not always taken into consideration by sociologists or media analysts) must be taken into consideration; on this level, Anthropology and Psychoanalysis have much contributed to a better understanding of expressions and dramatizations which very often take place in the media stages causing increased audience-ratings especially when they show crime or scandal scenes. These dimensions (important, but often neglected), are independent of the audiences' "level of education" or of a country's level of "development" (economic or technical) because they belong to what G. Durand (1960) had included in the category of the "Anthropological Structures of the Imaginary".[4] In fact, modernity has relied the idea of "rational communication" to the level of education and the level of (scientific and technical) development (according to the conviction that both "education" and "development" improve social life removing "lower instincts" – these instincts characterizing "uncivilized" humans or "underdeveloped" societies). Many analysts take it for granted that modernity is (has to be) obligatorily distanced from what is not considered "politically correct". This is a *constitutional myth of modernity* (still valid although not always convincing). Nevertheless, the media (either mass or social) very often project catastrophes and tragedies (which attract audiences as much as the presentation of the luxurious life style of the stars and influencers), thus expressing the contemporary imaginary (the storytelling of the research of survival, the relation between power and death and the relation to the "otherness"): what dimensions does this imaginary include? In other words, what is the "spirit" of contemporary societies, expressed by media worldwide?

In this attempt, we should have in mind the following issues:

1.1 *The* Archetypal Dimensions of the Imaginary

Many authors have already studied the influence of the "anthropological" (archetypal) dimensions of the imaginary (such as the fear of death) in any narrative dealing with basic guidelines of life. For instance, broadcasts present natural catastrophes in a detailed way, showing the impotence of humans towards any discontinuity such as seism, inundation, fire, nuclear disaster etc.; at the same time, they acknowledge the successes of science or technology (which replace religion as far as it concerns "human salvation") as the solution to this kind of problems. Still, because the main natural fear of any being, remains the fear of death, very often the artistic production which attracts audiences worldwide (science-fiction for instance) tries to explain (in different ways than those dictated by rational thought) this basic human inability. None of the contemporary narratives (either of the media agenda setting[5] or of beloved fictional stories)[6] escapes from this "standard".

---

4 Gilbert Durand (1960), *Les Structures Anthropologiques de l'Imaginaire*, Paris, PUF, published in English " The Anthropological Structures of the Imaginary" by Boombana Publications, University of Queensland, Brisbane, in 1999.

5 For instance in the 2021 Agenda the biggest role had the news for the Covid-19 Pandemic (again a threat towards life and a generalized fear of death), followed by Cyclone Seroja and Haiti Earthquake.

6 See for instance, "Game of Thrones", "King of the Rings", "Avatar" etc.

Enduring "complexes": George Horton Cooley[7] had remarked a century ago that in modernity, the function of "gossip" is realized by the media; the necessity to "gossip" (criticize other people and so "live" in and by others' lives) can be explained by Psychoanalysis. Diverse "impulses" and complexes can be observed in the frame of communication. Louis-Vincent Thomas (1978) had analyzed the "Butterfly Complex" (the desire to "live" through others' lives, by watching them, imitating the butterfly's rotatory eyes) the "Complex of the Executioner" (which means taking pleasure from others' suffers), the Complex of Minotaur (expressing the relief when a disaster happens elsewhere – even in the neighborhood but not in one's house – meaning that the danger is escaped at least for now on) etc. These "needs" are satisfied by the media (either mass or social media) showing that some ancestral phobias continue to "matter" and be present (either expressively or latently)[8] in the frame of social representations.

When the "agenda" of the "news" is analyzed, it is not possible to overlook the presence of these expressions (very frequent in popular emissions) even in the context of "serious" (political) narratives (J. Habermas[9] having pointed out the current ambiguity between "public" and "private" spheres).

1.2 *The "Spirit of the Time"*

The Spirit of the Time (described in E. Morin's major work with the same title)[10] has analyzed the profound cultural revolution which has been realized in the middle of the 20th century first in the western countries (and afterwards in huge parts of the planet because of the effects of globalization); this revolution concerned the transformation of practices and collective representations (still valid in the context of the contemporary societies). The emergence of this "ethical revolution" has induced common ways of acting and communicating which aliment and disseminate models and ideas turning around the importance of personal happiness. This Cultural Revolution is relied on the ideas of the importance of the biggest slots of time left for one's self and for individual happiness while the construction of a mediated universe has offered imaginary references which inspire individualist practices. Thus the "spirit of the time" nowadays suggests that the most important traits of sociality are

7 1918: *Political Economy and Social Process*, Journal of Political Economy 25, 366–374.

8 A further explanation of these complexes can be found in Louis-Vincent Thomas' works (*Mort et Pouvoir*, Payot, Paris 1978, *Civilisation et Divagations*, Payot, Paris 1979, *Fantasmes au Quotidien*, Méridiens, Paris 1984, *Anthropologie des Obsessions*, L'Harmattan, Paris 1988).

9 J. Habermas (1989), *The Structural Transformation of the Public Sphere,* MIT Press.

10 E. Morin, (1962) *L'esprit du temps*, Grasset, Paris.

individuality, self-realization "here and now", and self-centered practices (to get fun and so be happy).[11]

The above dimensions are in the core of diverse contemporary myths including individual happiness very much leaning on "modern life style" (including brand clothes, shoes, and accessories, health and nutrition products –to get thinner or improve body building, plastic surgery as a usual practice etc.). *Consuming for happiness* (where consume capitalism plays a central role) makes the need for "money" (in order to achieve all this promised paradise on earth) an essential goal. The "revolution of leisure" continues to dictate leisure values even in environments of economic crisis, war or pandemic disease. These contemporary issues (crisis of any kind) coexist with the media features promoting personal happiness based on consumption. Nowadays, the "self-promotion" (as "look") coexists with the "self-exposure" making public any individual expression (considered as central): in selfies, in Instagram or even in porn videos!

1.3 *The Power of Storytelling: The Narrative Spell Cast over Politics and Society*

Societies have always known how to cultivate the art of telling stories, art which is found in the heart of any social connection. Still, since the nineties, first in the United States then in Europe this art was invested by the consuming spirit of communication and of capitalism under the anodyne nomination of "storytelling". Behind the successful advertising of political campaigns are hidden sophisticated techniques of storytelling management or of digital storytelling in order to bewitch the modern mind of consumers as well as of citizens (Salmon, 2007); it seems like an incredible hold-up of the imagination which can be seen in the marketing of brands or the narration of politics!

Christian Salmon[12] argues that politics is no longer the art of the possible, but of the fictive. Its aim is not to change the world as it exists, but to *affect the way that it is perceived.* Christian Salmon looks at the twenty-first-century anatomizing the timeless human desire for narrative form, and how this desire is abused by the marketing mechanisms that bolster politicians and their products: luxury brands trade on embellished histories, managers tell stories to motivate employees, soldiers in Iraq train on Hollywood-conceived computer games, and spin doctors construct political lives as if they were a folk epic. It is

---

11 Joffre Dumazedier (1962),*Vers une civilisation du loisir ?* Seuil, Paris; (*1988*) *La révolution culturelle du temps libre,* Méridiens, Paris.

12 Christian Salmon (2007), Storytelling: La machine à fabriquer des histoires et à formater les esprits, La Découverte, Paris.

a "storytelling machine", more effective and insidious as a means of oppression than anything dreamed up by Orwell.

The dominant (media) discourses (such as stories about the vaccination against Covid-19[13] or the reporting of War in Afghanistan)[14] "communicate" the ongoing reality in almost the same stories in all countries rendering current myths about *remote existence* (work, education, entertainment) the substructure of the current culture. D. Lyon[15] argues about Covid-19 Storytelling: *Pandemic Surveillance allows governments and corporations to monitor the spread of the virus and to make sure citizens follow the measures they put in place. This is evident in the massive, unprecedented mobilization of public health date to contain and combat the virus, and the ballooning of surveillance technologies such as contact-tracking apps and population tracking. In a very real sense, COVID-19 has been a "pandemic of surveillance".* All these kinds of narration of the contemporary "politics" (such as public health or international security) coexist with the frame discourse of everyday lifestyle issues and personal happiness and fulfillment in close relation with consumer goods.

1.4 *The "Common Sense" in Fictional Productions*

When it comes to fictional productions provided by cultural industries, one realizes that the most popular films worldwide are those inspired by popular

13 Amongst the really numerous reports there was a big number of media stories about the number of deaths due to Covid-19 worldwide, but especially of the deaths of unvaccinated persons which often monopolized the broadcasts' news.

14 In his paper, *Reporting Afghanistan and Iraq: Media, military and governments and how they influence each other* Greg Wilesmith drew on his extensive experience with ABC as a reporter, correspondent and news manager to present a strong narrative of *how the media coverage of the two wars changed from being broadly supportive to much more critical.* In the short time he was in Oxford, Greg managed to interview several key players from the worlds of government, media and the military and to draw on a wide range of published sources. Greg Wilesmith argues that at first, Afghanistan was often overlooked or ignored because of Iraq. He draws out cases where media treatment did clearly influence the course of the wars, such as the extensive coverage of the two prisons Guantanamo Bay and Abu Ghraib. Thus, media coverage, had three key effects – weakening support for the Iraq war in the US and among coalition partners, inspiring insurgents throughout Iraq, and inflaming public opinion in the Muslim world thus acting like a magnet for foreign terrorists. As for Afghanistan, Greg argues that as media coverage of the war has become increasingly negative, 'the governments of the United States, the United Kingdom and Australia have constantly adjusted their narrative frameworks about what constitutes 'progress', while 'victory' is a term slipping into irrelevance, just as it did during the Iraq war. The author suggests that journalists should learn the lessons of the first wars of the 21st century'.

15 David Lyon (2022) *Pandemic Surveillance,* Polity, Cambridge, Memford.

interpretations of deep existential fears, often being part of what is called "common sense". The concept of "common sense" (in sociological terms) is not something different from "dominant social philosophy" (the dominant beliefs and popular philosophy teachings, also reported by the "classical" storytelling beginning with "once upon a time"). It is even easier to create stories in the field of everybody's beliefs. Popular cultural products always use the anthropological structures of the imaginary (archetypes of love or power and their relation to death); this is the recipe for success[16] for any cultural product (either completely "fictional" or reporting an imaginary but related to everyday reality plot).[17] The fictional productions symbolize (as usually myths do) real issues. There's a culture that nourishes human perception of reality through symbols (from ancient mythical creatures and rites through masterpieces of Renaissance to modern art and cinema) and cross-cultural symbols arise in popular culture today. Together with the "Spirit of the Time" these symbols lead to a certain understanding of reality and assist dealing with it.

The "storytelling myths" which massively express nowadays reality ("what is pandemic", what is security, how politics protect citizens etc.) essentially under the mask of science and technology are very often made of presumptions not easily perceptible to the average citizen. It is much easier for readers and viewers to perceive the part of fiction in cultural products (such as films and series); these ones also disseminate "common sense" (popular) ideas (praising the romantic love, making understand that the application of the law does not concern all the citizens or that abuse of power might be present everywhere, sometimes challenging the institutions etc.). Normally, these popular ideas do not contest a given reality, they nevertheless permit its' questioning.

In this volume examples of both "broadcasting" and "fictional" storytelling (either in TV, Press, or Blogs) are presented. The case studies concern Argentina, Brazil, Greece, Mexico, Peru and the United States. The first four chapters analyze TV broadcasting case studies (how Television content provides interesting elements to think about the contemporary ways of living in insecure settings in Argentina; how the Brazilian Media favor the privatization of universities, how business elites interfere with Brazilian media and how these media

16 The biggest filmic successes of the 21st century (so far) were Harry Potter (and the force of magic to change the unpleasant reality), the King of the Rings (full of legends about mythical beings and the struggle for power), The Pirates of the Caribbean (research of richness, power and love), The Titanic (again a love story in a frame of deluge) and Avatar (possibility of second life to surpass terrestrial terrors and/or disasters and of course again the stimulating power of love).

17 As the series which are analyzed in this volume.

frame homelessness); the fifth chapter interrogates the Covid-19 reporting in Peruvian Press while the 6th chapter analyzes how blogs (as bidirectional channels) play a crucial role in recycling myths and offering explanations of current turbulences based upon them, in Greece. Then follow three chapters on American and Mexican TV serials (police sitcoms and soap operas) where existential dilemmas are reiterated in contemporary myths. These case studies are an interesting sample of the contemporary media narratives and of how they reproduce and represent the popular mythologies.

All the above elements are present in media narratives (this is why media are the "reflection" of beliefs and ideas of current everyday life). Of course, in order to approach the question of "media influence", it is necessary to have in mind not only the circle of representations but also the reception process (which is not studied here). Nevertheless, the media discourse is an exceptional field of research on dominant mythologies in which people either absolutely believe, or compromise in order to be able to go on with their social life; and definitely important as the reflection of contemporary myths, which are explored in the following chapters.

CHAPTER 2

The New Criminal News

Narrative Modalities on Fear of Crime in Newscasts of the City of Buenos Aires, 2015–2019

Mercedes Calzado, Mariana Fernández, Yamila Gómez, and Vanesa Lio

1 The Production of Police News on Television: Introductory Remarks

How are police news constructed nowadays? What type of treatment is given to the voice of its protagonists? What criteria prevails in the programs when it comes to ascertaining what is newsworthy? What role do new technologies play? These are some of the questions that guide the present study. The aim is to analyze the content and form of the problem of safety as addressed by over-to-air news channels in the city of Buenos Aires. The goal is to determine, on the one hand, how urban crime is currently depicted by the main television news programs and, on the other, to explore the relation between narrative modalities and the citizenship practices of victimization and prevention of urban insecurity.

We begin with an understanding of the security issue as a field of dispute that extends over different layers of significance nested within each socio-cultural domain. In our contemporary societies, the language employed to address the topic of security by television news programs interpellates a subject at risk who is induced to take precautions against an enemy that is so omnipotent and bold that not even the police, with its vast network of video surveillance, is able to stop. Of course, this type of "contract" (Verón, 1985) does not contemplate those spectators who do not conceive of the security issue from the perspective of a punitive logic.

In recent years, Police news have played a leading role in the TV channels that are broadcasted in the City of Buenos Aires. In 2013 and 2014, according to surveys by the Ombudsman for Audiovisual Communication,[1] the main topic both in terms of news quantity and duration was, using their own classification,

1 The "Defensoría del Público de Servicios de Comunicación Audiovisual" (translated in this article as Ombudsman for Audiovisual Communication) is a government body created by the Law n. 26.55 of Audio-visual Communication Services (LSCA), to promote the rights of

that of "police and fear of crime" (henceforth without quotation marks). In 2013, coverage amounted to 18.7% of the total volume of information and 25% when calculated in terms of the total duration of all surveyed programs; in 2014, it was 17.4% and 23.3%, respectively.

In 2015, by contrast, given the context of national elections for President in Argentina and local elections for Mayor in the City of Buenos Aires, political news predominated and exhibited a greater time duration (20.7% of the total volume), displacing "police and fear of crime" news to a second place (14.9%). In 2016, the political issue maintained the first place both in terms of the quantity and duration of news (16.4% and 19.6%, respectively). The "police and fear of crime" category was relegated to a third place as it relates to quantity, but remained quite close to sports: this last category represented 12.3% of the total volume, whereas police news amounted to 12.2%.

However, as concerns the duration of news, the "police" category maintained its second place with 17.6%, quite close to politics and exceeding sports by seven points. In 2017, the predominant topic was politics, with numbers just under those of 2016 (7.1%). By and large, the news items revolved around judicial information concerning presumed acts of corruption attributed to former government officials and businessmen with ties to Cristina Fernández de Kirchner. In 2018, "police and fear of crime" news returned as the most widely covered topic (28.4% of total coverage), followed by politics (26.1%). In 2019, these two topics were once again the most largely covered by the news channels under scrutiny: whereas in terms of quantity of news "politics" (18.4%) was slightly ahead of "police and fear of crime" (17.1%), in terms of duration police news exceeded politics by an ample margin (27.1% against 17.2%). Thus, police news encompassed more than a quarter of the total broadcasting time of newscasts, displaying a recurring tendency over the years toward a greater extension in the treatment of information connected to the topic.

This central role of police news in over-the-air television newscasts raises a number of questions: How are the journalistic narratives on urban crime and violence constructed? On the basis of which thematic, rhetorical and discursive modalities are they built? What actors play the leading role? What impact do television news exert on the characterization of events? What newsworthy criteria is being employed? What treatment is given to the images? What type of TV viewer is being interpellated?

listeners and viewers. Its functions include the reception of complaints from the public and periodic reports on audio-visual content from television channels in Buenos Aires City.

With the aim of isolating regularities in the construction of police television news, we examine in an initial phase data from reports produced by the Ombudsman for Audiovisual Communication of Argentina for the period 2013–2019. Next, we conduct a quantitative analysis on the basis of surveys conducted during the first week of October, 2015 and the second week of October, 2019. From this analysis, we can observe the place occupied by police news in relation to the totality of news that were broadcast in the morning, afternoon, evening and night by news programs of the five over-the-air channels (both public and private) of the City of Buenos Aires: América, TV Pública, Canal 9, Telefé and Canal 13.

In a second stage, we conduct a qualitative analysis of the news items, forming a corpus of analysis on the basis of recordings from the primetime newscast that were broadcast during the above-mentioned weeks, and we proceed to select those news items which are categorized under the rubric of "police and fear of crime". With these criteria in mind, the corpus subjected to qualitative analysis ultimately consisted of 288 news items, of which 196 were classified under "police and fear of crime" as a primary topic and 92 were placed under the same rubric as a secondary topic. With the results from the database, we elaborated new categories that try to make a conceptual contribution to the literature about news in general and police-related journalism in particular. These conceptual categories are: news chain, news block, "anecdotal" police item, media characterization of crime, desresponsibilization through framing, news map of fear of crime, extended narration and aesthetics of objectivity.

The chapter is divided into four parts. First, we review some theoretical concepts and the principal antecedents in the study of news on crime. Then, we provide quantitative data to contextualize the corpus as well as the leading role played by police news in TV journalism. In a third section, we describe the main characteristics of police news as covered by newscasts from the Buenos Aires Metropolitan Area (AMBA), resorting to a group of themes and subthemes of classification that are frequently applied to allegedly criminal acts. In a fourth section, we map the ways in which stories about crime are typically narrated and we review their spectacularized dimension. Finally, in the conclusion, we summarize the main findings of the study.

2 Fear of Crime in the News: Conceptual Framework and Antecedents

Since the mid-1990s, fear of crime became established in Argentina as a media, political, economic and socio-cultural issue. The growth of crime, as evidenced by an increase of public statistics which helped define the agenda of debate, reached its peak in 2002 and started to decline from 2003 onwards; however, it never quite reached levels comparable to those of the early 1990s (Ministry of National Security). Through media coverage, the topic of fear of crime increased its visibility across the nation (Martini & Pereira, 2009). This reflected an objective increment of crime statistics that, nevertheless, was tainted with sensationalist and melodramatic traits that became a defining characteristic of journalistic discourses (Ford, 1994; Sunkel, 1985). In Latin America, there is a reiteration – with specificities associated with each jurisdiction – of the same symbolic-dramatic matrix, which portrays an image of the "other" and the "popular" as barbaric and dangerous (Martín Barbero, 1987). At present, the volume of information in TV journalism is dominated by police news, which take precedence over general information, politics and sports, a conclusion that can be drawn from data sets collected by the Ombudsman for Audiovisual Communication (2013–2019).

In Argentina, the thematic dominance of police news on television grew alongside deregulation of the local media system during the 1990s (Mastrini, 2005). The emergence and expansion of multimedia conglomerates (Becerra, 2010) was such that the same news item, with the same information sources and identical media treatment, was broadcast simultaneously in newspapers, radio, over-the-air television and cable TV. This transformation was also related to the emergence of cable news channels and the concomitant need to produce 24-hour audiovisual content. As a result, each police news story became a piece of information that was repeated throughout the day in all conceivable formats, thereby offering content that, with the rise of social networks, became even more interactive and repeatable (Paz Pellat, 2009). In light of this, we are currently witnessing changes in the mode of production and circulation of police information (Calzado & Lio, 2021). Debates surrounding the perception of fear of crime and the role played by the media were largely addressed by the specialized literature on the subject, which focuses particularly on the shaping by the media of an agenda of fear as well as the introduction of a topic that is capable of mobilizing and/or frightening citizens. The media representation of security issues has been analyzed by several research projects, both in Argentina (Baquero, 2017; Fernández Pedemonte, 2001; Lorenc Valcarce, 2005; Martini & Pereyra, 2009; Sánchez, 2014; Tufró, 2017; Vilker, 2008) and across Latin America (Bonilla &Tamayo, 2007; Lara Klahr & Portillo Vargas, 2004; Rey & Rincón, 2007). A large part of them focuses on the modes of enunciation produced by the written press (Howitt, 1998, Cohen & Young, 1978, the depiction of crime and the criminal, and the changes that were implemented in recent decades both in the formats and languages used to express the criminal question (Arfuch, 1997; García Beaudoux & D'Adamo, 2007).

Some studies, such as those conducted by Ericson et al. (1991), address the issue across different media forms, such as radio, newspapers and television. According to this research, violent crimes are a common theme in the popular media but tend to be ignored by quality newscasts. Other studies raise the question concerning audiovisual particularities (Focás & Galar, 2016; Silvera & Natalevich, 2012), or else the construction of a police genre via reality shows (Howitt, 1998, Barak, 1994,). However, few projects concentrate on the use of police narratives in news programs (Retegui et al, 2019; Calzado & Morales, 2021).

A broad review of the problem requiring a focus that transcends the written press is particularly relevant for our purposes, since, today, the information channels that are available to citizens tend to be multiple and the nature of police news cannot be explained solely from the perspective of newspapers. Indeed, print media has lost its central place in the public agenda in a context where audiences consume more information and interact through various media outlets. A little over 25 years ago, access to information consisted almost exclusively in reading the morning and evening newspapers, listening to radio programs and watching two news programs, both of them broadcast by over-the-air channels. In Argentina, this pattern was radically altered when, toward the mid-1990s, media deregulation facilitated the arrival of cable TV (Albornoz & Hernández, 2009). The scene was transformed even further with the arrival of the Internet a few years later and, subsequently, with the influence of social networks and cell phones (Becerra, 2015). Technological changes gave rise to a new journalistic dimension that can be measured in terms of the amount of news that was required by the media, the urgency of the broadcasts (Juntunen, 2010), the changes in coverage that resulted from new technologies (Di Próspero & Maurello 2010), and the type of experiences that subjects began to have with the consolidation of a complex news/journalistic ecology (Becerra, 2010).

On a global scale, although television continues to be one of the most widely used media forms when it comes to distributing information, some changes are already taking place. In Brazil, for example, 43% of information is conveyed by television, 44% by online sites (including social networks) and only 4% by print newspapers. These figures come from the Digital News Report (Newman et al., 2016), which is produced by the University of Oxford and the Reuters Institute. Surveys by the said institute indicate that TV viewers in Great Britain and the United States have been dropping at a pace of 3 and 4% each year since 2012, a reduction that is comparable to the decline that has affected print newspapers since the 2000s (Nielsen & Sambrook, 2016). According to a survey conducted by these same institutions in 26 countries, which encompasses more than fifty thousand people, television remains popular among those over forty-five years old, whereas younger people between eighteen and twenty four prefer social networks to inform themselves. Women tend to discover news through social networks rather than news websites. Facebook, according to this report, is the most popular social network for reading, discussing and sharing news (Newman et al, 2016).

This scenario has forced journalistic media to experiment with new formats and forms of organization. As concerns police information, the news programs analyzed in this research incorporated new formats, narratives and aesthetics as well as new resources and sources to construct the "criminal" case. These new forms of presentation involving police news and their thematization are supplemented by fragments of events captured by people with their cell phones (what is known as "citizen journalism") as well as by images from social media or security cameras, which are changing the guidelines of production in audiovisual journalism.

Hence, we arrive at a preliminary thesis concerning the sources of information. Historically, police news were constructed through data supplied by the police itself and by other judicial institutions, a process which was thoroughly investigated by studies that examine the indexing or ranking of these official sources (Calzado & Maggio, 2009). Classic works in the field, such as those by Hall et al. (1978), Cohen (2015) and Thompson (1998) address the manner in which moral panic is fostered by the media through the intervention of judicial and police sources that condition journalistic agendas. In Argentina, Caimari (2004), Gayol & Kessler (2002) and Saítta (1998) studied print media and, in some cases, also radio, from a historical perspective for the period corresponding to the first half of the twentieth century. These investigations expose the strong historical ties that exist between the media, the police and the justice system in our country, which are the traditional suppliers of information and the main sources that define the different ways of describing and categorizing deviant behaviors.

Now, as will be shown throughout the current analysis, in recent years there has been a "relative shift" in police news that paved the way for a strong presence of so-called non-professional private sources (Acosta, 2012; Calzado & Lio, 2021). To some extent, this process marks the entry of audiences as sources of audiovisual news through images captured by new information and communication technologies (Di Próspero & Maurello, 2010). Thus, audiences become active agents in the construction of meaning, which they assume, interpret and understand more or less critically. The way in which audiences produce information about public issues in various instances of social life exemplifies a new way of narrating events that tends to displace traditional media.

3 The Centrality of Police Stories in Newscast

Besides its emergence as one of the main public problems (Kessler, 2009), fear of crime has been gaining protagonism in hegemonic media outlets since the mid-1990s. The centrality of police news was made evident by the processing of survey data from the Ombudsman for Audiovisual Communication, which reflects all the news transmitted by over-the-air channels, both public and private, from the City of Buenos Aires over the periods specified by this study. During the first week of October 2015, 2,554 news items were recorded, of which 561 were included in the police category (21.96%). In turn, during the second week of October 2019, a total of 2,762 news items were recorded, of which 636 were classified as police-related stories (23.03%).

In addition to the volume of news, we observe a prevalence of the police genre with regards to news length. Thus, in 2015, the general average duration of news was 1:51 minutes, but the information classified as "police and fear of crime" exhibited an average extension of 2:12 minutes. In 2019, the average duration of news was 1:57 minutes, while the police category exhibited an average of 3:01 (a relative increase compared to the first survey). Another noteworthy aspect is the broadcast schedule of news programs: during the surveyed period, the midday and evening broadcasts (those with the largest audiences) presented a higher proportion of police news. In 2015, police news encompassed 25.6% of midday news, 28.6% of evening news, and 16.1% of morning broadcasts. In 2019, the proportion was 32.11%, 27.11% and 17.06% for midday, evening and morning newscasts, respectively, a situation that confirms the trend of the previous period. The analysis of thematic presence, duration and time slots expresses the visibility of the police topic and its media relevance.

However, the ways of expressing the relevance of police information are not exhausted by their quantitative aspects. On the contrary, the ways of presenting news involving fear of crime, and the place they occupy in the structures of news programs, provides an even more consistent sense of its predominance. Thus, news items classified under "police and fear of crime" are usually presented as a cluster and, particularly in the case of private channels, at the beginning of newscasts. When watching these programs, we observe that in the four private news programs the first information items involve "police and fear of crime" issues, whether as a primary or secondary topic. To this we can added that these news stories tend to last several minutes, often monopolizing the entire first segment of the program (and, in some cases, also the second). The news program transmitted by the only public channel was a notable exception, since the place given to police information is not so central. In general, there is no police news at the beginning of the program; instead, they are shown for a few seconds in the context of news compacts.

In turn, from the analysis of the manner in which news are presented, two types of groupings became evident. We call the first "chain news", and we understood it as the consecutive presentation of a series of stories. The news that are grouped in this way have similar discursive characteristics (for example, the use of comparable visual resources, voice overs, similar duration for each news item, uniform music style throughout the sequence). At the same time, the chain can also exhibit two different kinds of modalities: a global chain in which all the news included fall under the same topic (in this case, the police category), and a local chain in which police news are predominant but tend to alternate with information on other topics. The chains can be short (two or three news items in total) or long (especially when they include more than four news items).

The second type of grouping is known as the "block news" and consists of the presentation of various news items revolving around the same event, although they tend to display different perspectives and emphasize different aspects of it. For example, an initial story about a bank robbery can lead to a second story about similar episodes that occurred in recent months or years, and even to a third story where the specialists highlight the mechanisms of the criminal modality.

Both the chain format and the news block constitute hierarchical modalities: in the first instance because, far from being diluted in a larger context, the news item gains in strength when appearing as part of a series of news; in the second, due to the diversity of perspectives and the prolonged treatment of the event in question. Although they usually take place at the start of the program, the chain and block formats also stand out at other moments of the newscasts as well. In these cases, they use advance or preview techniques to locate the news item at the beginning of the program, a situation that leaves the viewer up in the air and ready for resumption at a later moment.

Finally, another aspect that underlines the centrality of police news is repetition within the same program: once a news item is addressed during the first segment, it is taken up in the following segment or segments (in some cases to update information, in other cases to reiterate the aforementioned occurrence). This is not about a news section per se, but rather, a prolonged treatment of a news item that spans over different segments within a program in a continuous or discontinuous manner depending on how the information emerges.

4 Police News as Spectacle

What do the media talk about when they allude to fear of crime? How do they thematize the events included in the informative segment under scrutiny?[2] The corpus reveals that, in general, police television news revolve around crimes against people and property, with the subtopics robbery and homicide being the most recurrent themes, especially in private channels. Drug trafficking, interpersonal conflicts and car accidents are also common. A striking detail becomes evident in this rather unoriginal list: the case of news items classified under the police rubric but addressed from the perspective of the strange and the bizarre. Indeed, one of the biggest curiosities in the construction of police television information are these minor events, not necessarily related to crime or large-scale police cases, which can be described as unusual, strange, bizarre and out of the ordinary. The journalistic coverage connects one aspect or aspects of these cases with the topic of crime, and from there the news story is classified as "police and fear of crime" information. Hence, a shift in the crime category takes place and the genre mutates into what we call an "anecdotal" police item. For instance, the story of a man who fell asleep inside his car because he was drunk is presented in terms of the weirdness associated with the fact that the authorities could not wake him up as well as the potential "risk" that the overall situation represents to his own life and that of others (Telenueve, 10/7/2015).

In this way, an expansion of the police genre begins to take place. On the basis of minor events, the news in question not only highlight the contravention or the hypothetical offence; they also combine it with entertainment.

2 When we began the surveying task, we adopted a matrix of categories to inform our observations. We sorted out the news classified as "police and fear of crime" according to whether they fell under: robberies, organized crime/drug trafficking, gender violence, homicides, kidnappings (including extortion and express modalities), hostage-taking, interpersonal conflicts (gang fights, car incidents, etc.), human trafficking, public policies and electoral campaign, economic crimes, lynching, and others. However, we left the analysis open to the possibility of new subtopics to be determined on the basis of statements from news programs. As a result, some of the categories belonging to the initial matrix did not appear at the time of reviewing previous subtopics (such as kidnappings or human trafficking) and, at the same time, new categories emerged which were linked to specific manners of constructing audiovisual police news in the present day (for instance, unusual or anecdotal news).

In other words, an event of low impact and little social relevance becomes news by virtue of its journalistic treatment, and so the news-making process becomes altered quite significantly: while the journalistic tradition dictates that the production of news must begin with an event (Rodrigo Alsina, 2005, in these rare occasions the news takes place despite the fact that the event in question does appear to be such, becoming what it is by virtue of the mere possibility of accessing it (for example, through images from security cameras, messages from social networks or other audiovisual materials).

The coverage of these rare events is not an isolated instance. A theft of plants from a flowerbed inside a building in a neighborhood of the City of Buenos Aires is narrated, amid laughter and jokes, using footage from the security cameras that captured the incident. The news is repeated in a sort of news segment that deals with other "unusual and incredible thefts" of plants, dogs and even dog houses (América Noticias, 10/7/2015). On the one hand, the act of theft is characterized as a quotidian experience that could be committed by anyone (perhaps an acquaintance or a neighbor) simply because it appears to be a "temptation". On the other hand, the presentation of the news emphasizes the extraordinary nature of such events: "There are thieves of all kinds: the clever, the bloodthirsty, and the bizarre," the host utters while the images are roll on.

"There are also silent, meticulous and audacious thieves," the host continues while interviewing the victim of a robbery which involved rope climbing and was referred to by the media as the "spider-man" modality (Telefé Noticias, 10/7/2019). This type of event is "curious" because of the "risky" nature of the robbery itself but, above all, because the apartment robbed was located a few meters away from the local police station. In these types of news the hosts often criticize the action of the police for being ineffective and/or untimely. A number of similar case (criminal acts that take place in the vicinity of police stations) was broadcast by different newscasts in which what predominates is the construction of a rhetoric of weariness as well as an emphasis on the victimization of defenseless citizens in the face of "audacious" and "cynical" thieves (Telefé Noticias, 10/10/2019).

This way of constructing news naturalizes fear of crime as the central feature of an ominous dynamic that will continue to haunt citizens indefinitely and against which the public must take necessary precautions in order to ensure its safety. The proposals for possible solutions from the perspective of the victims is a recurring discursive strategy employed by news media. In turn, newscasts promote alarm, monitoring and security systems as potential substitutes for the (ineffective) role of the police. These not only concern surveillance and controlling but, above all, are meant to foster a sense of tranquility and protection among citizens. These types of stories emphasize the importance of massively installing security devices (since neither private nor neighborhood alarms would be able to prevent robberies) and stress the "incredible impunity" (Telefé Noticias, 10/10/2019) with which, in their view, criminals act right in front of police cameras, reinforcing the sense of police inefficiency.

In turn, news programs classify stories related to other segments as "police and fear of crime" and, once again, magnify the police genre through a criminal framing of general information. As a result of this, a framework is produced which locates the presence of crime in anecdotal news stories, and police contents tend to be constructed based on events that, in principle, cannot be considered to be newsworthy information. Consequently, if on the one hand the police genre is magnified when framing events as being crime-related news, even though they are not, on the other hand, these anecdotal police stories also trivialize crime by depreciating both the act and the actors involved (victims, perpetrators and witnesses).

The ways of naming and narrating the events also define another characteristic of the media portrayal of crime. Police news often refer to criminal figures and modalities with varying levels of specificity, such as "entraderas" (robberies produced when a person is entering the home), "al voleo" (without a prior organization), hitmen, "motochorros" (thieves riding motorcycles), "mules" (women transporting drugs), "mecheras" (women who steal from other people or in shops), "pungas" (people who steal small belongings rather quickly), "piranha robbery" (attacks by multiple thieves), "spider men" (a robbery that involves escalation), "bicichorro" (thieves riding bicycles), "pibes chorros" (young thieves) and "abre puertas tarjeteros" (criminals who open doors using cards). These characterizations produce a novel displacement of legal terms and figures associated with crime that enable media typification which, in turn, serve to construct subjectivities and permit or block certain forms of relation with "others". In addition, these taxonomies, which emerge from and are reproduced by the media, constitute a discursive style that is distinctive of police news, with its own technical terms and others taken from common sense, all of which help to codify the criminal experience in novel ways.

In general, the actors invoked in the narration of police news are the victim and the perpetrator, although these figures undergo varying levels of characterization. The victim can be identified with a particular person, but it is also suggested that neighbors and even viewers can be potential victims. In fact, when the victim of a robbery refuses to appear on camera for fear of retaliation, the newscasts often rely on the testimony of a "neighbor-witness" who once suffered a similar robbery and, in this way, they exalt a general feeling of unease that is expressed by the common saying that "nobody wants to go out" (Telenueve, 10/11/2019). The staging of despair, and the fear of walking down the street, are communicated on the basis of a source that is not directly related to the event in question. This is a very recurrent strategy followed by news coverage.

In the case of interpersonal conflicts, the new programs shape the figure of the perpetrator using police sources. A notable case in our corpus is that of an act of discrimination committed in a school where the director of the establishment prevented the entrance of a student for having painted her lips, with the argument that the institution "is not a brothel" (Telenueve, 9/10/2019). The reporter on the scene, with a suspicious and accusing tone, interviews the adolescent who affirms that no violence was exerted against the director of the school, neither by her nor by her family. In spite of this, the newscast adopts a position through various tools such as the video graph or voice-over, conveying the opposite message: "Student and mother beat up the director", "the police suffered many hits, bites and kicks" (Telenueve, 9 / 10/2019). Here, if we take into consideration the concept of framing as the key mechanism through which the event is defined and constructed – which includes the selection concerning whose side of the story gives more relevance to certain aspects of the problem (Entman, 1993) – we can stress the promotion of moralizing valuations regarding gender femininity and, at the same time, a sexualizing portrayal of the adolescence by focusing the camera on her body. The purpose here is to make the viewer focus on the supposedly provocative way in which the young woman entered the educational establishment inappropriately dressed.

The figures of the victim and the perpetrator can appear directly in crimes such as robberies, or else be present indirectly through images or photographs, for instance, in cases of homicides. The family represents the voice of the victim and takes on a leading role in the plea for justice. However, when the homicides are aggravated by a public function (for instance, perpetrated by security agents), the news story tends to narrate the fact as an error resulting from "lack of professionalism" (Telefé Noticias, 10/10/2019). And although the voice of the decease's relatives is present in these cases, its version is often questioned. Thus, for example, one of the programs in our corpus characterizes the case of three policemen who fired nine times at a taxi driver in a Buenos Aires neighborhood as a "mysterious episode" (Telefé Noticias, 10/10/2019). Like so many others, the news is narrated using images captured by security cameras. Although the screen shows the police officers shooting when the man was already on the ground, the journalists debate and question the hypotheses of an excess in self-defense.

This type of journalistic coverage, which minimizes the responsibility of the police, also accounts for the differential treatment that the victims receive. To illustrate this point, let us consider how two similar news items are framed in substantially different ways. The first story is about a police vehicle that runs over a three-year-old boy, and the second about a football player who suffers an accident after leaning on a poorly shut door inside a balcony, which causes him to free fall from a sixth floor. In the case of the child, the desresponsibilization mechanism operates not just by emphasizing the tragic character of the event constructed in all the news programs analyzed, but also metonymically, that is, by means of a chain where two different news stories are characterized in the same way. "Another unexpected death" (Telenoche, 10/7/2019), says the host to refer to the case of the football player. The meaning that this tragedy produces operates by contiguity and is equated with the tragedy of the child run over by the two policemen. While in the news about the football player the building administration is held responsible for not checking if the door was adequately shut, in the case of the run-over child, the responsibility for the death falls on the father, who was next to him when "he escaped and ran across the street" (Telenoche, 10/7/2019), thus absolving the driver of the vehicle and characterizing the episode as "unfortunate".

The hosts put in play the pragmatic function of making a statement known and believed (Farré, 2004). If the homicide of the anonymous child is framed as a tragedy, the football player's accident is highlighted as a "double tragedy" (Telenoche, 10/7/2019) due to the victim's fame and the sudden interruption of his promising professional future. Thus, a valuation of the victims is produced in differential terms. This web of significance that tie the deaths of innocent victims (such as the soccer player) together with that of guilty victims (the child run over due to the irresponsibility of their parents) operates as a condition of possibility for the naturalization of practices of state agents leading to the death of people from popular sectors of society (Ríos, 2014).

In fact, if we compare the coverage given to this particular news item with that of two policemen who were themselves run over (Cinthia, deceased; Santiago, survivor) we notice that it is likewise classified as a "tragic event," but with a clear responsibility and a plea for justice that becomes politicized by making it extensive to other potential perpetrators: "The message [...] is directed at all those who kill behind the wheel," the voiceover states (Telefé Noticias, 10/7/2019). When the victim of a homicide is a security agent, a more weight is granted to the demand for justice. The agent killed in the line of duty is presented as a hero, yet the figure involved does not refer to any specific individual or specific event, but to prototypical models that convey sobering messages to the rest of society (Sirimarco, 2017).

The news analyzed also present, albeit as an exception, neighbors playing the role of "victimizers". When the "victims" retaliate on their own following a crime, the figure of the "vigilante" emerges, which combines the role of the victim with that of the perpetrator. When victims become victimizers, the figure of the perpetrator loses strength because it is believed to be justified by its retributive action. Without reflecting too much on the complexity of these roles, the news programs include headlines such as: "Neighbors of Flores almost beat a 'motochorro' to death. The police saved him after the victims themselves managed to stop him" (Telenueve, 10/5/2015). The news in question involves two crimes: the initial robbery and the severe beating received by the "motochorro", although the second is not framed as a criminal act. The same happens when news reports proceed to characterize the actors involved: those who perpetrate the lynching are treated as "neighbors" while the person who tried to steal is identified with the term "motochorro". In the average police news item, the perpetrators are associated with some figure that serves to illustrate a given criminal modality. But in the context of news involving double events such as these (a first crime followed by a second crime committed by the victim or a witnesses), there seems to be some discomfort on the part of reporters to call the neighbors "perpetrators". "What about the neighbors?" asks the host, and immediately explains the legal aspects of the matter, adding that "the law punishes lynching" (Telenueve, 10/5/2015). In other words, they warn viewers that lynching is also a crime, but they do not define the protagonists as criminals. Hence, a desresponsibilization of the perpetrator takes place through a kind of framing that fails to fully capture his or her role in the event.

Sometimes there is a difficulty associated with presenting a public person in the role of perpetrator. This tends to occur in the case of crimes carried out by celebrities, which in many cases are economic in nature. As Ojeda Segovia (2013) points out, the "non-violent execution" of these crimes "leads to a benign and careful treatment" by the media (p. 32). It is observed that, when the person involved is a well-known and popular public figure, and the news is not linked in principle to a political event, chances are that the story will be constructed and portrayed as a show: "Depending on the hierarchy of the characters, in the story there will be more or less spectacle, more or less mystery, and the objective will be to cancel the factual violence of the criminal act" (Ragagnin, 2005, p. 11). The treatment that this type of news receives puts the categories of "victims" and "perpetrators" in tension. In general, the news programs follow a logic of selectivity around white-collar crimes (Sutherland, 1999): much in the same way as the victim of economic crimes, with few exceptions, is seldom portrayed as a real person, the construction of news never places the person responsible in the role of criminal or perpetrator.

This procedure of desresponsibilization through framing is altered when the news exhibits a political nuance: in these cases, the question of how the perpetrator ought to be constructed are significantly exalted. However, we think that the stories about "corruption," in general, tend to deviate from the specific configuration of police news that we are concerned with in this article. Without a doubt, this is an interesting perspective to problematize, as suggested by some studies that examine the changes in the news agendas related to security in Argentina (Focás and Zunino, 2019). However, we think that crimes associated with corruption acquire characteristics that are different from those of police news classically defined; these characteristics include hybrid formats that incorporate elements from political news, investigative journalism and judicial news, all of which escape the particularities of police news.

5 "Hot" Zones, Hazards, and Potential Victims

A crime map is constructed across socially marginalized areas of the City of Buenos Aires and, secondarily, across suburban territory. In these areas, news events are picked up by news programs and often serve to stigmatize their inhabitants through a characterization of these territories as dangerous.

Now, although the newscasts are produced in the said areas, they have a national reach that is not made apparent by the content they present. Hence, the air channels focus almost exclusively on criminal events in the Gran Buenos Aires District and, from there, nationalize local news.

As for the way of presenting and constructing the crime map, it is interesting to note the differential characterization that occurs within these targeted areas, since not the entire city or province of Buenos Aires is classified as risky. There is a tendency to identify certain zones as dangerous or risky, characterizing their neighborhoods since news events. The Buenos Aires neighborhood of Constitución, for instance, is a synonym of danger and risk. In a chain of police stories that were broadcast by Telefé's newscast and are included in the corpus, the driver states: "Constitución is not a safe, warm and quiet place to go out. We who live and work in this area know this. The neighborhood is complicated" (Telefé Noticias, 10/5/2015).

Maps are also central when it comes to illustrating coverage and, often times, depicting journalistic statistics. The news of the drunk man who "fell asleep in the car and couldn't be woken up" (Telenueve, 10/5/2015), for example, is later expanded by the producers of the program as part of a more general analysis about the dangers associated with drunk driving. To illustrate this argument, they add a chart of the City of Buenos Aires where the neighborhoods with most positive tests for drinking and drivers are highlighted in red: Belgrano and Palermo. Hence, the maps determine the danger levels based on the contents of sockets annexed to the images. In another newscast by Telefé, when it comes to characterizing a humble area located in the southern neighborhood of Bajo Flores, in the City of Buenos Aires, the producers add a chart that illustrates what they call "the X-ray of a hot zone", emphasizing this instrument in headlines, video graphs and comments by hosts and columnists. The chart entitled "the narco map" depicts the geography of danger and disaggregates it according to the type of drugs that, they believe, is sold by immigrants of different nationalities living in the city slums: "In the sector of Paraguayans, cocaine and paco", and "in the sector of Peruvians, marijuana", the charts indicates (Telefé Noticias, 10/9/2015).

In this way, and on the basis of news events and statistics, they tend to build an image of the neighborhoods according to their presumed criminal characteristics. It is also interesting to note that these statistical and geo-referentiality procedures seldom rely on any sources, credible or otherwise. The data and the illustrations, by themselves, seem to function as sources, and in general the news avoid revealing where the information that supports their journalistic investigations comes from.

Returning to news about events that do not constitute crimes but are categorized under the rubric "police and fear of crime", we observe another quite novel discursive regularity that we call "extended narration". These news items convey a message of alarm despite the fact that the crime has not yet taken place or perhaps was less severe than communicated by the narrative. In a nutshell, the news programs present a non-news about a non-event and, on that basis, create a kind of futurology through long counter-factual debates about what could have happened if only what could have happened had, in fact, occurred. Nothing has happened, but it could have. The use of the conditional is frequently embedded in the journalistic story insofar as it is news built in a hypothetical register, moving away from the first journalistic requirement of a credible news story: that an event must take place (Clauso, 2007 Luchessi & Martini , 2004; Rodrigo Alsina, 2005. Instead, the newscasts present cases that alert about potential hazards and future risks, treating the non-event as if it had already happened. Hence, a double process makes possible worlds come true while at the same time generalizing those risks through an identification of the viewer with a potential victim ("It could happen to you").

This is the case of news that revolve around rumors or suspicions. For example, in a Telefé report entitled, "Fear in the university: suspect investigated", the origin of the story is not a complaint, but the remote possibility that such an event could happen: the hosts analyze a "rumor" about a man who was allegedly recruiting women for a trafficking network in the neighborhood of the Faculty of Social Sciences of the University of Buenos Aires. The hosts emphasize the dimension of fear and possible preventive measures based on the following question: "Does he look for women to prostitute them?" (Telefé Noticias, 10/5/2015). Through rumors, fear, and potential risks, a state of alertness and distrust is promoted as the prevailing characteristic of everyday life.

The modality of extended narration expresses a potentiality. Another news program in our corpus ranks as a primary news item a threat made to the owner of a restaurant who received an anonymous package with a grenade. Although the hosts communicate the information in terms of the dangers that the circulation of these weapons entails, simultaneously they report that the grenade was successfully deactivated and, consequently, the risk quickly becomes an anecdotal element of the story. However, on the basis of this information, they construct a series that gathers past similar cases – often separated by months or years – that had "discarded" grenades as their theme, grenades that were no longer functioning and were abandoned in a public highway (Telenoche, 10/5/2015). Although the danger does not seem to be imminent, the narrative stresses the dimension of fear and risk associated with the situation. In this way, they spectacularize these news stories through an extended narrative, which they create: the exhibition of objects, places, hypothetical harms, and the possibility of what could have been are not only resources that feed the television rhythm, but also elements that help materialize what in actual fact has not yet materialized.

Another side of spectacularizing police news has to do with the presence of specialists on the shows. These are individuals who possess knowledge or skills related to a particular discipline or topic, which in the newscasts translate into expert opinions on a given situation (Dodier, 2009). When it comes to key stories that extend over a long time in a single news programs, receiving a treatment that can last up to twenty or thirty minutes of airtime, the intervention of "experts" who are summoned to explain certain aspects of the news to hosts and viewers alike is a recurrent theme. The program producers appeal to the figure of the specialist (for example, a graphologist, a toxicologist or a lawyer) to provide a more technical and allegedly objective look, generally accompanied by a number of elements that support his or her scholarly character (the context of the interview can be a library, for example, and a number of materials and tools are deployed in connection to the news). In some newscasts, the assignment of roles also grants a place to the viewer, configuring him as a student to whom the expert is supposed to instruct about the how and why of the phenomena. In these kinds of exchanges, the hosts frequently assume the role of the viewers, pretending to be "uninformed" and asking the specialists for clarification to "understand" the subject matter. The experts, the fast thinkers or specialists of thought, as Bourdieu (1996) calls them, function as authority figures that are supposedly well informed about the subject.

It must also be noted that, even today, the news continues to be spectacularized through the classic plaques that function as blackboards and are used as a tool to provide contextual data, statistics, or else narrate the main events in the style of a chronicle. With this kind of staging, which is supplemented using images (for example, photos of weapons and drugs) and the demonstration or reconstruction of sequences of events by the specialists live on the floor, the news stories seek not only to inform, but also to entertain (Berrocal Gonzalo et al, 2014). The coverage uses fictional elements ranging from music that reinforces the tone with which the reporters seek to convey the story, whether in terms of action, suspense, fear, laughter and so on, to the editing of images and the use voice-overs. The result is that police news is narrated almost as segments of an action film, a mystery, a drama or even a sitcom, as in the case of the aforementioned "anecdotal police news" genre.

Another key component of the narrative is the images that become available because of massive access to audiovisual recording devices that, until some years ago, did not exist as such (security cameras, social networks, cell phones). These technologies engendered new ways of narrating events, giving rise to an aesthetic of "the real" that seeks to make mediations invisible and emulate "life itself" on the screens. Throughout Latin America, we find stories that revolve around the "really real" and display a potential that exceeds the narratives originating in the legal field, the state and institutional fields, even the police field (Alarcón, 2016, p. 14). As media products, these images seek an "aesthetic of objectivity" that, in the case of security cameras, is based on the presentation of videos footage as evidence and erases the marks that constitute them as intentional constructions (Gates, 2013). The loss of hierarchy that official sources tend to suffer leads to a situation whereby cameras are used in many cases as the main sources of material.[3]

We claim that a process of relative displacement of traditional sources is taking place due to the interplay that takes place between the police, the justice system and journalism. Three factors are modifying the dynamic among these institutions. First, the negative depiction of institutions involved in policies about crime (the police, the judiciary, the government, and other security forces) favors the emergence of new non-professional private sources and, in some instances, even the loss of reputation by those sources that were

3 As for the relative displacement of the sources of police news due to the impact of new information and communication technologies, we explored at length the work of Calzado & Lio, 2021.

traditionally considered official. Second, the technical capabilities provided by new technologies and media channels (social networks, mobile devices, video surveillance cameras) makes possible the appearance of new sources that take on the role of content providers, in our case supporting the narrative of police events. Third, the proliferation of communication channels through digital media and social network platforms promotes non-professional citizen practices, which in turn allows news producers to be on the hunt for more content (as well as updates on already announced facts), and to resort, whenever possible, to other alternative sources. This procedure constitutes a radical change in media practices to the detriment of more traditional ways of producing news. At the same time this combination of factors generates the aforementioned misclassification of events which are not necessarily connected to crimes or incivilities, or else have little impact or magnitude.

Also, in this search for novelty, the phenomenon called citizen journalism becomes magnified, which causes news content to become viral in social networks. Through these new media, social subjects reconstitute themselves as the primary creators of representations which are produced by themselves. We can think of a "double mediation" affecting police news, whereby it is no longer simply about the representation of the world by the media; instead, the mediation operates on a different level, with citizens "capturing" the world through their own cell phones or home surveillance devices. These captures and mediations are further mediated by the manner in which police news are subsequently conveyed by the mass media. What proliferates is the new forms of production by "common people" are photos and/or videos of police events recorded with everyday devices.

In the case of cell phones, their aesthetic characteristics (unprofessional videos shot with a hand-held camera and where parts of the image can appear obstructed by people or objects blocking the view) reinforces the idea that these stories revolve around "the real life", that they show what "really" happens in the *here* and *now* of news event. On the other hand, social networks are upheld as a means of accessing primary sources. In many cases, this ensures a direct path to statements made by the protagonists of the news, tracking their interventions in accounts or profiles from Twitter and Facebook. When faced with the impossibility of contacting the sources with the regular speed associated with traditional channels, the social networks guarantee a direct contact with the actors. Those social networks that are most closely tied to the circulation of photographs (such as Facebook or Instagram) also function as a repository or digital archive of images that serves to illustrate police news with photographs of the protagonists taken prior to the event.

In addition to the construction of police news through alternative sources, we should add the use of images produced by video surveillance systems (whether public or private), and their subsequent deployment in the media as representations of real events, a technique that omits the process of double mediation that we previously identified. The media also produce information from content that circulates on social networks and, as a result, the criteria of veracity are no longer defined solely by institutional sources but are now defined by the sense of immediacy generated by the images recorded with these devices or the "statements" of witnesses who communicate using posts on social media.

On the other hand, the information produced using these images in general does not appear to be very important: it refers to minor events relying on little data and very few informants. However, the visual content generated by new technologies takes on a decisive role in the newscasts as a result of the unique access to the material that the production of these programs enjoys. With the dramatization of news, a tension arises between, on the one hand, broadcasting of relevant stories that are difficult to access, and on the other, insignificant situations that rely on amateur audiovisual material (Baquerín de Riccitelli, 2008). Hence, the news tends to reinforce the notions of the "scoop" and the exclusivity that associated with the first-hand access to these images. A consequence of this process is the dispersion of the agenda both within each news program and across the broadcasts of the different channels. The aim is to sell viewers on the capacity for differential access to images as a way of "having the exclusive", rather than to pursue relevant news or a pre-existing agenda.

6 The Narration of Crime on Television: Reflections on the Construction of Police News and Its Relationship with the Prevention by the Public

The news programs foster prevention (and fear) among the public in response to urban violence by highlighting the way in which criminals act despite the surveillance measures adopted by the community. In societies at risk, citizens are addressed as the potential victims of crime, since this figure "makes biopolitical security work with a whole regime of novel affections" among which "compassion will be exalted by the media set-ups" (Gros, 2010, p. 290). The "carnality of suffering" shapes the subjectivity of our time (Calzado, 2015) on the basis of narratives about fear of crime in which pain is configured from the perspective of the victim. Thus, in the news, the predominant actor is the citizen and neighbor at risk.

"We cannot live here. We do not know what to do. Yesterday it was his turn. We are constantly communicating with our neighbors. Now we are going to install an alarm in the neighborhood, but it is terrible" (Telenueve, 10/7/2019), testifies a neighbor, and the reporter acts as spokesperson of the public demands to implement urgent measures. As Rodríguez Alzueta (2019) points out, this new system of organized neighbors consisting of citizens who otherwise participate very little in the public sphere constitutes an anti-political conception of community life and a police-based conception of security that journalists like to enthrone. In this regard, we have seen that the newscasts' reporters are always there whenever the neighbors summon them to echo their claims.

The discourses are directed at a viewer-victim whom journalists inform but are also meant to "alert" about possible "threats" and promote alternative defense mechanism – both communal and individual – when faced with "lack of policies". In police news, the hosts address viewers directly: "Pay close attention", they warn. The person interpellated must "pay attention" because he or she may be the next victim. Audiences are in danger because "anyone can steal from them", "a neighbor" and even someone they have known "all his life", as a report from the América newscast emphasizes (América Noticias, 10/8/2015).

Viewers are also held accountable for their own safety: they are interpellated as those who must assume an active role as concerns their personal security by adopting measures that will reduce "their own risk" (Telenoche, 10/9/2019). "The neighbors did everything to prevent the thefts, they put up several security cameras, they also set alarms, but it seems that nothing is enough because these events of fear of crime continue", says a reporter from the Telefé news program in reference to a series of thefts (Telefé Noticias, 7/10/2019). The emphasis on "fear" requires that the information be accompanied by images of robberies taken from security cameras. A voiceover gathers the neighbors as protagonists of the news. The "we" of concerned active citizens in the face of what is happening is opposed to an "other" that puts the "security of all" at risk. That "other" represents a tangible danger that "neighbors" must anticipate. Thus, in addition to the extended narrative, newscasts use the figure of the "other" to configure the addressee as a victim and editorialize the news in terms of prevention. In fact, in many cases, toward the end of the news segment, the newscast includes a series of advice or recommendations from the experts to the viewers. The newscasts function in this sense as manuals of appropriate behaviors that viewers must adopt to avoid becoming the latest victim.

They also construct the consumer of police news as someone who can recognize him or herself in the information, that is, as someone who empathizes with these specific situations and the various modes in which it is narrated. He or she is an addressee who sympathizes with the victim and his relatives, who is moved and surprised, who is just as furious and scared as the news reporters are, thus falling prey of the emotional appeal that is characteristic of private channels. In cases of homicides, the hosts editorialize the news by adding drama to the story, they appeal to emotion/shock, at times even using descriptions of images (visual or mental) that are almost morbid: they dwell on those "totally mutilated" bodies, or show the "violent marks on the asphalt". They stress that "two of the coffins are shut due to the state in which the bodies were left" (Telefé Noticias, 10/8/2015). The appropriate music, and the use of images showing the victims in happy moments are the last touches that shape a melodramatic narrative. Thus, by exalting to emotions and appealing to attitudes of prevention, the police stories seek to gain the sympathy of the addressee.

It is worth raising the question about the degree of representativeness of this victimizing perspective, which, although encompasses demands concerning the increase of security measures (armored doors, cameras, alarms), distrusts its utility as much as the effectiveness of policy-making institutions when it comes to increasing the feeling of safety and the protection of citizens within the community. What other voices are pushed aside as potential sources of police news? How are the news constructed when violence is carried out by security forces? At this point, the category of "desresponzability through framing" helps us review how the news surrounding a double event are framed (a crime against property followed by a crime against life carried out by the person attacked in the first place, with citizens present at the scene to witness the facts). These cases, whose protagonists are often "neighbors" playing the role of perpetrators, are not only presented as exceptional, but as an excess in the search for "justice by one's own hand" in a context of pressing fear of crime before which the State is typically absent. These are homicides in which the victims are characterized in highly stereotyped and selective terms according to social class, place of socio-territorial belonging and other professional profiles they could meet. These stereotypes also extend to the popular neighborhoods of the AMBA, whose geography is illustrated using the above-mentioned "insecurity maps".

The use of these fictionalizing mechanisms derived from dramatic art (Puente, 1997) is as recurrent as the victimizing social tie between news reporters and the consumers of information. This gives us an opportunity to reflect on the way in which the descriptive-referential discourse, characteristic of modern-day newscasts, was transformed through communication strategies built on a pact of verisimilitude implicating the "insecure", the "defenseless" and those neighbors who are "unprotected" by the security forces. The host joins the viewer on the basis of a feeling of identity that marks their belonging to a community of fear: a reality whose transparency is granted by images extracted from video surveillance cameras, cell phones and social networks, coupled with the urgent, chained and extended repetition of the imperative to feel safer.

The results reveal some guidelines concerning the prominence, characteristics, and new ways of constructing police news in over-the-air television. The regularities exhibited in this chapter permit us to review the current idiosyncrasy of audiovisual police news, both in relation to the modalities of other communication media, as well as the historical characteristics of this particular television format. In addition, the analysis allowed us to conceptualize some modalities on which police and/or fear of crime news on television are both configured and presented, such as extended narration, chain news and block news, media typification and anecdotal police news. At the same time, we witnessed the emergence of a new type of news constructed from images of security cameras and other technologies of daily use.

The road traveled thus far made it possible for us to detect the need to explore the media treatment of urban crime as it relates to instances of news production (Calzado & Lio, 2021) and the modes of interpreting police information that television audiences assume (Calzado, Irisarri & Manchego, 2021). We believe it is extremely important to attend to the relations that are constructed between the media and audiences. Television content provides interesting elements to think about the contemporary ways of living in insecure settings, but these contents cannot be explained by themselves, since they are part of a broader network of significance that helps explain them but at the same time transcends them.

References

Alarcón, C. (2016). Entrevista. Relatos periodísticos sobre "lo real-real". En Focás, Brenda y Rincón, Omar *(In)seguridad, medios y miedos: una mirada desde las experiencias y las prácticas cotidianas en América Latina.* Cali: Universidad ICESI.

Albornoz, L. & Hernández, P. (2009) "La radiodifusión en Argentina entre 1995 y 1999: concentración, desnacionalización y ausencia de control público". In Mastrini, G. (Ed) *Mucho ruido, pocas leyes. Economía y políticas de comunicación en la Argentina (1920–2007)* (pp. 261–290). Buenos Aires: La Crujía.

Arfuch, L. (1997). *Crímenes y pecados. De los jóvenes en la crónica policial.* Buenos Aires: UNICEF Argentina.

Baquerín De Riccitelli, M. T. (2008). *Los medios, ¿aliados o enemigos del público?* Buenos Aires: EDUCA.

Baquero, R. (2017) "El crimen de Brian". La legitimación de la baja en la edad de imputabilidad en el discurso del diario Clarín. *Question*, 1 (56), 1–17.

Barak, G. (1994). *Media, process, and the social construction of crime: studies in newsmaking criminology*. New York: Garland Pub.

Becerra, M. (2010) "Las noticias van al mercado: etapas de intermaediación de lo público en la historia de los medios de la Argentina". In G. Lugones y J. Flores (Ed.) *Intérpretes e interpretaciones de la Argentina en el Bicentenario* (pp. 139–165). Quilmes: Universidad Nacional de Quilmes.

Becerra, M. (2015). *De la concentración a la convergencia. Políticas de medios en Argentina y América Latina*. Buenos Aires, Argentina: Paidós.

Berrocal Gonzalo, S., Redondo García, M., Martín Jiménez, V., Campos Domínguez, E. (2014). La presencia del infoentretenimiento en los canales generalistas de la TDT española. *Revista Latina de Comunicación Social*, 69, 85–103.

Bonilla Velez, J. & Tamayo Gómez, C. (2007). *Los medios en las violencias y las violencias en los medios*. Bogotá: CINEP.

Bourdieu, P. (1996). *Sobre la televisión*. Barcelona: Anagrama.

Caimari, L. (2004). *Apenas un delincuente. Crimen, castigo y cultura en la Argentina, 1880–1995*. Buenos Aires: Siglo XXI.

Calzado, M. (2015). *Inseguros. El rol de los medios y la respuesta política frente a la violencia. De Blumberg a hoy*. Buenos Aires: Aguilar.

Calzado, M. & Morales, S. (2021) *Atravesar las Pantallas: noticia policial, producción informativa y experiencias de la inseguridad*. CABA: Teseo.

Calzado, M., Irisarri, V. & Manchego Cárdenas, C. (2021). "Flujos y tramas de experiencais: las noticias policials desde las pantallas porteñas". In: M. Calzado y S. Morales (Comp.) *Atravesar las Pantallas: noticia policial, producción informativa y experiencias de la inseguridad* (pp. 205–240). CABA: Teseo.

Calzado, M. & Lio, V. (2021) "Images of Crime: Empathetic newsworthiness and digital technologies in the production of police news on television in Argentina". In Wiest, J. (Ed.) *Theorizing criminality and policing in the digital media age* (pp. 109–128). Bingley: Emerald Publishing Limited.

Calzado, M. & Maggio. N (2009). "A veces pasa como si uno dijera llueve: la naturalización mediática de la muerte de delincuentes en enfrentamientos". In A. Daroqui (Comp.) *Muertes Silenciadas* (pp. 53–100). Buenos Aires: Centro Cultural de la Cooperación.

Clauso, R. (2007). *Cómo se construyen las noticias. Los secretos de las técnicas periodísticas*. Buenos Aires: La Crujía.

Cohen, S. (2015) *Demonios populares y pánicos morales*. arcelona: Gedisa.

Cohen, S. & Young, J. (1978). *The manufacture of news: social problems, deviance and the mass media*. London: Sage Publications.

Di Próspero, C. & Maurello, M. E. (2010). "Los periodistas y las nuevas tecnologías". In L. Luchessi (Comp.) *Nuevos escenarios detrás de las noticias: agendas, tecnologías y consumos* (pp. 51–71). Buenos Aires: La Crujía.

Dodier, N. (2009). "Experts et victimes face à face". En Lefranc, S. Y Mathieu, L. (Eds). *Mobilisations de victimes* (pp. 29–36). Rennes: Presses Universitaires de Rennes.

Entman, R. (1993) "Framing: Toward clarification of a fractured paradigm" Journal of Communication 43 (4), pp. 51–58.

Ericson, R., Baranek, P., Chan, J. (1991). *Representing order : crime, law, and justice in the news media.* Toronto: University of Toronto Press.

Farré, M. (2004). *El noticiero como mundo posible.* Buenos Aires, Argentina: La Crujía Ediciones.

Fernández Pedemonte, D. (2001). *La violencia del relato. Discurso periodístico y casos policiales.* Buenos Aires: La Crujía.

Focás, B. & Galar, S. (2016). Inseguridad y medios de comunicación: Prácticas periodísticas y conformación de públicos para el delito en Argentina (2010–2015). *Delito y sociedad,* 25(41), 59–76.

Focás, B. & Zunino, E. (2019). "Revisitando la agenda de la seguridad en los medios: un análisis exploratorio de los contenidos de las noticias policiales y de inseguridad durante el gobierno de Cambiemos (2015–2019)". *Cuestiones Criminales,* 2 (4), 2019, 78–104.

Ford, A. (1994). *Navegaciones. Comunicación, cultura y crisis.* Buenos Aires: Amorrortu.

García Beaudoux, V. & D'Adamo, O. (2007) Medios de comunicación de masas y percepción social de la inseguridad. *Boletín de Psicolocíga,* 90, 19–32.

Gates, K. (2013). "The cultural labor of surveillance: video forensics, computational objectivity, and the production of visual evidence". *Social Semiotics, 23*(2), 242–261.

Gayol, S. & Kessler, G. (2002) *Violencias, delitos y justicias en la Argentina.* Buenos Aires: Manantial.

Gros, F. (2010). "La cuarta edad de la seguridad". En Lemm, V. (Ed.) *Michael Foucault: neoliberalismo y biopolítica* (pp. 275–292). Santiago: Ediciones Universidad Diego Portales.

Hall, S., Roberts, B., Clarke, J., Jefferson, T., Critcher, C. (1978). *Policing the crisis: Mugging, the State and Law and Order.* Reino Unido: McMillan.

Howitt, D. (1998). *Crime, the media and the law.* New York: Wiley.

Juntunen, L. (2010). "Explaining the need for speed. Speed and competition as challenges to journalism ethics". In S. Cushion & J. Lewis (Eds.), *The rise of 24-hour news Televisión* (pp. 167–182). Oxford, Inglaterra: Peter Lang Inc.

Kessler, G. (2009). *El sentimiento de inseguridad. Sociología del temor al delito.* Buenos Aires: Siglo XXI Editores.

Lara Klahr, M. & Portillo Vargas, J. (2004). *Violencia y medios. Seguridad pública, noticias y construcción del miedo.* México D.F.: Instituto para la Seguridad y la Democracia.

Lorenc Valcarce, F. (2005). El trabajo periodístico y los modos de producción de la noticia: el tratamiento de la inseguridad en la prensa argentina. *Question*, 27, 1–22.

Luchessi, L. & Martini, S (2004) *Los que hacen la noticia. Periodismo, información y poder*. Buenos Aires: Biblos.

Mastrini, G. (2005) *Mucho ruido y pocas leyes: Economía y políticas de la comunicación en la Argentina 1920–2004*. Buenos Aires: La Crujía.

Martín Barbero, J. (1987) *De los medios a las mediaciones*. Barcelona: Gilli.

Martini, S. & Pereira, M. (2009) *La irrupción del delito en la vida cotidiana. Relatos de la comunicación política*. Buenos Aires: Biblos.

Newman, N., Levy, D. & Nielsen, R. K. (2016) *Digital News Report 2015. Tracking the future of news*. Oxford: Reuters Institute for the study of journalism.

Nielsen, R. K. & Sambrook, R. (2016) *What is happenning to television news*. Oxford: Reuters Institute for the study of journalism.

Paz Pellat, M. (2009) *Política 2.0, La reinvención ciudadana de la política*. México: Infotec-Conacyt.

Puente, S. (1997). *Televisión, el drama hecho noticia*. Santiago de Chile: Universidad.

Ragagnin, F.I. (2005). "El relato de las noticias sobre el delito de cuello blanco. La criminalidad de etiqueta". Revista *Palabra Clave de la Universidad de La Sabana*, 13, 46–61.

Ríos, A. (2014). "Estudiar lo policial. Consideraciones acerca del estudio de las fuerzas de seguridad y una apuesta", *Sociológica*; 87–118.

Retegui, L. Carboni, O., Koziner, N. y Aruguete, N. (2019). "Fuentes periodísticas, standing y rutinas de trabajo en las noticias del delito, inseguridad y violencia en los noticieros de AMBA". *Cuestiones Criminales*, 2 (4), 2019, 236–265.

Rey, G. & Rincón, O. (2007). *Más allá de víctimas y culpables. Relatos de experiencias en seguridad ciudadana y comunicación*. Bogotá: FES.

Rodriguez Alzueta, E. (2019). *Vecinocracia. Olfato social y linchamientos*. Buenos Aires: EME.

Rodrigo Alsina, M. (2005). *La construcción de la noticia*. Barcelona: Paidós.

Saítta, S. (1998). *Regueros de Tinta. El diario Crítica en la década de 1920*. Buenos Aires: Sudamericana.

Sánchez, M. (2014). Vivir en la inseguridad: Relatos sobre el delito y el control. *La trama de la comunicación*, 18 (1), 135–149.

Segovia Ojeda, L. (2013). "Tratamiento mediático de los delitos de cuello blanco o del poder". Revista *Chasqui* de la Editorial Ciespal, 122, 31–38.

Silvera, L. & Natalevich, M. (2012). La crónica policial en los informativos de televisión. *Revista Dixit*, 16, 4–12.

Sirimarco, M. (2017). "El "vigilante de la esquina". El rol de la nostalgia en la construcción de relatos policiales argentinos". *Antropología Portuguesa*, 34, 29–49.

Sunkel, G. (1985). *Razón y pasión en la prensa popular. Un estudio sobre cultura popular, cultura de masas y cultura política*. Santiago de Chile: ILET.

Sutherland, E.H. (1999). *El delito de cuello blanco.* Madrid: La Piqueta.

Thompson, J. (1998). *Los media y la modernidad.* Gedisa: arcelona.

Tufró, M. (2017). "Comunidades del miedo. Algunas observaciones sobre la construcción de los vecinos en la tematización de la "inseguridad" en Clarín". In S. Martini, & M. Pereyra (Comps.) *La noticia hoy. Tensiones entre la política, el mercado y la tecnología* (pp. 129–142.). Buenos Aires: Imago Mundi.

Verón, E. (1985) "El análisis del contrato de lectura, un nuevo método para los estudios de posicionamiento de los soportes de los media" en Les medias: experiences, recherches actuelles, aplications. Paris: IREP.

Vilker, S. (2008) *Truculencias. La prensa policial entre el terrorismo de estado y la inseguridad.* Buenos Aires: Prometeo.

CHAPTER 3

'Sex, Drugs and Communism'

Far-Right Narratives about Universities in Brazil

Gabriela Villen, Graziela Ares, Leda Maria Caira Gitahy, and Leandro R. Tessler

1 'Sex, Drugs and Communism'

The inauguration of the far-right former artillery captain Jair Bolsonaro as president of Brazil in January 2019, marked the consolidation of the strategy of dismantling[1] critical areas of public sectors (Mello et al. 2019; Ventura, Aith, and Reis 2021). Since entering office, Bolsonaro has undermined agencies and programs and freed the way for deregulation and intervention in essential areas such as environment, health, and education. Science-related[2] institutions are among those most affected.

This institutional destruction has been made possible by interconnecting acts and legal systems with widespread propaganda (Gitahy, Villen, and Ares 2020, 11). In accordance with the political agenda, the strategy relies on a 'disinformation ecosystem'[3] that exploits information disorder (Wardle and Derakhshan 2017, 20–41) which in turn actively strengthens this disorder.

The attacks against public education institutions, which is the focus of our research, began long before[4] the 2018 federal elections (Santos Junior 2016, 76, 115), but gained force[5] during this period (Amaral 2015; Cardoso 2020; Viana 2015). Throughout the campaign, Bolsonaro accused the former Workers' Party ('Partido dos Trabalhadores' – PT) administrations of imposing 'gender ideology'[6] in the public educational system and supporting homosexuality and

---

1 https://blogs.lse.ac.uk/internationaldevelopment/2019/07/02/bolsonaros-dismantling-in-brazil-a-threat-for-both-the-environment-and-the-economy/.

2 https://aterraeredonda.com.br/a-guerra-contra-a-ciencia/.

3 https://www.unicamp.br/unicamp/noticias/2020/08/20/o-ecossistema-da-desinformacao.

4 http://bibliotecadigital.tse.jus.br/xmlui/bitstream/handle/bdtse/4068/2016_santosjunior_vai_cuba_rede.pdf?sequence=1.

5 https://nacla.org/news/2018/11/06/specter-dictatorship-brazil.

6 'Gender ideology' is how conservative-religious groups accuse LGBTQIA+ activism of encouraging children to explore early sexualization and homosexuality. Bolsonaro has claimed to cherish conservative values and his campaign has widely appealed to polarize

immorality to impair the 'traditional family' and its values.[7] He has implicated his opponent, the former Minister of Education and PT candidate Fernando Haddad, in the distribution of a 'gay kit'[8] and baby bottles with penis shaped nipples[9] to public schools and nurseries during his tenure. Despite being proven false,[10] this disinformation was widely circulated throughout the campaign[11] and Haddad was associated with the sexualization of children, 'anti-heterosexuality' and 'anti-traditional-family values'.

Public higher education institutes and universities were also blamed for communist indoctrination and moral transgression. Bolsonaro's declarations[12] and 'mis-and dis-information' about education and public universities swamped social media with the help of engaged digital influencers.[13] At the same time, two other attacks gained momentum: 'Escola sem Partido'[14] ('School without party'), accusing teachers of the indoctrination of children from elementary school, and "Antes e depois da Federal"[15] ('Before and after public university'), which claimed that public universities turned students into leftists, gays, drug-addicts and perverts. These efforts aimed to mobilize fears and anxieties among traditional Christian families, creating an 'alterity' similar

the public debate on these matters (https://www.aljazeera.com/opinions/2018/10/31/bolsonaro-gender-ideology-and-hegemonic-masculinity-in-brazil).

7 https://www1.folha.uol.com.br/educacao/2018/10/motores-de-bolsonaro-escola-sem-partido-e-ideologia-de-genero-tem-raizes-religiosas.shtml.

8 'Gay kit' is the pejorative name used by conservatives to refer to a federal program in 2004 called "Brasil without homophobia" (https://novaescola.org.br/conteudo/84/conheca-o-kit-gay-vetado-pelo-governo-federal-em-2011) to promote LGBTQIA+ rights and tackle the violence and prejudice against these people. Directed at educators, the program included materials (https://nova-escola-producao.s3.amazonaws.com/bGjtqbyAxV88KSj5FGExAhHNjzPvYs2V8ZuQd3TMGj2hHeySJ6cuAr5ggvfw/escola-sem-homofobia-mec.pdf) to discuss the subject in the classroom. As a result of the criticism, the campaign and distribution of the material was suspended. In a television interview, during the campaign, Bolsonaro showed the Brazilian version of the French sexual education book for children "Le guide du zizi sexuel" and said that the book was part of the 'gay kit' distributed by Haddad to children at public schools.

9 https://slate.com/technology/2018/10/brazil-election-fake-news-whatsapp-facebook.html.

10 https://novaescola.org.br/conteudo/84/conheca-o-kit-gay-vetado-pelo-governo-federal-em-2011.

11 https://www.theguardian.com/world/2018/oct/18/brazil-jair-bolsonaro-whatsapp-fake-news-campaign.

12 https://www.universityworldnews.com/post.php?story=20181102101957300.

13 https://theintercept.com/2019/08/28/ranking-youtube-extrema-direita/.

14 dapp.fgv.br/en/polarized-debate-project-school-without-party-provokes-dispute-narratives-network-ideal-model-education/

15 https://www.facebook.com/Antes-e-Depois-Da-Federal-612362175631647/.

to the 'Cold War strategies' used by the Brazilian military dictatorship in the past (Brito 2020, 869, 879, 881; Cowan 2016).

Bolsonaro's election victory expanded and escalated this narrative, to the extent that it was fully integrated into official statements of the government and materialized in administrative and legal instruments. Our research investigated the interrelationship between the 'mis-and dis-information' narrative and the effective changes in educational public policies and programs. We examine how the Bolsonaro administration jeopardized social rights (Rampin 2020, 11) in public higher education during the first seven months of his tenure. The study covers the period since Bolsonaro's inauguration, in January, until the launch of a federal program for higher education, called 'Future-se',[16] in July 2019. Our research has monitored administrative acts, legal standards, and federal government statements and their synchronization with the spread of the narrative on social media. The aim was to understand how the 'mis-and dis-information' have circulated, impacted, and contributed to the government's higher education agenda.

The data collected were categorized into three groups, according to their sources, level of formality and legal enforcement.

The first group includes official statements from federal government representatives to the press or to the media, including social media. The Twitter accounts of the Ministers of Education Ricardo Vélez (January-April) and his successor Abraham Weintraub (April-July) and President Jair Bolsonaro (January-July) were monitored daily. Despite portraying the opinion of high-profile government officials, these statements have no legal value according to Brazilian law but are relevant for boosting debates and influencing public opinion. During their sequential tenures as Ministers of Education and until the launch of the 'Future-se' program in July, all 92 Twitter posts from Vélez and the 120 from Weintraub were selected, described, and analyzed individually. The sample included all 33 videos shared by the Ministers of Education that were transcribed, described, and analyzed. Among the posts examined, 30 items selected from Bolsonaro's Twitter account mentioned the words

16 "Future-se" ('be your future' in free translation) was created by the MEC to remodel the funding of public higher education by increasing the private contribution. The aim of the program was to increase the financial autonomy of universities and institutes by encouraging them to pursue sources other than public funds, such as via fundraising, sponsorship and entrepreneurship (http://portal.mec.gov.br/ultimas-noticias/212-educacao-superior-1690610854/78211-mec-lanca-programa-para-aumentar-a-autonomia-financeira-de-universidades-e-institutos).

<educação>, <ensino>, <universidade>, <MEC>[17] or the name of the Minister of Education in charge. Whenever further investigation into certain aspects was necessary, additional searches in the news were carried out using words such as <balburdia>, <contingenciamento>, and <Future-se>.[18] The institutional Twitter channels of the Ministry of Education, CAPES and CNPq were also monitored. Searches were also carried out in the news for any content or statements from authorities related to our research interests. The latter was grouped by subject, observing the repetition/replication of the content by news agencies.[19]

The second analysis group is social media dissemination. Its content consists mainly of narratives digitally spread by government supporters during the period in question. Searches on Facebook, Youtube, and Instagram used the same keywords. Using the first author's profile, 14 influencers were selected for sampling from YouTube's algorithm recommendations (see Table 3.1). The aim was to determine the identity of these far-right influencers, and how they use their channels and popularity to support the government agenda.

The third group consists of administrative acts and legal standards concerning education published in the government's official channels. In Brazil, any administrative or legal act is effective only after it is published in the Official Journal.[20] The data collected and analyzed in the two previous groups motivated further searches in the Official Journal, on official websites and in Federal Government documents. The inquiry analyzed a total of 107 documents in this data set.

---

17 Portuguese words for education, teaching and universities and the abbreviation for Ministry of Education (MEC), respectively.

18 Portuguese words for shambles (depreciatively used by Weintraub in one of his statements about public universities), contingency and the name of the financing program, respectively.

19 In journalism, one press release or one piece of news (n) may be partially or wholly published in several media (multiples of n). During the data collection phase, we needed to exclude repetitions or reverberations to tentatively isolate the root cause (n).

20 In our sample, nine measures announced in the news by government representatives (first group) could not be found in the Official Journal (third group). This could be a flaw in our research method, a breach of the Brazilian transparency legal requirements, or as a result of website changes (from "http://portal.mec.gov.br " to "https://www.gov.br/mec/pt-br ") implemented over the entire government.

2 Disinformation Ecosystem

The data analysis enabled the classification of the material into seven categories of 'mis-and dis-information' about higher education and public universities:

1. Productivism: return of social investment; mismanagement and corruption in public administration; higher cost-benefit ratio of fundamental and technical education; knowledge to generate income; training and preparation for the labor market;
2. Political-ideological: communist indoctrination; left-wing political parties' control and manipulation; anti-government; communists and rioters among human sciences students and professors; manipulative media;
3. Moral-religious: drugs; orgies and transgressive sex; family destruction; 'gender ideology'; paganism; corruption;
4. Individual liberties and privatism: defense of class-and merit-related privileges, loans and education vouchers; recording and denouncing teachers; financial autonomy of institutions;
5. Meritocracy and individual effort: enraged middle class over affirmative policies and welfare state to benefit minority groups;
6. Law enforcement and violence: the criminalization of drugs; anti-government demonstrations; communist coup; weapons;
7. Nationalism and patriotism.

Considered individually or jointly, the categories frame a narrative that public universities are dangerous places. The consumption and production of drugs and the indoctrination of 'useful innocents' (students) by communist professors aim to destroy the traditional-conservative family and their Christian values. Public universities are said to be a waste of taxpayers' money since society profits too little from their useless academic production and professionals who do not meet labor market demands. The students were portrayed as spoiled middle-class bums.

Simultaneously, authorities and their disinformation ecosystem work to disseminate carefully elaborated messages through official channels or their private social media accounts. Micro-targeted audiences[21] are chosen for their values and beliefs which make them easily influenced by the messages (Evangelista and Bruno 2019, 16–18). This behavior can be compared to seeding fertile soil since these groups legitimize and endorse the narrative and quickly share it throughout social media.

---

21 https://policyreview.info/articles/analysis/whatsapp-and-political-instability-brazil-targeted-messages-and-political.

A unique vocabulary[22] is created as long as one version of the facts is reproduced over and over by a group of profiles and becomes viral on social media. Whenever this version reaches the masses, it is almost impossible for a counterargument from opponents to obtain any impact (Malini 2020). In our research, we have observed a 'vocabulary universe' which includes the Portuguese equivalent for cultural Marxism, communism, gender ideology, manipulative media, shambles, taxpayer, labor market, indoctrination, and investment payback.

Going beyond government representatives, the narrative has spread to social media influencers[23] and anonymous bots[24] on WhatsApp. The online discourse is enhanced by images that depict academic members enjoying a lazy life at the taxpayers' expense, as a communist threat to Bolsonaro's government and its "God, motherland, and family" values.

April and May were critical months, due to unprecedented popular demonstrations[25] against government measures on education policies which created massive online traffic on social media. Many videos from that period and channels of government supporters were banned or deleted from YouTube for not complying with the platform's rules.

Table 3.1 describes the 14 influencers analyzed by our research and their main arguments.

Images, messages and videos carrying the same narrative simultaneously take over the capillarity of WhatsApp, the most popular social network in Brazil.[26] According to a WhatsApp monitoring[27] service, the most shared content on WhatsApp on May 8, showed naked students, thesis and dissertations with derogatory and offensive names and ironic drawings mocking humanities students. This was another of Bolsonaro's cyber militia attacks. Many groups associated with Bolsonaro, which seemed dormant after the elections, resurrected spreading messages with a force comparable to the year before, "when they operated at maximum capacity and with strong signs of massive triggered messaging".[28]

---

22 https://fabiomalini.medium.com/quando-tudo-parecia-ser-t%C3%A3o-distante-daqui-a-eclos%C3%A3o-das-narrativas-sobre-covid-19-23ef531b1be1.

23 https://saidapeladireita.blogfolha.uol.com.br/2019/04/03/quem-sao-os-10-maiores-influenciadores-de-direita-do-brasil/.

24 https://theintercept.com/2019/05/14/milicia-digital-bolsonarista-contra-universidades/.

25 https://www.theguardian.com/world/2019/may/31/students-protest-across-brazil-over-jair-bolsonaros-sweeping-cuts-to-education.

26 https://www.statista.com/statistics/798131/brazil-use-mobile-messaging-apps/.

27 https://theintercept.com/2019/05/14/milicia-digital-bolsonarista-contra-universidades/.

28 https://theintercept.com/2019/05/14/milicia-digital-bolsonarista-contra-universidades/.

TABLE 3.1 Social media dissemination: the sample of digital influencers

Influencer	Number of subscribers or followers	Short description	Highlights
Brasil Paralelo	Youtube: 1.86 Twitter: 0.27 Instagram: 0.97 (millions on 07/25/2021)	Video producer who aims to defeat leftist ideas in the cultural and educational battlegrounds.	Produced the movie "1964: Brazil between weapons and books", which is an alternative narrative for the Brazilian military dictatorship. The army saved Brazil from an imminent communist coup, but the culture was vulnerable and communism took it over.
LUIZ CAMARGO vlog	Youtube: 0.45 Twitter: 0.12 Instagram: 0.04 Facebook: 0.06 (millions on 07/25/2021)	He describes himself as a Christian-conservative dissatisfied person who talks about spirituality, politics, philosophy and others.	Humanities are occupied by leftists, and students are indoctrinated. . Inefficient management of universities and use of funds for propaganda. . Defends the focus on primary education and universities only for the 'intellectual elite'. . Higher education delays entry into the labor market and it is a "factory of imbeciles".

TABLE 3.1 Social media dissemination: the sample of digital influencers (*cont.*)

Influencer	Number of subscribers or followers	Short description	Highlights
Te atualizei @taoquei	Youtube: 1.26 Twitter: 0.55 Instagram: 0.50 (millions on 07/25/2021)	She describes herself as a mother, wife, sister commenting on politics. She mentions 'God, motherland and family' in her profile.	In April and May, she posted 03 videos accusing the universities of using public funds for mass maneuvers and demonstrations. She defends the use of funds in elementary education instead.
Carla Zambelli	Twitter: 1.20 Facebook: 2.60 Instagram: 2.00 Youtube: 0.53 (millions on 07/25/2021)	Congresswoman of 'PSL' (former Bolsonaro party) and top right-wing digital influencer	Protesting students confessed to ignoring motives for the demonstrations
Marreta Urgente	Youtube: 0.003 Twitter: nearly 0 Facebook: 0.05 Instagram: 0.003 (millions on 07/25/2021)	News website that is self-described as unbiased.	Published a typical Whatsapp fast sharing video where an anonymous person furiously denounces drugs, promiscuity, and indoctrination in federal universities. He says that none would like his kids at the federal university because professors turn them into drug users indoctrinated.

TABLE 3.1 Social media dissemination: the sample of digital influencers (*cont.*)

Influencer	Number of subscribers or followers	Short description	Highlights
Gabriel Monteiro	Youtube: 4.66 Facebook: 5.00 Instagram: 3.20 Twitter: 0.35 (millions on 07/25/2021)	A city councilman, military policeman, and member of 'Movimento Brasil Livre' ('Free Brazil Movement')	In May, he published a video of the demonstrations that starts with a picture of a bus on fire and a gun, followed by misinformed and manipulated protesters … He relates students' behavior to drug abuse, vandalism, loitering, banditry, and promiscuity. . Research in public universities is useless and poor.
Pau de Arara Opressor (no longer available)	Not available.	The name of this channel was a reference to a tool to torture people during authoritarian regimes in Brazil.	The 30% cut in universities' budgets was fake news. . In a video, speaking to the audience, a man states he is a professor at a Federal University who loves his institution and respects his work, but he is also a Brazilian who supports the contingency plan, social security reform, the anti-corruption package of Bolsonaro, and praises God.

TABLE 3.1 Social media dissemination: the sample of digital influencers (*cont.*)

Influencer	Number of subscribers or followers	Short description	Highlights
Gustavo Maultasch @Livres @eusoulivres	Youtube: 0.01 Twitter: 0.01 Facebook: 0.002 Instagram: 0.04 (millions on 07/25/2021)	Brazilian diplomat serving at the Brazilian consulate in Washington (United States)	Privatization is the way to resolve the administrative inefficiencies, useless academic production, and reprehensible behavior for higher education.
Arthur Moledo do Val @mamaefalei @arthurdoval	Youtube: 2.80 Twitter: 0.57 Instagram: 0.73 Facebook: 1.69 (millions on 07/25/2021)	State congressman in São Paulo of 'DEM' (Democrats political party) and member of 'Movimento Brasil Livre' ('Free Brazil Movement')	Public higher education favors wealthy students and promiscuous playboys. . Defends the funds to primary education. . Brazilian model does not allow private investment in the university, research is useless.
Italo Goulart	Youtube: 0.18 Twitter: 0.01 Facebook: 0.01 Instagram: 0.001 (millions on 07/25/2021)	Bolsonarista blogger about politics, religion, and sports. He says his reflections are interest-free, they are only for hobby and love for the truth.	"Indoctrination in Universities – Graduation, in the face!"(no longer available). . Quotes of Olavo de Carvalho and School Without Party. . Accuses Lula of being the leader of the largest criminal organization in history and shows a rector praising the former President in a celebration.

TABLE 3.1 Social media dissemination: the sample of digital influencers (*cont.*)

Influencer	Number of subscribers or followers	Short description	Highlights
Ana Campagnolo	Youtube: 0.32 Twitter: 0.004 Facebook: 0.28 Instagram: 0.72 (millions on 07/25/2021)	PSL state deputy in Santa Catarina. An avatar holds a gun in her profile picture on Twitter. Historian and teacher, she is the author of the book "Feminismo: perversão e subversão"('Feminism:Perversion and Subversion')	In one video she distinguishes budget cuts and contingency. . Defends the focus on primary education. . Blames the media and Bolsonaros' enemies for misinforming the population and obstructing the reforms that the country needs.
Bernardo P Küster	Youtube: 0.92 Twitter: 0.11 Instagram: 0.36 Facebook: 0.05 GAB: 0.02 (millions on 07/25/2021)	Officer of 'Brasil Sem Medo' ('Brazil without fear'), that it is self-proclaimed the most conservative news portal in the world. Essayist, translator, and journalist.	He defends the use of data and ranks to depict low productivity and useless academic research in public universities.

TABLE 3.1 Social media dissemination: the sample of digital influencers (*cont.*)

Influencer	Number of subscribers or followers	Short description	Highlights
Paula Marisa	Youtube: 0.64 Twitter: 0.33 Instagram: 0.16 Facebook: 0.33 (millions on 07/25/2021)	Her channel is a space to express her political incorrectness and she is an education expert, speaker, political commentator, anti-feminist, pro-guns, and conservative	Criticizes the cultural Marxism and indoctrination in universities with examples of courses and thesis. The solution is not public education.
Ideias Radicais (by Raphaël Lima)	Youtube: 0.65 Twitter: 0.09 Instagram: 0.06 (millions on 07/25/2021)	He defines himself as a libertarian, activist, and entrepreneur. He is the founder of Radical Ideas, a group to promote libertarianism in Brazil. He defends the minimum state.	There is a video that criticizes universal education. It claims that internships and homeschooling are more efficient, better connected to society, and less ideologically harmful.

SOURCE: ELABORATED BY THE AUTHORS BASED ON THE RESULTS OF THIS RESEARCH

3 Higher Education under Siege

The third data set, "administrative acts and legal standards", was divided into eight subject categories, as follows:

1. Budget and finance;
2. Dismissals and appointments;[29]
3. Opening/shutting down higher education programs;
4. Moral, ideological, anti-communist or religious;
5. Organizational efficiency;
6. Standards, structure, organization (competitions, selection processes, dismissals);
7. Private fundraising; and
8. Investigations into administrative irregularities.

Since Jair Bolsonaro's inauguration, Brazilian public universities were subject to a 'clean up' to 'end indoctrination' and to 'optimize taxpayers' money', according to Bolsonaro[30] and his ministers.[31] Budget instability[32] meant that the management of public universities and research institutions was not only unstable but barely sustainable after the budget cuts and constraints.[33] The direct intervention in the appointment of rectors, directors, and other professionals, despite local demands, had various consequences. One example is the fate of the National Institute of Educational Studies and Research.[34] Between January and July 2019, when the scope of this paper ends, four different

29 Rectors (or presidents) of federal universities are appointed by the Minister of Education from a list of three candidates (and one for federal institutes) suggested by the institutional representative body after voting by the academic community. Traditionally, the top-listed candidate is nominated; the Bolsonaro administration however has appointed allies or supporters who did not necessarily receive the most votes or even on the list.

30 https://gauchazh.clicrbs.com.br/politica/noticia/2018/12/na-vespera-da-posse-bolsonaro-critica-lixo-marxista-em-instituicoes-de-ensino-no-pais-cjqcbvtu200k301piy1zzwszl.html.

31 https://cjt.ufmg.br/en/2019/05/10/dismantling-of-education-the-anti-intellectualist-policy-under-the-bolsonaro-government/.

32 https://www.brasildefato.com.br/2019/05/14/confusao-em-dados-sobre-corte-nas-universidades-federais-e-proposital-diz-professor/.

33 https://www.brasildefato.com.br/2019/05/14/confusao-em-dados-sobre-corte-nas-universidades-federais-e-proposital-diz-professor/.

34 The Instituto Nacional de Estudos e Pesquisas Educacionais Anísio Teixeira – INEP (http://inep.gov.br/web/guest/about-inep) is responsible for the information, statistics, and systematic assessment of the Brazilian educational system.

people served as directors,[35] causing institutional instability and flaws[36] in the National Secondary Education Examination (ENEM) that year. Questions were leaked to social media during the exam and, later, a mis-correction affected the score of 3.9 million students, harming the reputation of the process. The attacks directed to groups such as civil servants, researchers and students gained the dimension of 'institutional harassment' (Mello et al. 2019). This has caused widespread distress and disturbed the operation of many sectors. Society's response to the repeated education budget cuts by the Ministry was seen in the form of public demonstrations all over the country. Protesters took to the streets[37] to denounce the general situation including that of public universities. Meanwhile, right-wing activists have reacted by 'reporting' online fake videos and images depicting protesters as violent, degenerated communist rioters. In opposition, the government supporters were shown as civilized, family-oriented, and patriotic.

Figure 3.1 presents the chronology of the statements and acts of the Federal government. It does not intend to exhaust the facts related to the period but rather give the reader a glimpse of how the agenda is driven and supported by 'mis-and disinformation'. The timeline shows how the narrative and actions take place simultaneously, in support of each other.

Since the period depicted in Figures 3.1 and 3.2, the narrative has been reinforced and the institutional dismantling has continued. Updated data on the subject confirms the budget cuts on public education and ideology-driven replacements of positions of trust in the civil service (Gussen 2021, 24–28). Since 2015, the Ministry of Education disbursement has decreased by 13.2 billion Brazilian Reais (BRL) and discretionary investments have been reduced by BRL 3.9 billion (54%), as indicated in Figures 3.3 and 3.4.

The distribution of posts in the Ministry among members of religious and military groups and followers of Olavo de Carvalho[38] has turned the office into an "ideological parish" (Gussen 2021, 25). Milton Ribeiro, the Minister of Education since July 2020, is a Presbyterian pastor committed to a conservative

35 https://g1.globo.com/educacao/noticia/2021/04/09/inep-servidores-divulgam-carta-em-que-pedem-protecao-de-tensoes-politicas-e-fim-de-trocas-sucessivas-de-comando.ghtml.

36 https://www.bbc.com/portuguese/brasil-51334141.

37 https://www.unicamp.br/unicamp/noticias/2019/05/17/comunidade-da-unicamp-protesta-contra-cortes-na-educacao-e-expoe-ciencia-na-rua.

38 Right-wing Brazilian writer and guru based in the United States since 2005. He calls himself a philosopher despite having no formal education in the field and not being recognized by his peers as so (https://brazilian.report/society/2018/10/23/guru-brazil-right-wing-olavo-de-carvalho/).

Month	Narrative	Action
JANUARY	War on Marxism.	Ricardo Vélez is appointed Minister of Education. His office includes defenders of 'family, church and traditional values' and homeschooling. The appointment of the Director of the National Institute of Deaf Education disregards the internal election process.
FEBRUARY	Moral and civic education and 'School Without Party'.	Schools are required to teach patriotism, praise government and national symbols under the monitoring of the Minister of Education. Monthly budget is reduced by 2.78% to comply with public expenditure targets.
MARCH	Budgetary optimization, improvement of performance and 'ideological cleansing' of public administration.	Decree cuts the Ministry of Education budget by 3.9% (BRL 5.8 billion) in 2019. Decree changes the rules to recruit civil servants and increases the outsourced positions in public administration. New rules encourage new 'Stricto sensu' professional graduation courses. The second most powerful position in the Ministry of Education is filled by a member of the military. No official records regarding dismissals and announcements made by the Minister on his Twitter account.
APRIL	No funds for 'useless' academic production and 'shambles' in campuses. Investment in elementary schooling is more effective than in higher education, hard sciences are more useful than humanities, and focus on "areas that generate an immediate return to the taxpayer". Students must denounce teachers for indoctrination. 'Cultural Marxism' should be banned from universities.	Neo-liberal and 'anti-globalist' Abraham Weintraub is appointed Minister of Education. Ministry announces 30% cuts in discretionary expenses of federal universities and institutes Bills to cancel the nomination of Paulo Freire as patron of Brazilian education and to regulate homeschooling in Brazil are proposed. Nominations of rectors of federal universities and institutes voted in by community elections are ignored or postponed.

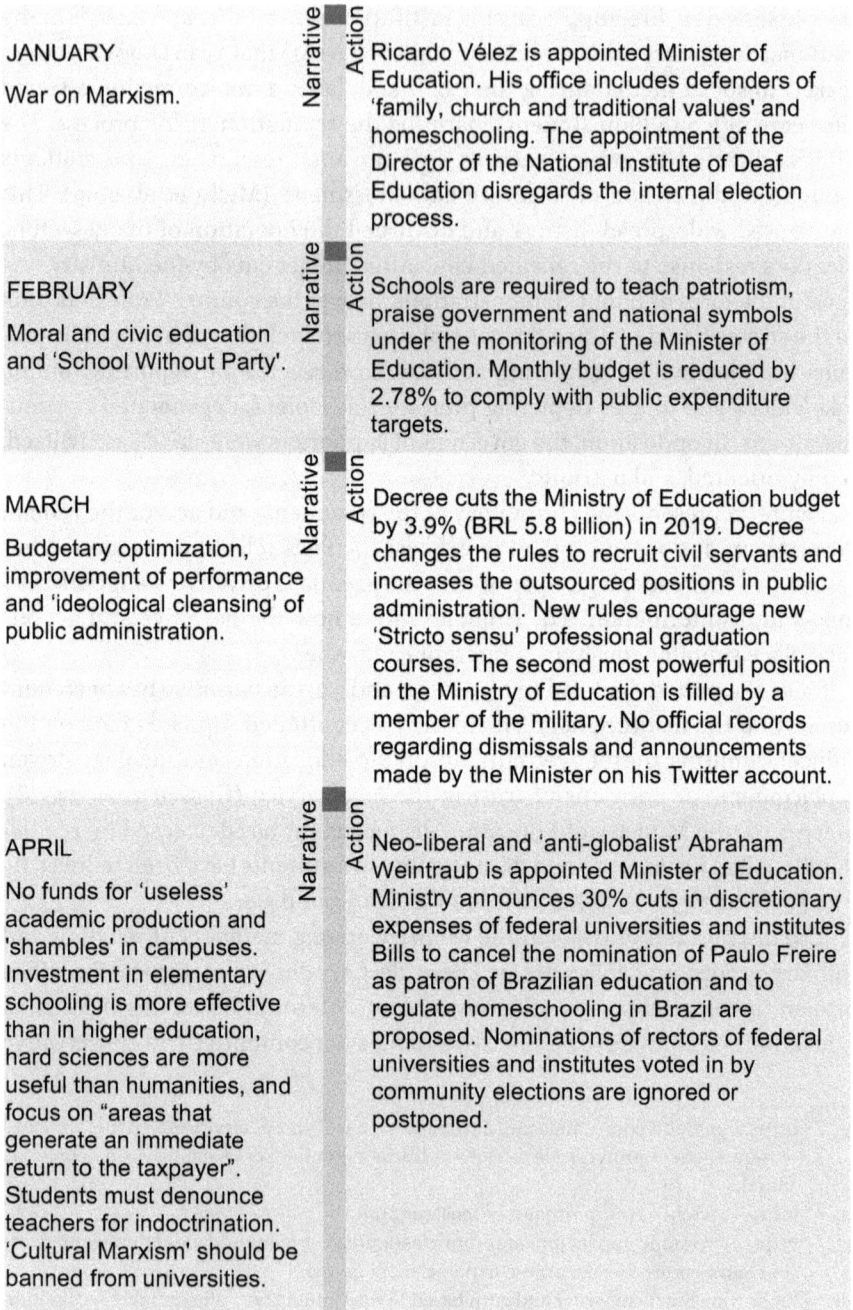

FIGURE 3.1 Timeline between January and April of 2019

Narrative	Action
MAY Protesters are 'useful imbeciles'. No budgetary cut of 30%, as announced by the media, but an 'unavoidable' budget restriction of 3.4%. Rectors are intolerant leftists. Universities are encouraged to seek financial autonomy via sponsorships and partnerships with companies and investors to complement their funding.	The entire education budget is affected by cuts. Suspension of 4798 graduate student scholarships. BRL 1.6 billion cut in education, announced on May 2 is revoked on May 22, after demonstrations. Phoneline set up to urge complaints to be made against members of public institutions accused of encouraging demonstrations. Another 11 nominations of heads of federal institutes and universities disregard the community vote. Decree allows the federal government to investigate and appoint the upper management of federal universities and institutes. Flexibilization of the standards to qualify higher education institutions.
JUNE Universities waste taxpayers' money. The government must protect children and adolescents from communism.	Contingency funds are released to research institutions (BRL 330 million) and federal universities (BRL 1 billion) to prevent suspension of activities. Despite the cuts, BRL 13 million of funds are directed to a new Academic Cooperation Program of Public Security and Forensic Sciences. Scholarships cut for low performance programs. The appointment of an additional three rectors disregards the preferences of the community.
JULY The federal program 'Future-se' does not mean privatization.	Decree permits Bolsonaro to nominate interim heads of federal educational institutions. Decree rules education credit. A bill is approved to rule the dismissal of low performers in civil service. The entrance exam of the University for Afro-Brazilian Lusophony International Integration for LGBTQA+ individuals is suspended after intervention from the Ministry of Education. 'Future-se', a federal program for higher education, is launched.

FIGURE 3.2 Timeline between May and July of 2019

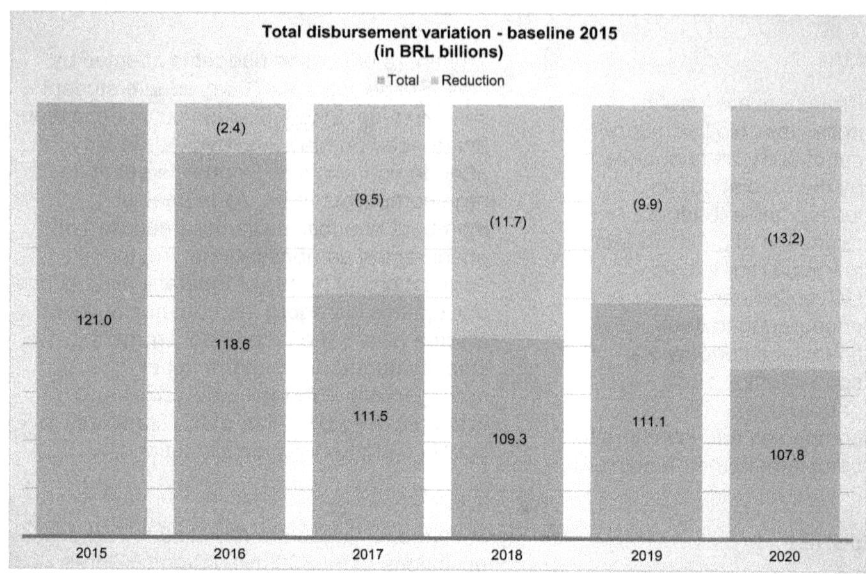

FIGURE 3.3 Total expenditure variation, baseline 2015
SOURCE: INTEGRATED SYSTEM OF FINANCIAL ADMINISTRATION OF THE FEDERAL GOVERNMENT (SISTEMA INTEGRADO DE ADMINISTRAÇÃO FINANCEIRA DO GOVERNO FEDERAL – SIAFI), CARTA CAPITAL (GUSSEN 2021, 25, 27)

and moralist agenda, and parts of the private education sector. Second and third tier positions were shared among 'School without Party' members, home-schooling supporters, and other ultra-conservative groups. The government is influenced by the concept of the minimal state personified by Paulo Guedes, the Minister of Economy, and the lobby of ultra-liberal investors that endorse the conservative agenda of the government in exchange for the mercantilization of education in Brazil (Gussen 2021, 26).

Our research reports that disinformation has been systematically and strategically used to legitimize the attacks on education and its institutions since Bolsonaro's inauguration. The budget restraints and the disarray of the Brazilian public educational system, including infrastructure and personnel, would not be possible without the threat of the Brazilian middle class's worst fear: the breakdown of its moral universe. In this sense, portraying public higher education institutions as places of sexual orgies, drug abuse, and communist indoctrination allows these attacks to take place. This is consistent with the neo-liberal expectations of the Brazilian economic elite and justifies the takeover of public higher education by the profit-driven private sector.

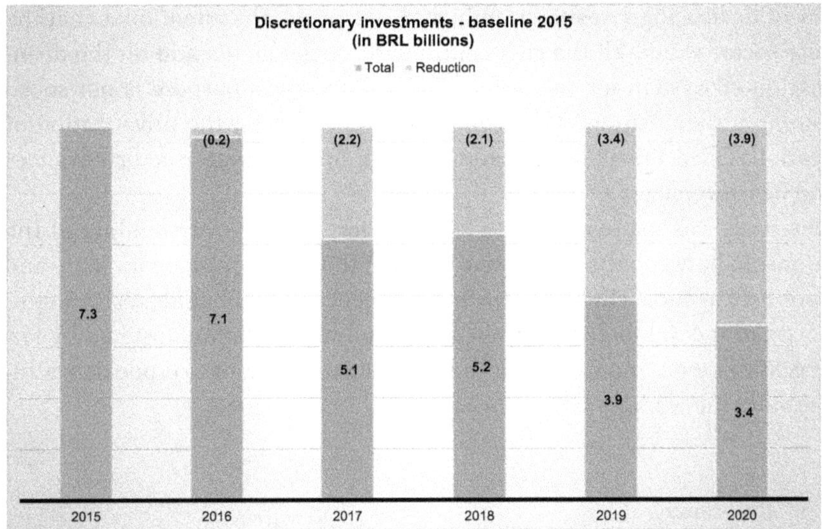

FIGURE 3.4 Discretionary investments in education in Brazil, baseline 2015
SOURCE: INTEGRATED SYSTEM OF FINANCIAL ADMINISTRATION OF FEDERAL GOVERNMENT (SISTEMA INTEGRADO DE ADMINISTRAÇÃO FINANCEIRA DO GOVERNO FEDERAL – SIAFI), EXPENSES UPDATED BY IPCA, CARTA CAPITAL (GUSSEN 2021, 25, 27)

The pandemic has worsened this situation. While classes were suspended from 2020 due to COVID-19, the government spent none of the BRL 1.2 billion budget on improving public school premises and, according to UNICEF, the delay and cuts to investments may cause setbacks and a situation comparable to 20 years earlier (Gussen 2021, 25). Many consider the situation alarming while others see it as an opportunity.

In her book "The Shock Doctrine", Naomi Klein (2008) describes how the neo-liberal approach of the 'Chicago School' has used and even created the crisis to replace the welfare state with private services since the 1970s. In the 21st century, a dictatorship or a natural catastrophe is no longer essential to create opportunities for intervention. The lack of regulation and new technologies make it possible for the masses to spread 'dis-and misinformation' and cause faster, wider, and more epidemic damage to public services. This is exactly what Bolsonaro has been doing.

Due to its high potential demand for education, Brazil is attractive to private investors. The for-profit market in the country corresponds to roughly 75% of the enrollment in higher education. However, the highest quality institutions are either public or non-profit. The Bolsonaro administration has enforced a policy of decreasing investment in higher education. His intention is that the private sector would fill the gap, counting on social media and on the disinformation ecosystem for validation. The government's purpose is not social welfare, but the creation of a favorable environment for the privatization of education. Once Brazilian education is torn apart, private sector advances would be irreversible.

Our study has made a humble contribution to the understanding of the relationship between the productive chain of the disinformation industry and the political agenda. However, much more needs to be investigated to better understand the link between propaganda and manipulation, fostered by far-right governments, and its translation into concrete actions to erode democracies around the world.

References

Amaral, Marina. 2015. "A nova roupa da direita". *Agência Pública – online*, June 23, 2015, sec. Reportagem. https://apublica.org/2015/06/a-nova-roupa-da-direita/.

Brito, Antonio Mauricio Freitas. 2020. "A subversão pelo sexo: Representações anticomunistas durante a ditadura no Brasil". *Varia Historia* 36 (October): 859–88. https://doi.org/10.1590/0104-87752020000300010.

Cardoso, Adalberto. 2020. *À beira do Abismo: uma sociologia política do bolsonarismo.* Rio de Janeiro: Amazon. https://www.researchgate.net/publication/344794093_A_beira_do_Abismo_uma_sociologia_politica_do_bolsonarismo.

Cowan, Benjamin A. 2016. *Securing Sex: Morality and Represssion in the Making of Cold War Brazil.* Chapel Hill: University of North Carolina Press. http://www.jstor.org/stable/10.5149/9781469627519_cowan.

Evangelista, Rafael, and Fernanda Bruno. 2019. "WhatsApp and Political Instability in Brazil: Targeted Messages and Political Radicalisation". *Internet Policy Review* 8 (4): 23. https://doi.org/10.14763/2019.4.1434.

Gitahy, Leda Maria Cira, Gabriela Villen, and Graziela Ares. 2020. "Science, Politics, and the Pandemic". In *Communication*, 15. Montevideo (virtual). https://www.researchgate.net/publication/345499595_Ciencia_Politica_e_a_Pandemia.

Gussen, Ana Flávia. 2021. "Na penúria e sem rumo". *Carta Capital*, July 21, 2021.

Klein, Naomi. 2008. *The Shock Doctrine.* 1st ed. United Kingdom: Penguin Books.

Malini, Fabio. 2020. "Quando tudo parecia ser tão distante daqui: a eclosão das narrativas sobre covid-19". Blog. *Medium* (blog). July 27, 2020. https://medium.com/@fabiomalini/quando-tudo-parecia-ser-t%C3%A3o-distante-daqui-a-eclos%C3%A3o-das-narrativas-sobre-covid-19-23ef531b1be1.

Mello, Lawrence Estivalet de, Josiane Caldas, José Antônio Peres Gediel, Liana Maria da Frota Carleial, and Yanick Noiseux, eds. 2019. *Políticas de austeridade e direitos sociais*. Curitiba: Kaygangue Ltda. https://www.academia.edu/40376249/Pol%C3%ADticas_de_Austeridade_e_Direitos_Sociais.

Rampin, Talita. 2020. "Desafios e perspectivas: as Ciências Sociais diante da Ascensão da extrema-direita no Brasil". In *Communication*, 15. Montevideo (virtual).

Santos Junior, Marcelo Alves dos. 2016. "Vai pra Cuba!!!! A rede antipetista na eleição de 2014". Mestrado, Niterói: Universidade Federal Fluminense. http://bibliotecadigital.tse.jus.br/xmlui/handle/bdtse/4068.

Ventura, Deisy de Freitas Lima, Fernando Mussa Abujamra Aith, and Rossana Rocha Reis. 2021. "A linha do tempo da estratégia federal de disseminação da COVID-19". Mapeamento e análise das normas jurídicas de resposta à Covid-19 no Brasil. São Paulo: CEPEDISA – Centro de Estudos e Pesquisas de Direito Sanitário. https://cepedisa.org.br/publicacoes/.

Viana, Natalia. 2015. "A direita abraça a rede". *Agência Pública – online*, June 22, 2015, sec. Reportagem. https://apublica.org/2015/06/a-direita-abraca-a-rede/.

Wardle, Claire, and Hossein Derakhshan. 2017. "Information Disorder: Toward an Interdisciplinary Framework for Research and Policymaking". Council of Europe report DGI(2017)09. Strasbourg: Council of Europe. https://rm.coe.int/information-disorder-toward-an-interdisciplinary-framework-for-researc/168076277c.

CHAPTER 4

The Business Elite and Media Worked Together?

Analyzing Both Narratives in the Brazilian 2016 Impeachment Process

Humberto Fernandes and Eduardo Barbabela

1 Introduction

In research on the political movements of the São Paulo business elite during the second term of Dilma Rousseff (2015–2016), it is common for the media to appear as a mechanism used by business groups to strengthen their specific point of view and exhaustively replicate it, influencing the opinion reflected in newspapers (Fernandes 2022).[1] The narrative embedded in the media discourse replicates the political perspective that antagonizes the left, considered political, and represented mainly by actors such as the Workers' Party and former presidents Luís Inácio Lula da Silva and Dilma Rousseff. The political left is also associated with characteristics such as corruption, immorality, and inefficiency, in opposition to a center-right position, as the business elite (banks, administrators, companies) define themselves, characterized as non-political and technical representatives, therefore considered as a new and a positive factor in renewing the Brazilian political system. The media narrative here appears as a critical point in this research, which is centered on business, making it possible to discuss the fundamental role of this same mass media and the mechanisms that built their narrative following the business elite position. We will analyze whether the media initially created such a position or channeled the business elite political discourse first, before absorbing and partaking in it.

In this sense, this work uses the *Manchetômetro* database to corroborate qualitative findings regarding discourse strategies in manipulative narratives. How do media narratives relate to business origin semantics? With the media

1 We want to express our great appreciation to Dr. Christina Constantopoulou for her invitation to participate in this publication. We would also like to thank Dr. João Feres Junior for kindly providing us with the database we worked on in this article. We are also thankful to Dr. Miguel Serna Forcheri for his supporting insights. To Prof. Joe Mitchel, M.Ed., we appreciate his high-quality proofreading services. Finally, we thank Dr. Fernanda Cavassana for her valuable and constructive suggestions for our work. Her willingness to donate her time so generously was greatly appreciated.

as a central object, how has its narrative been affected or impacted by socio-political events?

First, we must outline the main points in research findings about the media narrative discourse to explore the *Manchetômetro* database during the same research period (January 2015 to December 2016). Then, we will discuss the methodology in which two distinct methodological approaches combine to strengthen the hypothesis that the Brazilian media narrative during Dilma Rousseff's second term played a manipulative and strategic role of producing mistrust in institutions, hatred of the left, and towards anything qualified as political, in addition to making room for the rise of the extreme right. The following discussion will cover aspects between information, politics, and power, and challenges the supposed legality semantically within the impeachment process. The data analysis helps us to understand the efforts of the media and the business elite to manipulate and produce meaning for, through and along with public opinion.

2 São Paulo Business Elite's Narrative on Media

The analysis of the political discourse of the business elite in São Paulo[2] allows us to understand the practices of mobilization and articulation of this elite concerning the actors they relate with and the elements that make up their ideas and opinions. To this end, we will analyze seventy-one official notes and releases from Fiesp with direct mention of Dilma Rousseff or Michel Temer, between October 2014 and December 2016. Thirty of them belong to the political movement *Não vou pagar o pato*[3] and were published exclusively in newspapers (both in print and online), over six months, from October 2015 to March 2016. This fact demonstrates that newspaper (and media) narratives helped to channel the ideologies of the business elite and political goals of impeachment of the re-elected president. So far, there is nothing innovative about inferring that the media supports neoliberal narratives. However, the anomalies that this data presents are a result of the high rate of direct criticism of the executive

2 Following Diniz and Boschi (2003), the business-State corporate interaction remains, overcoming internal sectoral fragmentations, when convenient for the powerful representative minority, directly influencing public policies, as the authors point out and the course of Brazil's political destiny.

3 Brazilian everyday expression translated as *I will not pay for the duck*; it means *I will not be the whipping boy*, or *I will not pay for something I did not buy*, or, in the case herein, *I will not be economically responsible for the Government's financial deviances.*

in power and the disregard for other dimensions of the political-social reality. The supposedly informative narrative thus became, above all, politically ideologized.

The antagonism between the market and the political domain is apparent. Representatives of business and industrial elites place themselves outside the origins of the international crisis as if they had not been active and relevant agents for the historical and economic course of the country. Blamelessness is a crucial element in the demonization of government by other economic agents, hidden in the shadows of limited public opinion criticism.

It is not about how neoliberal the media discourse is, but how anti-political and anti-left its narrative becomes when playing a critical role in the crisis juncture at the national level. The appropriation of common-sense discourse from public opinion is grounded in the developmental rhetoric of the market, which is easily confused with social progress by statist discourse. Furthermore, this narrative is only compelling because it sustains an unequal state of political knowledge between the message sender and the mass audience.

When the political discourse of a collective is found both in official institutional notes and reproduced in newspapers and the media in general, it is possible to compare the two distinct audiences therein. It should be noted that there is a significant difference: while the official notes for members and international organizations reproduced highly technical, complex, and knowledge-based discourse, the notes reproduced in newspapers contained speeches delivered in a tone, which was easier to understand, seeking to strengthen the formation of a public opinion supporting that perspective. The narrative of the business elite displayed by newspapers during Dilma Rousseff's removal process is much more straightforward than the official launch notes for other business figures and intellectuals. Due to the speech simplicity, the anti-left and anti-political narrative of the media during the period between October 2014 and December 2016 has a more narrational character. Furthermore, precisely because of this, the narrative manages to reach the minds of ordinary citizens, whose heterogeneity and level of consciousness fits the tone of non-formal and non-complex discourse. This mechanism illustrates how Fiesp manages to influence the social representation of the politician by simplifying the political system, so multidimensional and complex, into a system of representation of a single culprit.

In addition to differing tones of speech and the dynamics of narrative, from the business elite point of view, it is evident that they started using newspapers to channel their political interests thirteen months after Dilma's re-election, and for only six months until the event had become remote by March 2016.

When Vice President Michel Temer takes over as interim,[4] the media no longer broadcasts the discourse of the São Paulo business elite, as they and Michel Temer are not only ideologically synchronized but also the Fiesp President, Paulo Skaf, and the Vice President-president are both co-affiliated within the same political party. The discursive antagonism between the retired and the new government represented a turn in the discursive-textual attributes given to the Temer government of positive meaning and effectiveness by the business elite. The public campaign "I won't pay the duck" acts as a symbolic tool for the construction of "antipetism" in public opinion, aimed at reaching an atomized and uncritical mass (Davis and Straubhaar 2020).

Although Fiesp defends the internationalization of capital, external contributions through favorable public policies, the inflexibility towards the demands of the working class, and the review and transformation of labor policies called "reforms," the general public was not a recipient of them during the Dilma Rousseff government. Instead, the reintroduction of the neoliberal agenda during Michel Temer's transitional government portrayed privatizations, open capital market policies with industry-friendly regulations consistent with increased competitiveness, and selective incentives for associative bodies which shape business action. All these points of concern were found in Fiesp's discourse at a horizontal level, into the business community, instead of also constituting the popularized textual content conveyed to the masses, through the mass media in general.

2.1 *Findings on the Business Elite's Political Discourse Strategies*

The tool of using third-party speeches and ideas to demonstrate one's own is evident in Fiesp's official discourse, with particular attention given to its function of adding social characters in its narrative, a strategy to make it appear as though more individuals share concerns, interests, and goals similar to their own. The discursive strategy of asserting oneself through the opinion of others, of personalities whose symbolic capital serves as a legitimizing instrument for mobilizing public opinion (academics, politicians, artists, activists, specialists, and professionals both national and international). An example of this strategy is in the speech of Fernando Schuler, a professor at the Insper Institute, pointing out the 'good relationship' between the executive and the legislative after Michel Temer's inauguration, spreading in a flow of public information the idea that this did not happen before, during the Dilma Rousseff government.

4 The impeachment process came to an end in August 2016, when the Senate had officially withdrawn Dilma, and Michel Temer rose from interim to President.

In recurrent passages, three objectives of discursive strategy stand out. The first is to promote the plural coexistence between social actors and different groups of power. The second being to build the social representation of an impartial, unbiased, diplomatic Fiesp, with its ideals. Thirdly, Fiesp's discourse shows that the Federation can play the democratic game through debates and divergences of opinions. However, separating the *informational content* from the three *strategic discursive objectives* aforementioned is fundamental to understanding Fiesp's political stance from its discourse. Throughout the research, contrary to the democratic and unbiased profile at the institutional (and economic) level, the *information content* included and promoted the antagonism guided by *otherness*, between 'us = good' (business, neoliberals, right-winged, traditionalists, nationalists) and 'them = bad' (politicians, progressivists, left-winged, pro-integration).

Concerning the tone of the speech and the key-analysis analyzed, the formal discrepancies within the mode of intentional enunciation between the Não vou pagar o pato group and the Fiesp-Rousseff (FR) and Fiesp-Temer (FT) groups are evident. In the first case, the speech is relatively informal, directed at 'you,' thus including the reader-agent in the speech, involving him directly in the mentioned facts. However, on the other hand, there is an eloquent formality regarding FR and FT groups with the public to which the official notes address. From this, we infer that at least two distinct discursive fields make up Fiesp's political engagement during Dilma Rousseff II: the highly experienced, professional, and technical audience for the FR and FT groups; and the uncritical and indignant reader is the most receptive to the intention of the sender of the first group message.

An important point to be highlighted in this research is the excessive simplification of the political system by taking advantage of the masses' lack of knowledge and political and social awareness. The speech defines the political as nothing more than "government," which is made up of the executive power, the presidency, and the ministerial body. It strategically distances other institutions and positions of a federal and tripartite democratic system, such as the legislative, the judiciary, and other social and political powers involved in the pluralist and complex multi-oligarchic system.

Thus, it is essential to check the symbolic construction of local semantics shared by public opinion through the available sociopolitical resources (actors, media, cultural capital, rubber ducks, public manifesto, agency, economic capital). In a way, Fiesp could fulfill its political objective of reducing the tax burden, ousting the president (not the government alliance that retained Fiesp ally Michel Temer), and preventing the reinstatement of the CPMF.

Communicative articulation is understood as a secondary post-mobilization moment. The symbolic elements already mobilized between different social actors ensure the integrated nature of the articulation itself. It appears in different ways such as coexistence, the strengthening of articulated results, the continuation of discussions, closing negotiations and agreements, which internally unite the collective actor, or externally with other collective actors, in processes of assimilation of its participants, not just at the subjective level, but also in bureaucratic-institutionalized forms of agreements.

We note the dissociation between popular and business demands, despite the supposed symbolic homogeneity of the anti-PT discourse and the demands for reforms that would benefit the business community more than the workers.

3 The *Manchetômetro* Database

The Laboratory of Media and Public Sphere Studies (LEMEP) qualitatively analyses the headlines of Brazilian major mass newspapers in a project called *Manchetômetro*. This permanent media coverage uses Sentimental Analysis for providing data on either negative, positive, neutral, or ambivalent semantics regarding a specific agent (in this regard, an institution, or a topic of either political or economic concern).

We will analyze the period from September 1, 2014, to December 31, 2016. Within this specific period, there are some critical moments of the impeachment process. December 2, 2015 was when the then president of the Chamber of Deputies accepted the request for impeachment. On May 12, 2016, the Federal Senate voted for the admissibility of the impeachment request, resulting in the removal of Dilma Rousseff from office and starting Michel Temer's interim period in the presidency. By August 31, 2016, the Federal Senate approved the impeachment of Dilma Rousseff. To assess media coverage in this period, *Manchetômetro* applied the sentimental analysis methodology (SAM).

Such methodology does build a measure to verify how coverage of a given fact, actor, or institution was carried out by the news, evaluating the trends and biases used, and influencing the image transmitted to the public of specific facts, characters, and parties. The sentiment each text portrays consistently seeks to answer the question: "the text in question expresses some position on the subject or the characters mentioned".[5] According to Feres Junior,

5 "Methodology of Manchetometro Project". *Manchetômetro* accessed on June 25, 2021. Available at http://manchetometro.com.br/quem-somos/#missao.

sentimental analysis studies can accurately demonstrate the media's bias, despite the subtleties present in journalistic texts (Feres Junior, 2016, 281). As Feres Junior highlights, SAM is the methodology that best responds to highly politicized coverage when evaluating the meaning of the text about the studied object (293).

We will use four sentiments in the study: neutral, contrary, favorable, and ambivalent. We will work with the texts published by the three printed newspapers studied by *Manchetômetro* – O Globo, Estado de São Paulo, and Folha de São Paulo – analyzing headlines, headlines, editorials, opinion articles, and columns. In this work, we used the variables: 'Politics,' 'Economy,' 'Federal Government,' 'Dilma Rousseff', and 'Michel Temer'; the last two condensed in a single President code in our graphics. For analysis purposes, despite the Temer government having officially only started in September, we consider the interim period also as part of the Temer government, given that despite the interim period, Michel Temer since May had appointed new ministers to his Esplanade and presented the new bases of his government that would remain after the end of the impeachment process. Finally, based on the coverage analysis, we will return to the discussions presented on Fiesp's notes and critically discuss the relationship between media coverage and the official position of the business community.

The choice to study print media is associated with its importance among opinion-forming sectors, economic, social, political elites, and decision-makers. In Brazil, the media structure is oligopolistic, and the primary news sources belong to the groups that own the largest newspapers in the country: O Globo, Folha de S. Paulo, and Jornal Nacional. On the internet, which could be an escape valve from this monopoly, there is no difference, as the news sites of these newspapers are the primary reference sources of news content, both for the mainstream media (other newspapers and magazines throughout Brazil) and for news sites and internet blogs. FIES published their notes in printed newspapers. Thus, we will analyze whether newspaper coverage followed or departed from the notes they also published.

The relationship between media and politics is a recurrent theme in works of political science and communication. In the United States, there is extensive academic interest in the subject. To name just a few renowned authors, we have Gaye Tuchman, Robert Hackett, Paul Weaver, Daniel Hallin, and Paolo Mancini. In Brazil, the field consolidated after the country's return to democratic rule. As a result, there is already an extensive bibliography on media and politics produced in our country, emphasizing studies on elections (Aldé, Mendes and Figueiredo 2007; Miguel 2002; Herédia 2008; Bezerra 2005).

According to some democracy theorists, the role of the press is to be one of the primary means by which citizens inform themselves not only to exercise their rights but also to better express their concerns about society and the State (Christians, Ferre and Fackler 1993). Other theorists, using the ideas of negative freedom, understand the press as the guardian of society in the face of possible abuses of power by the government.

The media study does not propose to discuss media stimuli but about how disputes between different perspectives are processed, with the political consciousness of each emerging from this confrontation. Thus, the objective of this type of study is to analyze the process of communicative interaction, relating it to the constructed meaning and how it affects the other, allowing us to consider "the perspectives of the media and affected subjects from the perspective of interaction" (Cal 2014, 92–93).

The media is not a neutral information channel but an institution holding relationships with other social actors, in addition to having its codes of conduct and economic interests as essential and influential factors in its decisions on the agenda (Feres Junior et al., 2015; Lycarião, Magalhães and Albuquerque 2015). Therefore, analyzing the media thematization process allows us to better understand its construction and to question existing positions and practices, and which in turn allows us to politicize the topics covered and interact with the subjects involved and the redefinition of the issues.

In a democratic society, the role of the media is not to be merely an objective information service but also to issue an opinion, as long as it contemplates the most significant possible number of positions and opinions in its different means of communication. Thus, it would be what Nelson Traquina calls a 'market of ideas' (Traquina 2012). This dependence intensifies when we adopt a liberal-pluralist position for which the offer of alternatives is necessary so that the reader/spectator can exercise their free choice, as in the market (Sartori 1994; Miguel 2002).

We must highlight, as Rousiley Maia does, the importance of people in society by feeding both the information and the discourses that circulate within it, in addition to creating new spaces for subjects to produce a "sense of themselves, of the relationship with others, which often intertwines with entrenched institutions and cultural patterns" (Maia 2012, 209). Furthermore, as the author herself states, the material presented can transform everyday relationships, dramatizing conflicts, relating them to values, and, above all, politicizing lived experiences.

The objective of media vehicles with this type of coverage is to convey an image of impartiality, that their job is to expose reality 'as it would be.' The discussion about journalistic partiality leads to a series of questions, both theoretical, about the roles of the press and the mass media in contemporary democracy and history, about the social construction of the productive routines of journalism, and the very notion of objectivity. Several authors highlight the socially and historically constructed character of these values incorporated into a journalistic discourse that they end up naturalized without realizing the difficulty in defining them.

The act of taking a stand carried out by the media is not a problem in itself (Traquina 2012). In democratic societies, the media is not expected only to offer an objective neutral information service to its user, but also to issue an opinion on the issues addressed. However, for society to function well, different forms of media must consider positions and opinions in a 'market of ideas.' Thus, this action becomes genuinely democratic. The importance of contemplating differing opinions is based mainly on the great relevance in constructing reality through speeches, generating knowledge, and answering simple questions (Sousa 2002).

Reality shows us a different panorama of this democratic ideal, in which the marketing appeal has priority in newspaper decisions regarding the perspectives that are published (Lycarião, Magalhães and Albuquerque 2015). Significant forms of media will tend to all use textual and visual formats to influence the reader's opinion on the subject covered (Aldé 2004). They seek to shield themselves from criticism regarding the possible partiality of their coverage, claim to base their journalistic production on two values: objectivity and impartiality – values present, even in some journalistic manuals within newsrooms, to reinforce this position (Feres Junior et al., 2015).

There are some indications of the partiality conveyed that we could notice: the repetition of signifiers, such as themes and expressions of value (Hackett 1999), the insistence on covering some facts, the omission of some themes considered embarrassing to their allies, and the recurrence of lies (Breed 1999); Chomsky and Herman 1979). Another mechanism capable of helping to perceive the partiality of media coverage is the presence of the naturalization of opinions in the texts, presenting them as if they were global, which contributes, at the same time, to the discourse of impartiality, disguising the ideological framework used by the media (Hackett 1999). According to Luís Felipe Miguel and Flávia Biroli, this last feature ignores existing social conflicts and makes it impossible to broadcast voices that do not share the vision presented by the media (Miguel and Biroli 2010).

The news does not start from a vacuum that would allow journalistic means to inform reality – which ignores the differences that surround us – without being influenced by it. Even if the news came from the void, journalists can quickly reproduce the intentions of their producers. Another necessary

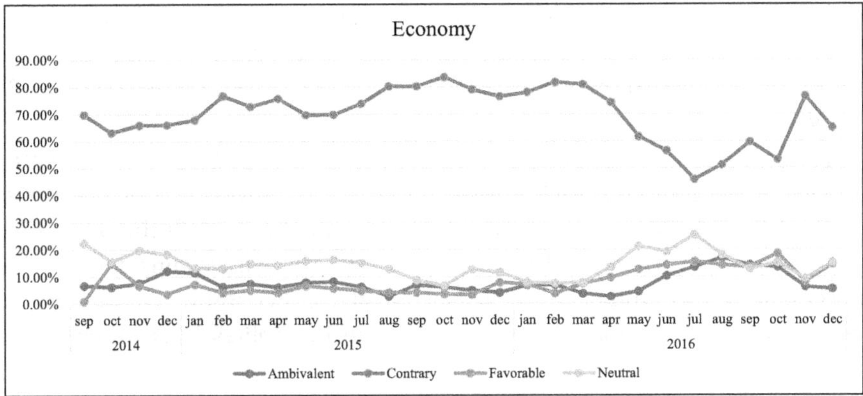

FIGURE 4.1 Sentimental analysis of media coverage about economy

deconstruction carried out by media studies concerns the understanding of a division in printed newspapers between the content of 'opinion texts' and the content of 'news texts,' helping to explain the position taken by the media (Peake and Eshbaugh-Soha 2008).

According to Peake (2007), two possible motivations for the positions are sociological and economic. According to sociological explanation, the sum between the environment in newsrooms and the development of an organizational, political culture drives some biases over others through periodicals (Barrett and Barrington 2005). The economic bias, on the other hand, highlights that the audience is an essential factor to be considered in decisions, given that, as the newspaper is also a marketing product, the relationship of the journal with the reader-customer is an essential fact for its maintenance (Peake 2007; Lycarião, Magalhães and Albuquerque 2015). Thus, journalistic coverage offers a good proxy for political communication in our society, that is, for evaluating the general relationship between media and politics, despite the significant transformations that society and the media itself have undergone.

3.1 *Manchetômetro Data Analysis*

The graphs below represent the set of texts analyzed. It is essential first to highlight some facts of the relevant timeline for the analysis: the 2014 election period, which had both the first and second rounds in October 2014, the decision of the president of the Chamber of Deputies, Deputy Eduardo Cunha (PMDB-RJ) in accepting the request for impeachment in December 2015, and the removal of Dilma Rousseff in May 2016, until the process was closed on August 30, 2016, with the impeachment vote and the qualification of Michel Temer as president of Brazil.

The chart above (Fig. 4.1) highlights the coverage of the economy since September 2014. As shown in chart 1, the economy had predominantly negative coverage, with more than 50% of the texts being negative, except for July 2016. However, we can notice that the negative coverage was more prevalent than 60% of negative texts, except for between June to September 2016. Therefore, the economy graph does not change its eminently adverse coverage profile of the Dilma I and II governments, being modified only with the beginning of the Temer government. This fact is quite interesting if we consider that the second administration of Dilma had as Minister of Economy, Joaquim Levy, a representative of the market, in a nod to the business elites. In an official note, Fiesp stated that:

> Since his nomination by President Dilma Rousseff in November 2014, Finance Minister Joaquim Levy has been a tireless advocate of cutting government spending. However, in his favor, it should also be said that he has never denied that, in addition to cutting spending, the government could resort to raising taxes to get the public accounts out of the red.[6]

Despite this seeming articulation, this business official note also states that Joaquim Levy would favor re-implementing the national CPMF tax, which goes against Fiesp's interests to overrun this new taxation. Furthermore, it highlights expressions as '*economy in flames*' and mentions that "as has happened before, Dilma always prefers to pay to see. The problem is that, in the end, she sees, and we pay".[7] Thus, compared to the coverage of the economy, we can see that even though Dilma had signaled a certain willingness to bring business figures and industrialists closer, the narrative persisted in connecting the president herself to the economic crisis, under the national oppositional articulation.

The policy coverage represented in Figure 4.2 highlights that the policy throughout the analyzed period was considered a percentage more hostile than any other valence. This representation reinforces the understanding we presented above that associates politics with negative characteristics such as corruption and immorality. The politician then becomes a negative character, strengthening the argument that associates the left's negative aspects with corruption. In turn, this same discourse strengthens the argument of center-right characters who present themselves as technical actors outside the field of politics, distinguish themselves from these characteristics, and this negative

6 "A conta vai sobrar para você de novo", *Época*, September 29, 2015, http://www.naovoupagaropato.com.br/deu-na-midia/a-conta-vai-sobrar-para-voce-de-novo/.

7 (*Época* 2015).

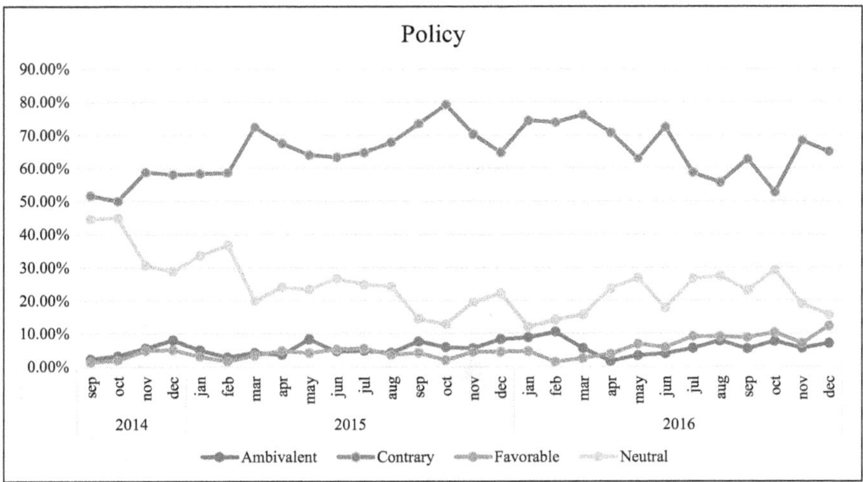

FIGURE 4.2 Sentimental analysis of media coverage about policy

coverage. Fiesp's notes strengthen this type of interpretation by trying to differentiate economic issues from political issues. According to Fiesp president Paulo Skaf himself,

> We have to separate the political crisis from the economic one. The political crisis is in the political arena. We must have separate tracks. The political crisis continues on its track until it is solved, and the economy continues on its separate track to resume growth.
>
> SKAF 2016[8]

It strengthens the argument that the business elite has produced certain elements present in the media narrative, alongside other narratives that demonized all that is related to the political. It also takes advantage of low political cognition levels amid public opinion, so that civil society believes that the economy would function without political interactions and articulations. On the positive side, economic agents such as the private sector, enterprises, and those who work in business roles, would lead progress and development when the systemic political crisis would be politically produced.

The federal government's coverage (Fig. 4.3) demonstrates a clear distinction between the Dilma II government and the Temer government. While the

8 "Sindicouro participar de Encontros de Empresários com o presidente Michel Temer", *SINDICOURO*, June 23, 2016, interview by Paulo Skaf, https://www.Fiesp.com.br/sindicouro/noticias/sindicouro-participar-de-encontros-de-empresarios-com-o-presidente-michel-temer/.

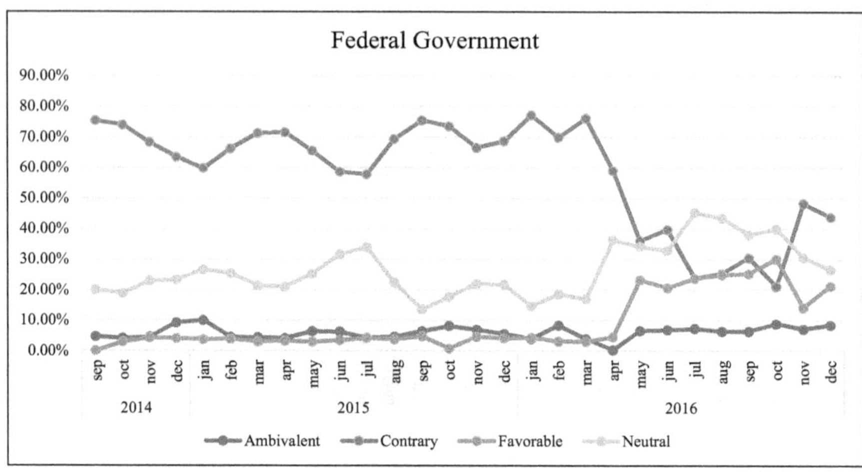

FIGURE 4.3 Sentimental analysis of media coverage about the federal government

Dilma II government had predominantly negative coverage, with only three months (June and July 2015; and April 2016) with percentages of contrary valences lower than 60% of all texts that mention the government of Dilma Rousseff; the Temer government's coverage, in turn, presents a much more balanced coverage, with a coverage period with more excellent neutral coverage than negative coverage. This fact speaks to Fiesp. As his notes point out, "Temer enters with more credibility than Dilma,"[9] and

> [...] research captured the sentiments of the industries before the opening of the impeachment process of the ousted president Dilma Rousseff. [...] there is a greater optimism today among the representatives of the companies with the government of interim president Michel Temer [...].[10]

Many other official notes from Fiesp address the ease in articulating with Michel Temer in contradiction to Dilma's irreducibility and acute adverse effects on the economy.

9 "Na Fiesp, governador de Mato Grosso defende reforma política", *Agência Indusnet Fiesp*, May 17, 2016, https://www.Fiesp.com.br/noticias/na-Fiesp-governador-de-mato-grosso-defende-reforma-politica/.

10 "Investimento da indústria deve recuar 50%, mostra estudo da Fiesp", *Agência Indusnet Fiesp*, June 13, 2016, https://www.fiesp.com.br/noticias/investimento-da-industria-deve-recuar-50-mostra-estudo-da-Fiesp/.

If we look at the period before the opening of the impeachment process, we note that there is eminently negative coverage by the federal government during the entire period. However, once we reach March 2016, with the beginning of the activities of the Special Impeachment Commission, and political movements and news agencies begin to report the victory of the impeachment process for Dilma Rousseff, the coverage of the Federal Government reduces the negative aspect. Thus, we can see that the last months of the Dilma Rousseff administration had its lowest negative rates of political coverage, in a transition towards a new coverage for the interim government of Michel Temer, which had a different coverage, with more of a positive, less neutral coverage than negative. Media coverage, however, resumes its most negative trend only in November when the then Minister of Culture, Marcelo Calero, resigned from his post, accusing government secretary Geddel Vieira Lima of pressuring him to release work pertaining to a listed project in Bahia. The case resulted in Geddel's dismissal.

The coverage of the personal code on the president of the Republic (Fig. 4.4) presents us with exciting movements over the months studied. First, during the final months of 2014, there is a time when coverage of Dilma Rousseff, still during Dilma's first term, is more neutral than negative, a brief period of media truce with the president, probably a reflection of the period. This was during the election, when the president ran for and won the 2014 presidential elections against the candidate Aécio Neves. Once the Dilma II government officially began work in January 2015, the truce ended, and the negative coverage persists at 50% until the president's removal.

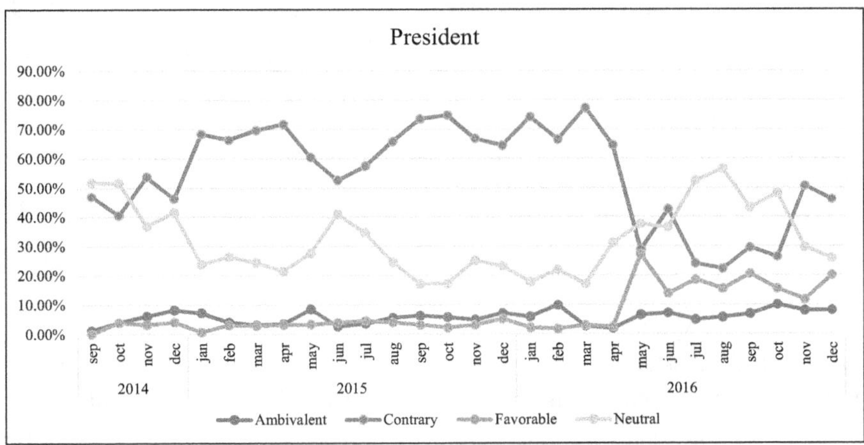

FIGURE 4.4 Sentimental analysis of media coverage about the president

In turn, the media coverage of the Temer government, since the interim period, had experienced a different treatment, with a higher percentage of neutral stories than the contrary, except for two moments: June 2016, when the then Minister of Tourism, Henrique Alves resigned after investigations by Operation Lava Jato accusing that Alves had received money from bribes, and November and December, when the case of Geddel, a minister close to President Temer, was still reverberating.

The coverage of the representative of the federal executive reflects the same movement as the coverage of the federal government. During the presidential transition, there is a reduction in negative coverage, replacing a more neutral coverage in the first months, which resumes its preference for the opposite coverage at the end of the year, even if at a lower percentage than that in Dilma Rousseff's period of leadership. As the *Manchetômetro* has previously highlighted (Sassara et al., 2017), the mainstream media acted differently with the two presidents: while the PT's second term had its coverage in perspective closer to the watchdog logic, that is, from a more critical media to power, the Temer government, since its first interim moment, had less negative coverage, demonstrating some goodwill and the realization of coverage often known as 'the honeymoon': coverage which makes room for the government to propose and present its agenda to society, with a reduction of initial criticism.

Thus, we can see a clear distinction in media coverage between the two terms, especially in the specific coverage of the president and the government itself. The Dilma II period has more negative coverage than the Temer government, which could signify that the PT's government would be worse than its vice president's. However, opinion polls indicated that society did not share this opinion and the Temer government set rejection records throughout its short period. Fiesp's official notes also demonstrate the same distinction between the presidents, as Michel Temer's mandate period showed no negative criticism towards the government.

We can see the image conveyed by the media reflects more the business elite view than the society's perspective, which does not agree with the analysis of both concerning governments.

4 Discussion

This data from *Manchetômetro* matches the four distinct moments in the Brazilian business elite's discourse during Rousseff's second mandate. First, negative approaches towards the federal government plummeted as soon as Dilma Rousseff was removed from office in May 2016, followed by Michel

Temer's rise to the presidency, three months before Rousseff's impeachment (graph 1). Second, the March 2016 peak on the media discourse against the Workers' Party (graph 2) follows the change in Fiesp's demands from being a critic of new national taxation policies to a direct and public defender of Dilma Rousseff's withdrawal. Not to mention that favorable mentions to the Workers' Party are close to nonexistent.

These changes show that, despite the small number of official communication samples researched, other data confirms the inferences regarding the role of big media in generating a narrative that is not in accordance with actual social development. The demonization of what is political comes hand in hand with the necessity to highlight any resemblance of 'neutrality' and 'correctness' (as in opposition to 'corruption') from the message, thus antagonizing any reference to social, redistributive, and political meanings, including those of public policies, in a semantic relation to the political left, to the Workers' Party, to Lula, and Dilma Rousseff.

As Adalberto Cardoso (2020) puts it, the current rise of the extreme-far right in Brazil began during the mass protests of 2013. In 2013, the right-wing, namely neoliberal, authoritative, and conservative forces, have started to manage public opinion based on [1] particular, personal, interest goals which are hidden by [2] manipulative, antagonistic discourses over [3] uncritical and politically lower social classes. Discourses of anti-communism have managed to demonize social policies in terms such as 'red threat,' 'Venezuela,' 'dictatorship,' and 'corruption.'

This study highlights the politicization of the 'Car Wash' (*Lava Jato*) legal process, which discursively grounded the connection between the Workers Party, former presidents Luiz Inácio Lula da Silva and Dilma Rousseff with corruption events in the state oil company Petrobrás. The term 'corruption' was the main discursive element to influence political protests (Cardoso 2020, 148), which have also been fundamental over 'high taxation' in 2015, followed by 'impeachment' in 2016, using 'mediatic bombardment' and "great support from the media". These elements have been constructed from the São Paulo business elite's political campaign and succeeded in guiding the public opinion of an unsatisfied civil society lacking political cognition.

According to Cardoso, "the novelty in the June 2013 mobilizations was the presence of working-class segments enlivening the protests. However, they became more clearly middle class from 2014 onwards, as the mobilizations' demands over the impeachment of Dilma Rousseff increased" (Cardoso 2020, 158). Nevertheless, as the combinations of both data show, the narrative distributed over the media did not lose its 'popular targeted' and 'working-class aimed' discourse despite the change in the social identity of political manifestations.

On the contrary, it generates a sense of general clamor attributed to a middle-class mobilization, in as much as it denounces the state of manipulability of the middle classes, especially employing fake news and misinformation (267). For instance, the extreme far-right Bolsonaro, who achieved power in 2020, has increasingly used this same disinformation pathway (Viscardi 2020; Maranhão Fº et al., 2018).

Even though the entire political destitution process has centered around fair, juridical legal *impeachment*, the social and political literature has brought the notion of *a coup* as a break from democratic legitimacy. Terms such as 'parliamentary coup' (Santos and Szwako 2016; Dijk 2017; Santos and Guarnieri 2016; Cardoso 2020), 'neoliberal coup' (Souza 2016; Roque 2017), 'soft coup' (Bohl et al., 2016; Chomsky 2016), and including 'mediatic coup' (Caballero and Sola-Morales 2020) have widely expressed the right, neoliberal coalition against Dilma Rousseff and all that is political, and is therefore corrupt. It notably indicates a pervasive, lurking political articulation whose actions question the legitimacy imprinted on the emerging media discourse, from this politicized (and concealed) false-based juridical procedure. Most of these authors point to the antagonistic relationship between Dilma Rousseff (PT) and her vice-president Michel Temer (PMDB), who remained in power despite having been part of the re-elected political alliance (PMDB-PT) which allegedly had executed illegal action.

In this regard, the political-discursive essence of this centered-right-far-right oligarchic arrangement, including the media itself, denounces a disruption of democracy employing suscitating hatred from lower and middle classes during the Brazilian systemic crisis throughout Dilma Rousseff's second mandate. Hence, this narrative had the power to subvert legalities by operating social strata's imaginary, opinions, and informational grounds so that they would support an ideologized, biased juridical process.

The anti-democratic narrative has favored the new government, especially regarding the allegation of corruption towards Michel Temer, which was disregarded both by the courts and the media themselves.[11]

---

11 "[...] many argue that the alleged corruption was being directly used against Rousseff for the purpose of throwing her out of office. Like Collor, Rousseff became widely unpopular among Brazilians and became the scapegoat for Brazil's multiple crises [...] Curiously, the Senate, with the approval of the President of the Supreme Federal Tribunal, split its impeachment vote into two: (1) whether to convict Rousseff; and (2) whether to deprive her of her political rights for eight years. On the second question, the Senate voted 42 to 36, with three abstentions. With the requisite two thirds majority lacking, Rousseff has retained her political rights [...] Temer swiftly named an all-male, all-while cabinet upon

5 Conclusion

The heterogeneity in keys of discourse relates to the different publics Fiesp aims at communicating, introducing the discursive aspect that underlies manipulation strategies, which moves reason and passion in a mass society. Thus, from the moment that Fiesp and popular classes are different social agents, with different capitals, discourses, and contexts – especially within the power system – it is essential to analyze entrepreneurial thinking. In addition to this, it is arguably even more critical when it has the capacity and possibility to convert its economic capital into political and social capital through influence through a public campaign in the mass media.

Regarding the impeachment process, what was supposed to be a legal-juridical stance was, in fact, an accord among the center and right-winged elites, including the business and the media, which appears as their narrative, and whose discourse denounces an anti-democratic movement concealed by an allegedly legal, legitimate juridical process. Hence, terms like 'parliamentary coup' or 'mediatic coup' only show a fraction of the 'national agreement' against Rousseff, which had also involved other institutional stances such as neoliberal intellectuals, local and sub-national political movements, among others. The media narrative, armed with the seeming legitimization from political and market agents, have managed to worsen general distrust in state institutions by demonizing the political, linking it to corruption and the left. The challenge now would be to re-establish trust in institutions as well as get democracy back on track.

As shown by Fernandes (2022), the *Não vou pagar o pato* campaign, from the business elite and mediated through mass newspapers and online media, achieved to represent a popular and generalized sociopolitical demand to withdraw the former president despite the clear middle-class, white, conservative, and military-grounded movement aesthetics. The *Manchetômetro* database has corroborated the discriminatory treatment given by the media to the two presidents from the PMDB-PT alliance and reinforced the mechanisms through which the media narrative manages public opinion insofar as the

---

gaining a seat to the presidency and is as unpopular, if not more, than Rousseff herself. The attorney general of Brazil has now charged Temer with receiving money from the massive meatpacking firm JBS, which itself is already implicated in a corruption scandal. The charges have already been delivered to a Supreme Court judge who referred the question of whether Temer should be tried by the Supreme Federal tribunal to the lower house of parliament. A two thirds majority vote is needed to waive Temer's immunity. On August 2, 2017, the Chamber of Deputies rejected the bid to waive Temer's immunity by a vote of 238 against, 198 for". (Rattinger 2018, 153–156).

public lacks political cognition and critical questioning over the information conveyed.

Let us not mention the philosophical stamp of 'economic time' and 'political time' that operate at different speeds and at separate times. However, we cannot separate the political and the economic dimensions in practical social reality. This research has raised a handful of issues concerning complex space-time social configurations, which overlap and show intensity in moments of crisis, such as the recent Brazilian one. The passage of time demonstrates the legal process, with the 'juridical timing' which instituted new bodies of authority through the supposed constitutional procedures – after one year, there was the presidential impeachment. As for the 'political time,' over articulating the national agreement to destabilize the balance of power and promote new ideological institutions, it can be traced from the 'Brazilian Spring 2013', intensified with Dilma's re-election, and which had not yet culminated in consensus as Michel Temer rose to power. The 'economic time' is the fastest and tends to be altered by the actions of individual investors, for an economic crisis can be generated and solved faster than other crises – note the positive reaction in the face of the change of government after three months. The 'cultural time' has not yet changed through history. Therefore, it still depicts a crisis of knowledge and critical reasoning from the masses, historically reproduced by these institutions and actors who hold the capacity (reasoning, means, and legitimacy) to manipulate public opinion through media narratives.

References

Aldé, Alessandra. *A construção da política. Democracia, cidadania e meios de comunicação de massa.* Rio de Janeiro: Editora Fundação Getúlio Vargas, (2004).

Aldé, Alessandra, Gabriel Mendes and Marcus Figueiredo. "Tomando Partido: Imprensa e política nas eleições de2006". *Politica & Sociedade* 10, (2007): 20–28. DOI: 10.5007/%25x.

Barrett, Andrew and Lowell Barrington. "Bias in Newspaper Photograph Selection". *Political Research Quarterly* 4, 2005.

Bezerra, Heloisa D. "*Cobertura jornalística e eleições majoritárias: proposta de um modelo analítico*". Ph.D. thesis, Research University Institute of Rio de Janeiro (IUPERJ), Rio de Janeiro, 2005.

Bohl, Alexandre, Juan Chavarro, Raiesa Frazer, Rachael Hildebrand and Emma Tyrou. "Soft Coup in Brazil: A Blow to Brazilian Democracy". *Council on Hemispheric Affairs*, (May 2016). Available at https://www.coha.org/soft-coup-in-brazil-a-blow-to-brazilian-democracy/.

Breed, Warren. "Controle Social na Redação: Uma Análise Funcional". In *Jornalismo: questões, teorias e 'estórias'*, organized by Nelson Traquina. Lisboa: Editora VEJA, 1999.

Cal, Danila. "*Configuração política e relações de poder no trabalho infantil doméstico: tensões nos discursos dos media e de trabalhadoras*". Ph.D. thesis. Federal University of Minas Gerais (UFMG), Belo Horizonte, 2014.

Caballero, Francisco S. and Salomé Sola-Morales. "Media Coups and Disinformation in the Digital Era. Irregular War in Latin America". *Comunicación y Sociedad*, e7604 (2020): 1–30. DOI: 10.32870/cys.v2020.7604 Available at http://www.comunicacionysociedad.cucsh.udg.mx/index.php/comsoc/article/view/e7604/6222.

Cardoso, Adalberto M. *À beira do abismo. Uma sociologia política do bolsonarismo*. 1st ed. Rio de Janeiro: Amazon, (2020).

Chomsky, Noam. "Noam Chomsky: Brazil's President Dilma Rousseff' Impeached by a Gang of Thieves'". *Democracy Now*, May 17, 2016. Available at https://www.democracynow.org/2016/5/17/noam_chomsky_brazils_president_dilma_rousseff.

Chomsky, Noam and Edward S. Herman. *The Political Economy of Human Rights, Vol. 1: The Washington Connection and Third World Fascism*. Montreal: Black Rose Books, Boston: South End Press, (1979).

Christians, Clifford, John Ferré and P. Mark Fackler. *Good News: Social Ethics and the Press*. New York and Oxford: Oxford University Press (1993).

Davis, Stuart and Joe Straubhaar. "Producing Antipetismo: Media activism and the rise of the radical, nationalist right in contemporary Brazil".. *International Communication Gazette* 82, no. 1 (February 2020): 82–100. DOI: 10.1177/1748048519880731.

Dijk, Teun A van. "How Globo Media Manipulated the Impeachment of Brazilian President Dilma Rousseff". *Discourse & Communication* 11, no. 2 (April 2017): 199–229. https://doi.org/10.1177/1750481317691838.

Diniz, Eli, and Renato Boschi. "Empresariado e estratégias de desenvolvimento". *Revista Brasileira de Ciências Sociais* 18, no. 52 (2003):15–33. Redalyc, https://www.redalyc.org/articulo.oa?id=10705202.

Feres Junior, João. "Em defesa das valências". *Revista Brasileira de Ciência Política*, no. 19, (2016).

Feres Junior, João, Eduardo Barbabela, Miguel Lorena, Márcia Cândido and Luana O. Sassara. "Testando a hipótese do contrapoder: A cobertura das eleições de 1998 e 2014". *Annals from IV Congresso do Compolítica* (IV Compolítica Congress). Rio de Janeiro, 2015.

Fernandes, Humberto. "Political-Discursive Behavior of the São Paulo Business Elite in the Crisis that Ended Dilma Rousseff's Second Term (2014–2016)". *Middle Atlantic Review of Latin American Studies* 6, no. 1 (2022): 58–96.

Hackett, Robert A. "Declínio de um paradigma? A parcialidade e a objetividade nos estudos dos media noticiosos". In *Jornalismo: questões, teorias e 'estórias'*, organized by Nelson Traquina. Lisboa: Editora VEJA, 1999.

Herédia, Leila. "*A retórica da capa: a reeleição de FHC e de Lula na primeira página de O Globo e FSP*". Master's thesis, Research University Institute of Rio de Janeiro (IUPERJ), Rio de Janeiro, 2008.

Lycarião, Diógenes, Eleonora Magalhães and Afonso Albuquerque. "Jornalismo parcial feito para vender: a decadência do padrão 'catch-all' pelas leis do mercado". *Annals from IV Congresso do Compolítica* (IV Compolítica Congress). Rio de Janeiro, 2015.

Maia, Rousiley C. M. The News Media as a Forum for Civic Debate. In *Deliberation, the media and political talk*, edited by Rousiley C. Maia. New York, NY: Hampton Press, 2012.

Maranhão F°, Eduardo M. A., Fernanda M. F. Coelho and Tainah B. Dias. "'Fake news acima de tudo, fake news acima de todos': Bolsonaro e o 'kit gay', 'ideologia de gênero' e fim da 'família tradicional'". Revista Eletrônica Correlatio 17, no. 2, (December 2018).

Miguel, Luis Felipe. "A eleição visível: a Rede Globo descobre a política em 2002". *Revista Dados* 46, no. 02, (2002).

Miguel, Luis Felipe and Flávia Biroli. "A produção da imparcialidade: a construção do discurso universal a partir da perspectiva jornalística". *Revista Brasileira de Ciências Sociais* 25, n. 73, 2010.

Peake, Jeffrey. "Presidents and Front-page News: How America's Newspapers Cover the Bush Administration". *The Harvard International Journal of Press/Politics* 12, 2007.

Peake, Jeffrey and Matthew Eshbaugh-Soha. "The presidency and Local Media: Local Newspaper Coverage of President George W. Bush". *Presidential Studies Quarterly* 38, no. 4, 2008.

Rattinger, Alexandra. "The Impeachment Process of Brazil: A Comparative Look at Impeachment in Brazil and the United States". *University of Miami Inter-American Law Review*, no. 129, (2018). Available at: https://repository.law.miami.edu/umialr/vol49/iss1/7.

Roque, Tatiana. "Sous la Destitution de Dilma Rousseff un Coup d'Etat Neoliberal". *Regards*, May 12, 2016. Accessed May 03, 2021. Available at: http://www.regards.fr/web/article/sous-la-destitution-de-dilma-rousseff-un-coup-d-etat-neoliberal.

Santos, Fabiano and Fernando Guarnieri. "From Protest to Parliamentary Coup: An Overview of Brazil's Recent History". *Journal of Latin American Cultural Studies* 25, no. 4 (2016): 485–494. DOI: 10.1080/13569325.2016.1230940.

Santos, Fabiano and José Szwako. "Da ruptura à reconstrução democrática no Brasil" *Saúde debate* 40 (December 2016). DOI: 10.1590/0103-11042016S10.

Sartori, Giovanni. *A Teoria da Democracia Revisitada: O Debate Contemporâneo*. São Paulo: Editora Ática, (1994).

Sassara, Luna de O., Lidiane Rezende Vieira, Eduardo Barbabela and João Feres Júnior. "De Dilma a Temer: o cão de guarda e a Lua de Mel". *Manchetômetro*, April 24, 2017. Available at http://manchetometro.com.br/2017/04/24/de-dilma-a-temer-o-cao-de-guarda-e-a-lua-de-mel/.

Skaf, Paulo. "Sindicouro participar de Encontros de Empresários com o presidente Michel Temer", *Sindicouro*, June 23, 2016. Available at https://www.fiesp.com.br/sindicouro/noticias/sindicouro-participar-de-encontros-de-empresarios-com-o-presidente-michel-temer/.

Sousa, Jorge Pedro. *Teorias da Notícia e do Jornalismo*. Chapecó: Argos, (2002).

Souza, Jessé. *A Radiografia do Golpe*. Rio de Janeiro: Leya, (2016).

Traquina, Nelson. *Porque as notícias são como são*. Ed. Insular, (2012).

Viscardi, Janaisa M. "Fake news, verdade e mentira sob a ótica de Jair Bolsonaro no Twitter". Trab. Ling. Aplic. 59, no. 2, (May-Aug 2020): 1134–1157 DOI: 10.1590/010318137158916202005 20.

CHAPTER 5

Crime or Commiseration

The Contingent Framing of Homelessness on Brazilian Television

Pedro Paulo Martins Serra

In this chapter, we present a framing analysis of television news that reveals how homeless groups are represented on Brazilian broadcast television. For this we analyzed the prime-time coverage of the following newscasts: Jornal Nacional (Rede Globo, the most-watched television network in Brazil), SBT Brasil (SBT), Jornal da Record (Rede Record), Jornal da Band (TV Band), Jornal da Cultura (TV Cultura – public television network), and Repórter Brasil (TV Brasil – public television network).[1]

This chapter is organized as follows: first, the framing analysis methodological question will be addressed, and then, we will move to the case study *per se*, which is divided in two parts. In the first, we will present the results of the news framing analysis, and in the second, we will interpret the results.

The main event chosen for analysis is the repossession of the Hotel Aquarius in downtown São Paulo, on September 16, 2014, an action that degenerated into mass confusion that spread downtown and involved confrontations with the police. To illustrate how the homeless are represented in significantly distinct ways according to, for instance, occurrences that lead to their inclusion in the news agenda, we will offer a counterpoint at the end of the article based on an analysis of the main TV network in Brazil (Rede Globo) news coverage of a fire and the collapse of a downtown building in São Paulo in 2018.

1 Methodology

Analyzing the representations of vulnerable groups requires the identification, from among the events reported in television newscasts, of those capable of

1 T.N.: In order, translated names of the main Brazilian newscasts: Jornal Nacional (Rede Globo) – National Newscast (Globo Network); SBT Brasil (SBT) – SBT Brazil (SBT); Jornal da Record (Rede Record) – Record Newscast (Record Network); Jornal da Band (Band TV) – Band Newscast (Band TV); Jornal da Cultura (TV Cultura) – Culture Newscast (Culture TV); Repórter Brasil (TV Brasil) – Brazil Reporter (Brazil TV).

revealing meaningful aspects of the distinct ways in which these groups are represented on television. To accomplish this, we analyzed news coverage of an event that pitted excluded social groups against the police in the context of the defense of private property. This type of material is of great interest, for it allows the analyst to evaluate whether news coverage focuses on the dramatic and episodic aspects of the incident – the emphasis here being on the confrontation against the police, but also on the acts of vandalism and their immediate impacts on everyday life in downtown São Paulo – or if in some way it presents contextual and/or structural elements that were the root cause of the reported events. Moreover, this type of material, which stages the clear opposition between police and civilians, provides input for an analysis in terms of favoring one group over the other.

At first, the methodological procedure consisted of repeatedly viewing sample videos and identifying pertinent news story elements to which framing analysis could be applied. Aiming to prevent any risk of subjectivity, that is, a selective approach by the analyst, pointed out as a specific analytic weakness that will be tackled next (Harsin, 2015: 49), excerpts of these news stories are highlighted and transcribed in the footnotes of this article. The methodology considered pertinent to this type of content analysis is framing analysis.

> Framing essentially involves *selection and salience*. To frame is to *select some aspects of a perceived reality and make them more salient in a communicating text, in such a way as to promote a particular problem definition, causal interpretation, moral evaluation, and/or treatment recommendation* for the item described.
>
> ENTMAN, 1993: 294; italics in the original

Although this definition is useful as a starting point, this methodology requires a more precise definition, even more so because the concept of framing is utilized with distinct meanings (Cappella; Jamieson, 1997: 39; Nelson et al., 1997: 222–223). It is important to make a distinction between two types of framing. The first is "news framing", used by journalists in news production (called "news angle" in news jargon), which is the favoring of some aspects of news instead of others. The second, "interpretive framing", is related to the kind of reading or interpretation deduced from news stories. It can come from comments made by journalists themselves or, more commonly, from the statements of various actors consulted during the reporting work and included in the final edition of the news story. Brought up by actors involved in the broadcast events (such as police officers, people directly involved or witnesses), specialists or even political leaders, interpretive framing includes "the definition of problems, evaluations of causes and responsibilities, and recommendations for treatment" (Porto, 2004). Within the scope of this chapter, we will distinguish between three kinds of interpretive framing: one relating to problem definition, another to event causes, and another envisioning problem solutions.

2 The Repossession in Downtown São Paulo on September 16, 2014

On September 16, 2014, a group of homeless families (the number ranging from 80 to 200 according to the news), members of the Frente de Luta por Moradia[2] among other movements, were forced to move out of a hotel building located in downtown São Paulo that they had occupied for six months. There was a confrontation: the occupiers threw objects out of the windows, the police used rubber bullets, stun grenades and tear gas; vandalism and looting also occurred in the area. The exact circumstances leading to the confrontation are not clear. What is clear, though, is that many groups joined the homeless, and as reported in the newspapers, as well as in most of the newscasts from the networks in our sample, two police chiefs interviewed in these reports referred to them as "opportunist groups". This possible confusion regarding the identity of those involved in the conflict offers interesting material to the scope of this work, for not mentioning the opportunist groups led the audience to wrongly ascribe the entire responsibility for the acts of vandalism and aggression to the evictees.

At the same time, because it was related to public administration matters, that is, the housing policy of the city of São Paulo, a violent event downtown, in plain sight, gave journalists unique images capable of arousing public interest, especially when it concerns television newscasting. Emphasis on the conflict, mainly through the predominance of episodic framing (i.e., limited to the immediate factual aspects), is common in television news for it allows the staging of attractive audiovisual resources, even approaching the filming esthetics of action movies.

Some of the criteria that we consider relevant for this analysis are the vocabulary employed when referring to the homeless or to reported events, the actors asked to speak, and whether or not there was any interpretive framing in the reports. We will see throughout the framing analysis how these and other elements played a role in the six Brazilian TV networks.

2 T.N.: Battlefront for Housing.

3 News Framing: The Homeless from the Criminalization Perspective

The first aspect to be addressed relates to the vocabulary employed by television news when referring to the events. Table 5.1 shows that SBT Brasil and Jornal da Band[3] were the only ones that chose the term "war" to describe the events. This suggests a dramatic approach to news framing that tries to appeal to the emotions of the audience. The SBT Brasil was the only sample that used dramatic background music and special visual effects, such as video editing resources, i.e., speeding up or slowing down moving images.

TABLE 5.1 News framing – dramatization

Television newscast	Mentions "war"
Jornal Nacional	no
SBT Brasil	yes
Jornal da Record	no
Jornal da Band	yes
Jornal da Cultura	no
Repórter Brasil	no

The degree of violence in plain sight during the clash in downtown São Paulo, the damage left behind by the confusion (burning objects in the streets, looted stores, destroyed pay phones and a bus set on fire), and the impact on commerce and public transportation led most of the television news to adopt dramatic and episodic news framing, focusing on the extraordinary and violent character of events and their consequences to store owners and passersby. In some cases, this framing dominated the entire duration of the report segment. Jornal Nacional (Rede Globo) is such an example. After presenting the report recorded during the day, in which scenes of violence and plundering were abundant and predominant, they went back live to show the visible signs of vandalism. Moreover, Rede Globo was alone in entering the building after the eviction, drawing attention to "lots of dirt", "broken furniture, unwound fire hoses and a stockpile of coconuts, like the ones that were thrown out of the

3 TV Band is the forth-most-watched television network in the country; SBT ranks between the second and the third position.

windows", elements contributing to the construction of negative representation of the homeless.

It should be noted that both public TV broadcasts – TV Cultura and TV Brasil, which are significantly smaller than the others in terms of audience and resources – used far fewer images of the confrontation and the vandalism, relying more on interviews with witnesses and actors who were involved. Thus, that coverage relied less on dramatic and episodic news framing.

It is also interesting to observe the selection of the dramatized aspects: there is a tendency, at least by the three programs with the largest audiences – Jornal Nacional (Rede Globo), Jornal da Record (TV Record) and SBT Brasil (SBT) –, to consider any injuries caused to police officers before those inflicted upon the homeless (see Table 5.2).

The images reviewed show that there were injured police officers, as well as injured homeless. Most television news focused on injured police officers (Jornal Nacional, SBT Brasil, Jornal da Record, and Jornal da Cultura). At Jornal da Band, when the report narrative states that "at least six people were hurt", but without any further details, the recorded images show an injured civilian carried by two officers, leaving no doubt that civilians were among the injured, but at the same time portraying the police positively. Only one newscast (Repórter Brasil – TV Brasil) highlighted injuries to passersby and homeless, while information on injured police was not given.[4]

In the Jornal Nacional coverage, the report ends with information about journalists of the Rede Globo team, (the network where it is aired and, by far, the main TV network in Brazil) who were injured during the filming. The inclusion of this material illustrates a corporative and self-referential journalistic attitude from the broadcaster. One of them, injured by a rubber bullet, leaves no doubt about the fact that the shot was fired by a police officer. Nevertheless, nothing is said about the police action. The only coverage suggesting

4 One could expect that the framing of these events on TV Brasil (Repórter Brasil) and TV Cultura (Jornal da Cultura), both public television networks, would be similar. But an important difference between them should be noted. Whereas federal-level institutions manage TV Brasil (thus, with no relation to the police of the State of São Paulo), TV Cultura is managed at the São Paulo state level. Therefore, at TV Cultura, the image of the São Paulo's police force is an issue. It is also important to note that the State of São Paulo has historically been governed by the right wing PSDB party, as was the case in 2014, whereas the Partido dos Trabalhadores (the left wing Workers' Party) had been in power at the federal level since 2002. Given that 2014 was a presidential election year, this political shift between the two TV networks should be considered.

TABLE 5.2 News framing – identification of the injured

Television newscast	Mentions injured homeless	Mentions injured police officers
Jornal Nacional	no	yes
SBT Brasil	no	yes
Jornal da Record	no	yes
Jornal da Band	"injured people"	"injured people"
Jornal da Cultura	no	yes
Repórter Brasil	yes	no

Note: In spite of not expressly referring to injured homeless, the report says the confrontation "left some injured", showing images of an injured man with no uniform

inappropriate conduct from São Paulo police officers is that of Repórter Brasil (TV Brasil).[5]

From the point of view of news producing routines and the immediate working conditions of reporters, a hypothesis emerges: information referring to police officers is "easier" to obtain than information referring to the homeless. Indeed, institutions like the police and firefighters are a source of privileged information in the task of television reporting.

Up to now, we have exclusively tackled the primacy given to the aspect of conflicting in the reporting. We shall now move on to the way the homeless are presented. First of all, it could be inferred that the terms used to describe the homeless vary from one television newscast to another.

The choice of the term "invasion" rather than "occupation", for instance, brings a symbolic meaning. The latter, though it does not suggest the legitimacy of the homeless presence, is distinguished from the first, which highlights the illegitimate aspect of the people inside the abandoned building and

5 The report says: "This man living in the occupied building states that he was shot by a rubber bullet fired by a police officer when trying to leave the building with his son. He and other homeless, children included, were at a taxi stop when they were struck by stun grenades thrown by the military police". The testimony of an interviewee is also elucidating. Carla Rissatto (tattoo artist) says: "This was the option I had from the cop, it was my choice. Go and be hit by a stone or get shot by some rubber bullets".

TABLE 5.3 News framing – terms used in reference to the homeless

Television newscast	Homeless qualified as
Jornal Nacional	"invaders"
SBT Brasil	"occupation", "residents", "women carrying infants"
Jornal da Record	"occupation", "residents", "families with children"
Jornal da Band	"invaded hotel", "residents"
Jornal da Cultura	"occupation", "residents", "families", "children"
Repórter Brasil	"occupiers"

TABLE 5.4 News framing – identification as 'opportunistic vandals'

Television newscast	Identification as opportunistic vandals (by whom)
Jornal Nacional	no
SBT Brasil	yes (riot police commander)
Jornal da Record	yes (police commander and reporter)
Jornal da Band	yes (riot police commander)
Jornal da Cultura	yes (reporter)
Repórter Brasil	no

denotes an approach that especially aligns with the building owner's point of view. Only Rede Globo chose to call them "invaders" (see table 5.3).[6]

Another meaningful element of how the homeless are represented is the use of the term "families". All television newscasts used the term when quantifying the building occupiers (figures of 80, 130 and 200 families are mentioned). In this case, significant weight cannot be given to the specific framing or decisions made by the television news teams, as it would have been difficult to have done so differently. Not taking the report excerpts attempting to quantify the groups into account, only two television newscast described the group as "families" (Jornal da Cultura[7] and Jornal da Record).[8] They also highlighted

6 Jornal da Band spoke of an "invaded hotel", and then referred to them as "residents". The term "residents" was present in the coverage of most newscasts, except Jornal Nacional and Repórter Brasil.

7 "...homeless families and military police started a conflict".

8 "Families resisted and the uproar ended up spreading out across the region".

the presence of children among the evictees. SBT, on the other hand, without using the terms "family" or "workers", specified that among the people arrested many were "women carrying infants".[9]

The next aspect relates to the identification of those responsible for damages and of the individuals involved in direct confrontation with the police, which, in terms of the news stories analyzed, is linked to information about opportunistic vandals (see Table 5.4).

Four out of six newscasts analyzed reported that confrontations did not occur only between police officers and evictees. In SBT Brasil and Jornal da Band the information was lifted from the same section of the interview with José Balestiero, PM riot police commander.[10] The Jornal da Record reporter[11] does not link evictees to police confrontation, as emphasized by the section from the interview with Nivaldo César Restivo,[12] also identified as the PM riot police commander. In the Jornal da Cultura it is the reporter that is doing the explaining.[13]

There is no such explanation in Jornal Nacional (Rede Globo) and Repórter Brasil (TV Brasil), allowing an interpretation of events that attributes attacks on police officers, as well as the acts of vandalism and material losses, exclusively to the evictees. This is a point in common between both newscasts, but they differ in other significant aspects. In contrast to the Jornal Nacional, the Repórter Brasil report spent little time broadcasting shocking images of acts of vandalism and direct confrontation, acknowledged the injuries of the homeless and did not use the term "invader" to describe. Repórter Brasil also stands

9 These words were seen in the recorded images of a police station, showing women and children sitting down in a police station courtyard. The fact that SBT, a TV network based in São Paulo, was the only one broadcasting such images allows consideration of the hypothesis that other teams were not present on the ground, and that the exclusivity of this information broadcast by them precisely results in the possession of those images – strengthening the thesis of the police and their place of significance as sources of information – and, naturally, the decision to broadcast them. Possession of exclusive images can also explain the reasons through which Jornal da Cultura, also based in São Paulo, was alone in showing a woman crying and warning to the presence of children in the building.

10 José Balestiero (PM riot police commander): "This is done by vandals, who are opportunists, taking advantage of this moment to break the law and riot".

11 "According to the police, protests started with the building eviction. But those responsible for the riot would be groups not related in any way to the residents".

12 Nivaldo Cesar Restivo (riot police commander) "We see that there are many opportunists. The fluctuating population in the region nowadays is very large, so not everyone involved in these acts of vandalism are part of the movement evicted from the building today".

13 "These vandals were infiltrating among the residents and went out into the streets downtown".

out by pointing out a case of assault during the riot involving a person wearing a press vest, showing a less corporative journalistic attitude.[14]

All of the television newscasts analyzed refer to confusion, confrontation or arrests resulting from the repossession action.[15] Only the Jornal Nacional (Rede Globo) news report lead[16] and one of the SBT news stories allow one to interpret that the homeless alone had confronted the PM: "Repossession action in downtown São Paulo motivates confrontation between PM and homeless" and "PM and homeless clash during repossession"., respectively. However, unlike the Rede Globo coverage, SBT speaks of vandals and opportunistic demonstrators.

4 Interpretive Framing

Once the analysis of news framing is complete, we move to interpretive framing analysis. Even if news framing has the effect of favoring a certain interpretation of events, it is useful to consider, analytically, that presenting a definition of the problem, a causal interpretation and a recommended solutions comes from a distinct type of framing. The reporter or anchor, actors such as representatives of the social movement, specialists, witnesses and political leaders can contribute to interpretive framing. Observing who is asked to comment and has their statements included in reports is, thus, a crucial element in an interpretive framing analysis of a journalistic report.

Most reports showed images of the occupied building facade where the red flag of the Frente de Luta por Moradia could be seen.[17] Nevertheless,

14 "Down the theater stairs, a woman was assaulted by a man after throwing a plastic bottle at a group of police officers. He was dressing a press vest and was not arrested, unlike many homeless who taken to the police station".

15 TV Brasil: "Repossession creates confusion in downtown São Paulo", Rede Record: "Repossession ends in confusion in downtown São Paulo", TV Cultura: "Vandalism, brawls and arrests in downtown São Paulo during repossession of a building occupied by 200 homeless families", TV Band: "Downtown São Paulo has confrontation during repossession", SBT: "Repossession in São Paulo ends up with 70 arrests".

16 In television news jargon, "lead" is the report's introduction, which synthesizes the news and announces the opening of the report.

17 According to the Ponte Jornalismo website, an alternative media outlet, the occupation was conducted by the Movimento pela Reforma Urbana (Homeless Movement for Urban Reform – MSTRU) alongside the Frente de Luta por Moradia (Struggle for Housing Front – FLM) and the Movimento Sem-Teto do Centro (Downtown Homeless Movement – MSTC). Source: <http://ponte.org/reintegracao-de-posse-leva-caos-e-sofrimento-ao-centro-de-sp/> accessed 01/20/2018.

TABLE 5.5 Interpretive framing – direct sources

Television newscast	A movement representative was allowed to speak	Police allowed to speak
Jornal Nacional	yes (the coordinator of the Central dos Movimentos Populares)	yes
SBT Brasil	no	yes
Jornal da Record	yes (lawyer representing families)	yes
Jornal da Band	no	yes
Jornal da Cultura	yes (unidentified occupier)	yes
Repórter Brasil	yes (Frente de Luta por Moradia representative)	yes

Note: T.N.: Popular Movements Central

information about this movement being the occupation organizer was only directly broadcast by SBT Brasil,[18] and indirectly by Repórter Brasil, which asked a direct representative of the movement to speak and give her version of the facts (see Table 5.5).

The diversity of sources representing the homeless may reveal the difficulty in identifying and accessing legitimate representatives of the movement, and the diffuse leadership of the movement demonstrates the difficulty in identifying spokespersons. The newscasts that expressly named some social movement as the occupation organizer were SBT Brasil and Jornal Nacional. However, the latter attributed the occupation to the Movimento Sem-Teto,[19] a broad denomination not corresponding to the name of any of the specific movements involved.

In pursuit of a more systematic analysis, we will distinguish between three levels of interpretive framing analysis: problem definition, event causes, and solutions.

The framing of the problem definition does not refer to the reasons for the confrontations, but to the underlying housing-based problem. Only Jornal da Cultura,[20] which spoke of the housing deficit, presented a problem

18 "Frente de Luta por Moradia, responsible for the occupation, (...)".
19 T.N.: Homeless Movement.
20 A public television network.

TABLE 5.6 Interpretive framing – disagreement between homeless and the police

Television newscast	Disagreement is mentioned
Jornal Nacional	yes
SBT Brasil	yes
Jornal da Record	no
Jornal da Band	no
Jornal da Cultura	no
Repórter Brasil	yes

definition: "The housing deficit in the city of São Paulo is currently at 230,000 housing units. At least 90 vacant lots and buildings, most of them privately owned, are occupied by homeless workers".

In addition to the reluctance of those families to leave their current place of habitation, the direct reasons for confrontations, which we have depicted as interpretive framing referring to the causes of the event, seem to have involved misunderstandings related to an agreement concerning the number of trucks available for eviction. As many newscasts stated, this was the third repossession attempt, the first two having been suspended for failure to reach an agreement to make trucks available to transport the belongings of the evictees (see Table 5.6).[21]

Information about this disagreement is meaningful for the analysis, as to some extent the occupiers' reaction could have been motivated by noncompliance with a previous agreement. Jornal da Cultura does not explicitly mention the agreement, saying only that: "The delay in parking the moving trucks provoked misunderstandings". In Jornal da Record, although the report also does not mention the disagreement, there is the information, through an interview with the "lawyer representing the families", that there was a mediation

21 The text of the Jornal Nacional report, for example, says: "Invaders had been warned of eviction but refused to leave. They claimed there were not enough trucks for removing the furniture. Two prior repossession attempts had already been suspended for this reason, but this time the building owner and the PM said there were 40 moving trucks. As no agreement was reached, the police decided to enter the building. Confusion ensued".

problem.[22] In the only interview granted by a Frente de Luta por Moradia representative broadcast by the television newscast in the sample analyzed, Repórter Brasil (TV Brasil) reports that in fact an unfulfilled agreement was in place.[23]

Finally, on the interpretive framing of the solution, its total absence in five out of the six newscasts analyzed stands out. The only one tackling this aspect was Jornal da Cultura. This one was set apart by mentioning the stance of the São Paulo City Hall concerning the renovation of the building to transform into housing.[24]

5 The Homeless from the Commiseration Point of View: The Wilton Paes de Almeida Building Collapse Affair in 2018

Four years later, in 2018, the Wilton Paes de Almeida building, listed by CONPRESP,[25] abandoned since 2003, and occupied for years,[26] collapsed due to a fire. The issue of occupations in downtown São Paulo was entering, once again, the television newscast agenda.

By analyzing the Jornal Nacional coverage of May 1, 2018 (the collapse happened at dawn that same day), continuities and discontinuities related to the 2014 coverage are seen.

The news stories did not refer to them as "invaders", as the same newscast had referred to the occupiers of the Hotel Aquarius in 2014.[27] Because of the

---

22 Juliane Avance (lawyer representing the families) the family's lawyer: "Also because the judge did not mediate this situation. Judges currently let the military police mediate the repossession situation. This is our current problem".

23 Ivanete Araújo (Frente de Luta por Moradia representative): "There was an unfulfilled agreement when they arrived here at the door. The authorities said they would repossess the building anyway".

24 "City Hall states that transforming the old hotel occupied by the homeless workers into a people's habitation is not doable because of the costs. With the amount spent to renovate the building, which has around 100 apartments, it would be possible to build three habitation complexes".

25 The Civil Council for the Preservation of Historical, Cultural and Environmental Property of the city of São Paulo.

26 A report devoted to the matter, broadcast by Fantástico on 05/06/2018, stated that the building had been occupied since December, 2014, while a report broadcast on the 05/01/2018 edition of Jornal Nacional said that the occupation started in 2006.

27 Within the whole body of news stories devoted to the matter, a total of more than 20 minutes were dedicated to references to abandoned buildings that "ended up invaded by social movements", but the residents of the occupied buildings are not even once

tragic nature of the fire, terms such as "victims" or simply "residents" were used to describe the occupants.[28] Indeed, the tone was clearly one of commiseration,[29] and the homeless were portrayed as hardworking people, emphasizing that they study and work. A statement from the interview with 16-year-old student Leandro Bueno Araújo closed one of the news stories: "Yes, I am going to school tomorrow. With my head up because the world is not for weaklings". Praise of the heroism of the firefighters[30] was also evident, similarly to the relative adherence to the police officers' point of view in the 2014 coverage.

As for the social movements, the treatment was negative, backed by accounts from some residents, according to whom the Movimento Luta Social por Moradia[31] was charging some of them rent and building management and maintenance fees. This time the homeless were depicted as victims both of the fire and the social movements.[32] In an excerpt, reporter Gabriela Azevedo talks about the precariousness of the residents' living conditions. Without mentioning factors like unemployment, high levels of social inequality in Brazil, the housing deficit in São Paulo, or even the responsibility of public authorities, her comments suggest a causal relationship between this precariousness and the social movements.[33]

Predominant episodic framing also marked this coverage, which can be measured by the shorter video dedicated to sources that dealt with the less immediate aspects, like broader housing issues and responsibility for the

described as "invaders". In the Fantástico (a Rede Globo news magazine show) coverage, while the anchor Tadeu Schmidt speaks of an "invaded building", both during the report and in the text published on the website, "occupied building" is used whereas "invaders" are never mentioned.

28 As in one of the news story headlines: "In eight seconds, building collapses and leaves residents desperate".

29 It speaks of "despair" and "pain".

30 Live, reporter Roberto Kovalick highlights "the firefighters are going to spend the night working tirelessly in despite of all this smoke" and puts on a serious face when saying "firefighters will use their own hands to look for survivors". The closure of an interview with Fire Brigade sergeant Diego da Silva also stresses the corporation's heroism: "We will always try to fight until the last moment. Both with my life and my mates' lives, even the victims' lives. We never give up, we will always fight until the end".

31 T.N.: Social Struggle for Housing Movement.

32 As is suggested by one of the relatively long – by newscasts standards – news story (03′47″): "Victims said they paid rent to live in the now collapsed building".

33 "Long before the collapse, the building residents were already living with insecurity and precariousness. Many of them said that they paid to live here and lived among threats of eviction and the tragedy that just happened".

building conditions (01′25″),[34] as compared to the set of sources that dealt with the rescue operation and the collapse itself in great detail (03′12″).[35]

Another common narrative in the coverage in 2014 and 2018 was the privileged approach given to the property administration aspects of the Hotel Aquarius, a privately-owned hotel, and the Wilton Paes de Almeida building, a building of recognized architectural and historical value and a federal government property, respectively. In 2018, this aspect was evident in a journalistic angle based on the issue of public property preservation.

Surprisingly, among the news stories comprising the edition of Jornal Nacional that day, the only one speaking of a "housing crisis" was not referring to the city of São Paulo. The decision of Rede Globo to mention the housing issue in a news story about New York City housing policies sounds strategic. The news story[36] gave the floor to Brenda Rosen, from NGO Breaking Ground, that defended offering housing as a less expensive alternative than leaving people on the streets and paying for health and safety costs. The set of news stories broadcast in that Jornal Nacional edition did not bring, however, an equivalent interpretive analysis concerning the Brazilian case.

When discussing the housing policies of other countries, the main TV network strategy was to deal indirectly with the housing issue without addressing the materiality of the situation underlying the occurrences reported on national soil. In this way, even if abstractly, since it is not directly related to those groups in Brazil, Rede Globo raises the broader theme of housing policies directed at vulnerable populations. Resorting to American reality seems to suggest recognition of interest in such policies, but not as part of the reality of a country like Brazil. From this comes a certain dissimulation of the housing problem in an urban center like São Paulo; the general question is brought up, but the specific one is not put in the agenda.

6 Closing Comments

The data presented helps to go beyond an understanding attributing television news coverage features to inherent traits of the television format,[37] as it shows

34 Political leaders (30″ in total), the Federal Government Property superintendent (35″) and members of the social movement (20″).

35 Firefighters (2′30″ in total), forensic expert Lorenço Trapé Neto (16″) and civil engineer Júlio Timmerman (26″).

36 Entitled "In New York, law compels City Hall to find housing for the homeless".

37 For a discussion on technological determinism, the reader can refer to Raymond Williams (2016).

differences among the respective TV networks. Indeed, the set of analysis results shows a predominance of journalistic coverage generally broadcasting social movement representations in a negative on commercial TV networks, as different from those broadcast by the public networks. Both public television networks stood out for their coverage: only Jornal da Cultura offered an interpretive framing relative to the problem definition and to the solution, and Repórter Brasil was alone in directly interviewing a Frente de Luta por Moradia representative and revealing questionable police behavior.

The distinct ways of covering the homeless can also be explained through the social distance separating the morphological composition of newsrooms and their respective audiences on one hand, and the homeless groups, on the other. Moreover, the repossession of the Hotel Aquarius, by bringing to light the private property occupation matter – unlike the Wilton Paes de Almeida building fire incident, a landmarked building – concerns the economic interests of those acting in the housing market, i.e., real estate owners, such as well-paid members of the TV network teams themselves, as well as portions of their audience, especially when dealing with TV networks, such as Rede Globo, whose audiences have a relatively high purchasing power.

Analysis results showed how hard it is, however, to generalize conclusions when identifying specific forms of coverage particular to each media outlet, for the analyst faces partially contradictory data. Thus, it is necessary to state that television news content is determined not only by the TV network editorial line, world views held by journalists involved, the political context and the target audience, but also television news fast production work routines, dictated by the immediate context of news production.

Jornal Nacional represented the homeless in an especially negative way. Other studies have pointed out the moralistic bias of Rede Globo in journalism that frames social movements unfavorably. This was the case in a content analysis conducted in 1997, concluding that framing used by Jornal Nacional when covering the MST portrayed "the homeless as violent, irresponsible and not worthy of trust" (Aldé; Lattman-Weltman, 2000: 108). This study also analyzed SBT television news, describing the network coverage (as that of the Jornal Nacional) as "dramatic", highlighting "elements of danger" and "confrontation".

Our analysis came to the same conclusion: SBT, a less prestigious TV network than Rede Globo, focused on shows addressed to a more popular audience. It was the only one using music and dramatic graphic effects to show the conflicts, dedicating most of its time to broadcasting violent images.

A plethora of factors explains the differences in representations of the homeless broadcast by television newscasts in 2014 and 2018.

On the one hand, the nature of the occurrences reported and the programs. In 2014, it was, above all, the conflict, the acts of vandalism, and their repercussions for the everyday life of downtown São Paulo that seem to have justified the repossession resonance in newscasts, based on a criminalizing bias of the homeless and a reading of facts favoring the property owner's point of view. In 2018, the tragic dimension of a fire and building collapse of huge proportions, with material – an architectural landmark disappearing from the city – and human losses – the disappearing of residents in the building debris –, prompted TV networks to adopt a perspective of commiseration for the homeless groups.

On the other hand, the political scenario. The repossession held in September 2014 happened less than a month before presidential elections in which the leftist Partido dos Trabalhadores[38] (PT) was running for its fourth consecutive presidential term. The broadcasting of negative representations of social movements could be considered to have been influenced by pervasive attitudes of rejection towards the PT launched by the biggest media outlets, something likewise felt by many layers of Brazilian society.

In 2018, also a presidential election year, the gradual proximity of the Rede Globo editorial line in relation to themes concerning the defense of oppressed groups like Blacks and the LGBT was advancing, while competing TV networks envisaged a more conservative audience. This movement, which grew deeper during the second half of the 2010s, while the political ascension of Jair Bolsonaro and his agenda of attacking those groups was being affirmed, can also contribute to understanding the less negative ways in which the homeless were seen in 2018 at Rede Globo.

References

Aldé, Alessandra; Lattman-Weltman. Fernando. "O MST na TV: Sublimação do político, moralismo e crônica cotidiana do nosso 'estado de natureza'".Contracampo [online]. 2000, no 5 [20-03-2017]. Available at https://periodicos.uff.br/contracampo/.

Cappella, Joseph; Kathleen, Jamieson. (1997), "Spiral of Cynicism", New York, Oxford University Press.

Entman, Robert, "Framing: Toward clarification of a fractured paradigm", Journal of Communication [online]. 1993, vol. 43, no 4 [12-03-2017]. Available at https://online library.wiley.com/journal/14602466.

38 T.N.: Worker's Party.

Harsin, Jayson. "Cultural Racist Frames in TF1's French Banlieue Riots Coverage", French Politics, Culture & Society [online]. 2015, vol 33, no 3 [10-03-2017]. Available at https://www.berghahnjournals.com/view/journals/fpcs/33/3/fpcs330303.xml.

Nelson, Thomas; Zoe, Oxley; Rosalee Clawson. "Toward a psychology of framing effects" Political Behavior [online]. 1997, vol. 19, no 3 [12-03-2017]. Available at http://citeseerx.ist.psu.edu/viewdoc/summary?doi=10.1.1.466.4209.

Porto, Mauro. (2004), "Enquadramentos da mídia e política", *in* A. C. Rubim, *Comunicação e política: conceitos e abordagens*. Salvador, Edufba, pp. 73–104.

Williams, Raymond. (2016 [1974]), *Televisão*: tecnologia e forma cultural. São Paulo, Boitempo.

CHAPTER 6

Immortal and Happy! Myths about Vulnerability in the Press

José A. Ruiz San Román, Enrique García Romero, Jaqueline García Cordero, Lucía Acuña-Pedro, and Miranda Claudio Cornejo

The greatest problems, inquiries and facts of our existence can be seen through humanity's stories: happiness, vulnerability, fear, progress, self-improvement, immortality and so on. Each era has had its own ways of expressing the strength of these catchy yet disconcerting experiences. However, there is a narrative that appears frequently: in the face of uncertainty and fear, stories have been fundamental for representing, understanding, coping and building one's own existence and reality as a whole. Civilizations have forged its foundations through and thanks to the human capacity of storytelling and thinking. Every society and each individual is built around stories that are transmitted from one generation to the next, and although, apparently, they are not related, they always lead to the same place, to the origin of everyone and everything. "Humanity allows itself to be guided not by its reason, but by the desire, the need to know the origin and root of beings and things (...) if science fails to provide a convenient or satisfactory explanation, humanity will turn to its heart and imagination" (Commelin 2017, 8).

For the Hellenes of Antiquity, myths are fantastic stories or so, of a greater or lesser quality from which moral lessons can be learned, in other words, they depict proposals for achieving plenitude and happiness of oneself and the community. Even though logic reasoning and fantasy seem to be opposed, and may appear as antagonistic realities, as seen through this book, they may also result complementary. This is the case of some narratives expressed by myths.

Mythos, whose meaning is words (Jennings 2004), speech or story shared through oral tradition (Grimal 1998), have been part of every civilization throughout the world's history. Nevertheless, Greek culture gave humanity a remarkable collection of sources that are kept under the name "classical mythology", these stories have become a reference and an endless source of inspiration (Cardona 2018). Classic myths are, in a way, living stories because "a myth is not an independent reality but one that evolves according to the historical and ethnical conditions" (Grimal 1998, 17), if interpreted and understood from the right perspective myths hold and protect information that even nowadays gives us light about our past, present and future. It is not daring to affirm that myths, even today, accompany, guide and forge us.

1 Classical Greek Mythology on Vulnerability and Happiness

Greek mythology shows vulnerable beings who in order to face their weaknesses aim to progress, to make an improvement. Not even heroes, nor gods in myths are exempted from experiencing this multifaceted human condition that coexists in cotidinity because "there is no invulnerable human life; human life as such is vulnerable. Birth and death mark the vulnerable transitions in which the interrelated dependency, fragility and the bundle of possibilities ahead and behind become real" (Günter and Heike 2017, 17).

Human willingness to overcome vulnerability has been depicted differently according to the era and culture. In the case of our Greek ancestors, it was in myths where the fear of the passing of time was more latent. Grimal's (1951) compilation in Dictionary of Greek and Roman Mythology will be used to raise several examples.

Although the desire for immortality is the final longing of the human race, it must always be accompanied, in order to be fully enjoyable, of beauty and youth. Forever young and forever beautiful, a diachronic, universal, unattainable and cursed quest. The stories of elderly people trapped in young bodies and fine faces that hide the darkest of secrets are endless. One of the very first testimonies and contributions to Greek mythology about the Fountain of Youth can be found in Book III of The History of Herodotus of Halicarnassus (Herodotus 2018):

> [3.23] The Icthyophagi then in their turn questioned the king concerning the term of life, and diet of his people, and were told that most of them lived to be a hundred and twenty years old, while some even went beyond that age – they ate boiled flesh, and had for their drink nothing but milk. When the Icthyophagi showed wonder at the number of the years, he led them to a fountain, wherein when they had washed, they found their flesh all glossy and sleek, as if they had bathed in oil – and a scent came from the spring like that of violets. The water was so weak, they said, that nothing would float in it, neither wood, nor any lighter substance, but all went to the bottom. If the account of this fountain is true, it would be their constant use of the water from it which makes them so long-lived.

Traditionally, from a western perspective, longevity has always been related to exotic places, its customs, rituals, and, in this case, to particularly wonderful places such as a fountain and its water.

If, instead of enclaves with supernatural powers, eternal life is searched through gods' favors, we must be careful what we wish for. In the myth of Eos, goddess of the dawn, and Titono, a mortal, we are shown an impossible love between two incompatible lineages. Nonetheless, and exceptionally, Zeus granted Eos' wish to give Titono immortality with a trap: Eos forgot to include in her request that her husband was also given the gift of eternal youth. Consequently, an old and ill Titono was finally locked at her palace.

As for beauty, there are some historical facts about how even in the midst of wars or poverty, people were concerned about the care of their physical appearance. Probably it was the upper classes, the wealthy ones, who spent more time and money for those purposes, but all of them did. Among the most famous ointments is the one provided by Aphrodite to Phaon. Phaon was a poorly graceful boatman who transported, without asking for anything in return, Aphrodite, without knowing that the passenger was the goddess of love herself, since she was disguised as an old woman. She, grateful for the gesture, gave the man an ointment that turned him into a beautiful creature, who even managed to charm Sappho, who ended up killing herself after the rejection of Phaon.

A person will not always be young nor always be beautiful, and based on those who have been, humans will always feel discouraged to be so. If we persist trying, the Moirai will set limits, whilst Clotho (from the Greek κλώθω, "to spin") waves the thread that will be our life and Lachesis (from the Greek λαγχάνω, "cast lots") allocates our future. At the end, scissor in hand, awaits the unavoidable Atropos (from the Greek ἄτροπος, "inevitable").

The loss of youth and beauty are the prelude to the final chapter of life. If humans were to know their fatal ending in advance, the distress would be elongated, however if the loss was unexpected, it would feel all of a sudden. Truth is we, humans, will never be ready to accept that one day we are no longer going to be here, thus will not be concerned about the clock. Fear of death is perhaps the most understandable and common dread, it has a different nature, out of all other phobias: we fear death from plurality and acknowledge its enforceability. In Greek antiquity death was already an abundant thought and it was seen and represented through three main branches: how to avoid it, how to rescue someone from it and how to triumph over it.

It is no coincidence that the name of the hero who tries to dodge death is *Akhil(l)eús* the contraction of *Akhí-lāu̯os* whose etymological meaning is directly related to pain and grief (Nagy 1999) since the origin of the term vulnerability comes from the Latin word vulnus which means wound, blow, sting, disgrace or affliction (Feito 2007). Achilles, son of the goddess Thetis, was the result of a forced marriage between her and a mortal, since despite having suitors such as Zeus and Poseidon, they were warned that if a child were to born as a result of their relationship with the goddess, they would be replaced. Thetis, resentful, kills her first six children, but saves the seventh who received the gift of invulnerability by being submerged in the lake Styx held by the heel, the only part of him that the holy water did not touch (Zukerfeld and Zonis 2005).

Achilles goes to war accompanied by his friend Patroclus, and throughout the battles, he kills thousands of warriors, including Tenes, son of Apollo, Hector and Pentesilia, the Amazon warrior with whom he was in love. Nonetheless, the sudden but announced end of Achilles comes from Paris's hands, son of Priam, who with the help of Apollo manages to wound him lethally by shooting an arrow in Achilles' only vulnerable body part, his heel (Zukerfeld and Zonis 2005). However, Achilles' true vulnerability, contrary to what is believed, was not the heel, the Iliad is the story of the progressive breakthrough of the human in the demigod.

"His excellence is not found in his achievements alone (…) His virtue lies in part in his responses to his vulnerability, and his eventual acceptance of the inevitability of death and the loss of honor and of friends as part of living well" (Berzins 2013, 19). It is Achilles who, having the possibility of choosing between having a long life without remarkable events and living a short but heroic life, chooses to die soon but giving Troy and Patroclus, who was assassinated, glory and honour. Reaffirming that Achilles' virtue and strength was not the result of the absence of fear, but of his fragility (Berzins 2013). Perhaps the most heroic feature of a human being is his ability to cope with life knowing that the end is imminent, and still, fight every day to have one more.

A universally known rescue from the dead is κατάβασις (from the Greek κατά, "below", and βαίνω, "go") of Orpheus. It is probably the most famous katabasis along with Homer's Odyssey. The descents to hell, as any other contact with the dead, overall have a premonitory and catastrophic overtone, these interactions between both worlds should be meticulously done, because for the Greeks the living and the dead shall not be together.

The most accepted tradition tells us that Eurydice, Orpheus' wife, while escaping from Aristaeus dies from a snake bite. Orpheus, desperate for the sudden loss of her woman, descends to hell charming with his lyre all the obstacles that were presented to him in the journey. The gatekeepers of the underworld, Persephone and Hades, agreed that Orpheus could guide Eurydice back, with the proviso that he must not look at her until they have reached their destination. Orpheus accepts, but just about to achieve it, giving into the uncertainty of being deceived by the guardians or having lost her in the journey, he turns to verify if it was her, losing Eurydice for a second time and on this occasion, forever.

When speaking about the victory over death, we are faced with myths such as that of Asclepius. Son of Apollo, educated by the centaur Chiron, a scholar in different artistic branches and professor par excellence of mythological childhoods, of whom a young Asclepius learned so much, that achieves the discovery of a cure for death through the use of the blood on the right side of Medusa, the gorgon, thus having the power of resurrecting numerous figures. Zeus, enraged because Asclepius' action misaligned the natural order and defied divine force, killed him with one of his rays.

These three narrative categories, the avoidance of death, the rescue from the death and the victory over death, are traversed by the same notion: the inability to assume its unavoidable condition, especially that of those who are loved by us, and the mistake that doing so represents for both the living and the death. Previously, Thetis, unable to accept the mortal condition of her heritage by having a human father, subjected several of her children to procedures that aimed to foster her perpetuity, all unsuccessful and lethal for them, also leading to the failure of her marriage with Peleo. Moreover, Orpheus not only could not rescue Eurydice, but made her die again and found his own death for having crossed the border between the world of the living and the death. Finally, Asclepius obtained the severest punishment for his arrogance, death itself.

Death and old age are presented to us as the most inescapable destiny that can only be delayed but not avoided. In Classical Antiquity, in the absence of material means to extend our existence, we resorted to narratives with rituals and magic, but only to discover their ineffectiveness and emphasize acceptance as the only method to overcome our natural mortal condition. In modernity, these "retardants" are the scientific and technological advances, which Thetis could only have dreamed of, that have become more resistant and effective, fueling the pride of Asclepius, without realizing that we are our own Orpheus and our own Eurydice, and that we too have an Achilles heel.

Although vulnerability is inevitable, it is not an unalterable condition, since there are several factors that may intervene in its perception and experimentation: "hence, this is the key that holds the moral obligation of a preventive, healing, social, economical, or any other kind of action that could potentially minimize, palliate or avoid this favorable conditions for damage, those vulnerable spaces" (Feito 2007, 11). Said moral obligation or commitment, as a result of uncertainty, triggers a series of actions and events that generate changes within all spheres of society (Riesco 2014), in other words, vulnerability unleashes progress.

Cycles are part of human existence, whilst one human dies another is born, and that is the continuity that allows each generation to take up what the other did not conclude. *Gressus* is the passive participle of *gradi* whose meaning is walking, taking steps, therefore, the word progress or *progressus* means going forward (Rodríguez 2006 as cited in Rivas 2008). To make progress one must move forward and in order to advance it is fundamental to know where to go. The actions that aim to overcome vulnerability draw from the real community, the one we have, to the ideal community, the one we aspire to build, and it needs freedom, good will and the responsibility and solidarity with others in order to be sustained. Consequently, progress has the firm duty to contribute towards the realization of all human beings and to the preservation and proliferation of its species (Rivas 2008).

Prometheus, in ancient Greek, means forecast or prospection (Luján 2010) and it is, precisely, the name conferred to the titan who gave humans, depending on the version, all of the good and bad, their misfortune and salvation. The Greek myth of Prometheus has two main variations Hesiod's in the "Theogony" and in "The Labors and Days", and Aeschylus' in "Prometheus in Chains". In the former, the titan is anything but a hero and in the latter, he is who creates the idea of progress in humanity. Hence, the myth of Prometheus could be the story of each person (García 2006).

In the sacrifice that formalizes the covenant between men and gods in Mecona, Prometheus deceives Zeus by dividing an ox into two parts, within the first part were the meat and the entrails wrapped in the skin of the animal, in the other, the animal's skeleton surrounded by fat, the purpose was tricking the father of gods into thinking the second part contained the meat. So it was, Zeus chose the second option and as he realized he was being fooled, he decided to punish humans by hiding the fire from them. Prometheus manages to mislead him once more and steals the hidden fire to return it to men, this rebellious action unleashed Zeus' rage and, as a punishment, he sent the first woman to earth with the purpose of releasing all evil and misery contained in a jar (García 2006).

Prometheus' good deed, giving back the fire to humanity, is key to understanding progress. Fire allowed men to cook their food and expand their territories. In addition, fire is a defense instrument, it encourages the development of techniques that fostered agriculture and this, in turn, technological, social and cultural growth (Mora 2010). Moreover, by returning fire to men, Prometheus became their creator, since fire gave them spirit and wisdom, attributes that drove humans to find their liberty and in doing so, developing their maximum potential, making men similar to gods (García 2006). Nevertheless, fire heats, but also burns, illuminates, but also sweeps away, as progress does.

Progress has limits and those boundaries lie in wisdom's dual force, for whoever dares to defy vulnerability, even with progress, awaits a lifetime of disappointment. The consolation, then, is knowing we are capable of being part of something greater than ourselves, something that transcends our finite existence: "Today science and technology are ahead of social needs, which is not necessarily reasonable nor beneficial. These advances (…) are human products that have merit and deserve respect, as long as they contribute to the freedom and wellness of humanity" (Riesco 2014, 35).

Have we really known how to use Prometheus' fire?, or have we fallen into the pride that led Asclepius' knowledge to feel that we have power over death? Are we close to achieving immortality?, or are we just ignoring that not even Achilles was invulnerable? Have we managed to find a fountain of eternal beauty and youth?, or have we forgotten, like Eos did, that time always takes what belongs to him? Have we crossed the limits of what is humanly possible like Orpheus?, or are we simply trying to change the course of what Lachesis has already written for us?

Without a doubt, one of the narratives that underwent the greatest changes in the modern era has been human vulnerability. No one is ever ready for crises nor for death, even if they think they are, and yet we keep fighting our own Troy, challenging fate with the only weapon that has always allowed us to move forward, knowledge and humility in the face of the unknown.

2 Science, Technology and Happiness

Classical literature is not the only way to approach the myths that still shape us about vulnerability, immortality, and progress. At other times in history, enduring myths have been created and consolidated that continue to influence us. A good example is the cultural and ideological environment of the late 18th and 19th centuries that brought new political and philosophical approaches.

Rationalist thinking, characteristic of the Enlightenment, insisted on the ability of human reason to solve problems. A powerful idea was sweeping the intellectual world: the use of rational thought will make us happy.

It is indisputable that fostering rigorous scientific research advances society. The application of new scientific knowledge to concrete and tangible improvements in transport, food production, health care, etc. has improved the lives of millions of people. The decisive factor is the application of the so-called scientific method.

In the same period of history, philosophy, by contrast, underwent a serious crisis. On the one hand, it has been moving away from the quality of the golden age of scholastic thought that took place in the distant 13th century. In later centuries it is difficult to find thinkers of the stature and intellectual capacity of Thomas Aquinas or Bonaventure. Old disputes, to a large extent sterile or already sufficiently resolved, are repeated. It seems that there is little to add to what has already been said or, what is worse, that what has already been said has little to contribute to the contemporary world.

The best students begin to be more interested in scientific knowledge than in philosophical knowledge. It seems logical because disciplines like Physics are making remarkable advances. More and more invariable physical laws are known by which matter is organized and the movements of the celestial bodies farthest from the Earth can be predicted with surprising precision or it has become possible to support buildings standing with little support and remarkable security.

In those years the situation seems to be able to be summarized in that the Sciences advance with benefit for humanity. And Philosophy seems stagnant, boring and dying.

The situation leads thinkers to wonder about the causes of science success. And the answer ends up being concretized in what has been called the "scientific method", which consists of looking for invariable laws in nature through empirical research, through trial and error. And, from these laws and from those investigations, to extract new hypotheses that will have to be contrasted again with new empirical tests. And so on, true and proven knowledge about reality accumulates.

This way of proceeding has led Physics to discover stable laws on the resistance of solid bodies or on the dynamics of fluids that have made it possible to predict the movements of the planets or to construct safer and more comfortable buildings. Confidence in science is growing more and more. Even, in some cases, with a touch of exaggeration. It is precisely these cases of exaggerated confidence in the ability of Science that are of interest to us at the moment.

Some authors begin to refer to a certain "scientist excess". Some of the great novels of the 19th century reflect this in a masterful way. Chapter 2 of Dickens's novel "Hard Times", entitled "Killing Innocents" is an ironic denunciation of the exaggerated scientific zeal of the moment.

In the following text Dickens shows the dialogue between a teacher proud of his scientific training and a girl who claims with naive innocence the role of the imagination.

'So you would carpet your room – or your husband's room, if you were a grown woman, and had a husband – with representations of flowers, would you?' said the gentleman. 'Why would you?'

'If you please, sir, I am very fond of flowers,' returned the girl.

'And is that why you would put tables and chairs upon them, and have people walking over them with heavy boots?'

'It wouldn't hurt them, sir. They wouldn't crush and wither, if you please, sir. They would be the pictures of what was very pretty and pleasant, and I would fancy

– "Ay, ay, ay! But you mustn't fancy,' cried the gentleman, quite elated by coming so happily to his point. 'That's it! You are never to fancy.'

'You are not, Cecilia Jupe,' Thomas Gradgrind solemnly repeated, 'to do anything of that kind.'

'Fact, fact, fact!' said the gentleman. And 'Fact, fact, fact!' repeated Thomas Gradgrind.

'You are to be in all things regulated and governed,' said the gentleman, 'by fact. We hope to have, before long, a board of fact, composed of commissioners of fact, who will force the people to be a people of fact, and of nothing but fact. You must discard the word Fancy altogether. You have nothing to do with it. You are not to have, in any object of use or ornament, what would be a contradiction in fact. You don't walk upon flowers in fact; you cannot be allowed to walk upon flowers in carpets. You don't find that foreign birds and butterflies come and perch upon your crockery; you cannot be permitted to paint foreign birds and butterflies upon your crockery. You never meet with quadrupeds going up and down walls; you must not have quadrupeds represented upon walls. You must use,' said the gentleman, 'for all these purposes, combinations and modifications (in primary colours) of mathematical figures which are susceptible of proof and demonstration. This is the new discovery. This is fact. This is taste.'

DICKENS, 1854

Dickens's clarity, finesse, and irony require no further explanation to show the risks of exaggerating the role of Science.

3 Pandemic and Vulnerabilities

The pandemic that appeared in 2020 spread awareness of vulnerability throughout the Earth. The pandemic and the consequent awareness of vulnerability challenged the idea of humanity in continuous progress thanks to science and put disease, pain, crisis and death on the public agenda.

The dictionaries reveal the relationship between vulnerability and being exposed to the possibility of being attacked or harmed, either physically or emotionally (Real Academia Española 2019). Concepts such as "injury" or "damage" stand out, that is, vulnerability understood as a greater propensity to be damaged to some extent.

Leading thinkers argue that vulnerability is not a minority trait of a few people. On the contrary, it is an irredeemably human condition, extensible throughout different cultures and historical periods. In reality, if we do not constantly perceive that vulnerability, it is due to a learning of concealment that allows us to live with fragility. We hide our finitude, revealed to a different extent according to everyday events. However, in the course of life, vulnerability would be revealed as a process of maturation.

> Vulnerability is thus universal in the space-time world, but the consciousness of it is not. From the experience of living, we are realizing, as if it were a natural education, not a formal one, that we cannot do everything, that we can fall, that they can hurt us, that we are at the expense of the unexpected, of misfortune that can break in at any moment. We live experiences that place us fully in the awareness of vulnerability
>
> TORRALBA 2010, 29

Karl Jaspers (2012) talks about the human capacity to transcend and go beyond the consciousness of vulnerability because the person is capable of observing the finiteness of the other inhabitants of the universe, but in contrast to other animals he tries to explain it, he it reveals against, generates an "open vulnerability" as a path of salvation.

Martin Pallares (2014), from a philosophical perspective, stresses that the Western philosophical tradition, aware of the finitude that characterises us, would be traversed by human ontological fragility. However, he points out:

> (...) It can be said that modernity, characterised by absolute knowledge, grand narratives, the power of reason and technology, is today in a period of questioning. Reality sharpens the questions that arise from medical-scientific advances, the fragility of nature, the unlimited consumption of limited resources and the inequity in the distribution of the products of the capitalist system; it calls for a deepening of our idea of vulnerability.
>
> PALLARES, 2014, 65

Vulnerability began to play a role in science. It was not enough to point out that all human beings are vulnerable, but certain attributes needed to be identified as indicators of vulnerability for instrumentally effective research.

> Vulnerability was introduced into the field of human research as a characteristic attributed to certain categories of the population considered more exposed and less able to defend themselves against abuse and mistreatment by others. The need for such protection was evidenced by history, as the number of clinical trials undertaken grew enormously in the first half of the 20th century, involving unprotected or institutionalised groups of people. Orphans, prisoners, the elderly and, later, ethnic groups considered inferior, such as Jews and Chinese, were affected. Ethnic minorities, the socially disadvantaged and women were also connoted as vulnerable
>
> CAVALCANTE and SADI 2017, 312

In order to distinguish between vulnerability that affects all people and other specific vulnerabilities with social causes, it has been useful to use the concept of "social vulnerability":

> Situations that generate social vulnerability in research in peripheral countries include: low research capacity in the country; socio-economic disparities in the population; low levels of education; inaccessibility to health services; and specific vulnerabilities related to gender, racial and ethnic issues, among others.
>
> CALVACANTE and SADI 2017, 316

Segura Martina (2020), in relation to pandemic times, points out that the disease, on the one hand, made everyone equal in the face of the natural inclemency, especially in the early days of the disease. As time went on, it became clear that not all population strata suffered equally from the process, because the pandemic has also shown the fragility of social structures. There is a "group vulnerability" which refers to the capacity of a community to cope with the inclemency. The group vulnerability of the community is coupled with the vulnerability of each individual within the community.

Cardona (2001), from the perspective of environmental studies, considers vulnerability as "the internal risk factor of a subject or a system exposed to a threat corresponding to its intrinsic predisposition to be affected". In other words, if a community has sufficient organizational capacity to be able to adapt to a situation that poses a risk to itself, it will have more opportunities to manage it and therefore it will be less vulnerable than another society that lacks this capacity.

From various perspectives, the communitarian aspects of vulnerability have been emphasized. Castel (1995), from the sociology of work, uses the concepts of integration and exclusion: In the exclusion zone, individuals are disaggregated, with no social ties to support them. Kowarick (2009), a social geographer, emphasizes vulnerability as the inability to exercise basic social rights when social assistance systems do not protect citizens. From gender studies, the term patriarchy is used to refer to "a system of sexual domination that is, in addition, the basic system of domination on which the rest are built, such as those of class and race" (Varela 2019, 31)

The evolution of thought has also been reflected in the media. In the same way that we have seen how myths related to the progress and power of science were dominant in the past and, slowly, over time, they were colored by the awareness of personal vulnerability, collective vulnerability and the weaknesses and limitations of science, the media have also modified their stories during the pandemic, as we are going to see.

The pandemic has reminded us that, despite medical advances, nature follows inexorable mechanisms. Some effects can be mitigated. Life expectancy can be lengthened. Science has been able to end some diseases that caused death throughout history. But, at the same time, it has given us the false illusion of being able to control the uncontrollable.

> Modern Scientific Capability has profoundly altered the course of human life. People live longer and better than at any other time in history. But scientific advances have turned the processes of aging and dying into medical experiences, matters to be managed by health care professionals. And we in the medical world have proved alarmingly unprepared for it.
>
> GAWANDE 2015

In some way, the pandemic has come to remind us that our destiny, no matter how much we want to hide it inside hospitals and residences, is death. The late surgeon Sherwin Nuland, in his classic book *How We Die*, lamented, "the necessity of nature's final victory was expected and accepted in generations before our own. Doctors were far more willing to recognize the signs of defeat and far less arrogant about denying them" (Gawande 2015).

Have there been changes in the press when addressing the ideas of progress, scientism and vulnerabilities? A case study on the Peruvian El Comercio.

In this part of the chapter, we try to see if the pandemic caused by COVID-19 has caused changes in the media discourse on the myth of progress, on scientism and on vulnerabilities. In order to reach this objective, we have carried out a qualitative content analysis, focused on a relevant newspaper published in one of the countries most affected by the pandemic: Peru.[1]

Founded in 1839, El Comercio is one of the oldest newspapers in Peru. It belongs to the most relevant media group in the Andean country: Grupo El Comercio, owner of newspapers such as El Comercio, Perú 21, Trome, Gestión and Depor, as well as television networks such as Canal N and América TV. El Comercio has a liberal editorial line, with a center-right focus in the economic and political spheres. According to data from the Peruvian Company for Market Studies and Public Opinion, El Comercio is one of the most widely read newspapers in Lima and throughout Peru.

The dates selected for the content analysis of the editions of El Comercio have been two periods of one month each. First, from January 15 to February 15, 2020, dates that represent the pre-pandemic era. On March 11, 2020, the World Health Organization classified the COVID-19 outbreak as a pandemic, having spread to more than 100 countries in the world simultaneously. Peru decreed a mandatory quarantine as of March 16, 2020. Secondly, we have selected the editions of El Comercio corresponding to January 15 to February 15, 2021, when almost a year had passed since the declaration of the new coronavirus health crisis as a pandemic.

To carry out the content analysis, the sixty editions of the newspaper El Comercio have been consulted, in order to make available to the reader interesting examples that allow to verify or reject the hypotheses raised. Journalistic texts related to the following topics have been analyzed: pandemic, vaccines, science and technology. The content analysis carried out is not quantitative, but qualitative and descriptive, focused on the headlines, subtitles, summaries and issues addressed by journalistic texts. In some cases, paragraphs of the texts that are of interest have been selected to test or reject the hypotheses.

3.1 *Have There Been Changes in the Treatment of the Idea of Progress?*

The first research question is the following: Have there been changes in the treatment of the idea of progress by the press? The hypothesis that arises is that, due to the COVID-19 pandemic, there is more distrust of progress in the analyzed newspaper, but not a radical change.

1 According to Worldometers, Peru is the country in the world that, proportionally, has suffered the most from the consequences of the COVID-19 pandemic: 5,919 deaths per million inhabitants. Retrieved on September 2, 2021 from: https://www.worldometers.info/coronavirus/.

Regarding the first block of newspapers analyzed, published before the pandemic, on February 10, 2020, El Comercio included an article by Elmer Huerta, presented as a public health specialist. The headline was: "A glimpse into the genetic detection of cancer"; and the subtitle: "Imagine being able to determine that in about 15 years you are going to develop a malignant tumor. This is not a crazy idea". The text made reference to a series of articles published by the journal Nature on the relationship between genetics and cancer.

That same day in February 2020, El Comercio published a short news item titled "They develop a new technique to analyze the lunar soil". And the next day, another brief news item with the headline: "A new spacecraft is heading to study the sun".

A year later, on January 19, 2021, El Comercio published a short story with the headline "Experts study the use of fungi to make clothes". The article informs about "a scientific team, in which experts from a Spanish university collaborate, demonstrated that fungi have properties that allow external stimuli to be processed, so they could be used in the manufacture of clothing, electronic devices and in construction".

On that same page, the Peruvian newspaper published a longer article, titled "Are we going to Mars?", by Tomás Unger, presented as a scientific popularizer. The subtitle of the text was: "Sending a crew to this planet implies having suits and habitats that protect people from the extreme Martian conditions". Among other issues, the article pointed out that "there are various plans for a rocket that, in addition to arriving at Mars with a crew, carries enough fuel and a vehicle (capsule or habitable space) for the return. NASA has hired several private companies to present possible solutions".

On January 31, 2021, El Comercio published a testimonial from a Peruvian volunteer from the Johnson & Johnson vaccine trials. The text was included in the National section, with the following headline: "The investigation does not give immunity". In his story, Ronny Isla explained that he got infected with COVID-19 during clinical trials. "Even though I was infected-despite the care I had-it is not possible to conclude that I have received a placebo or a vaccine" said the volunteer.

On February 1, 2021, the Lima newspaper published in the World section a chronicle titled "Disasters that marked NASA". The subtitle was: "Today marks the 18th anniversary of the Columbia shuttle explosion, which followed the Challenger explosion in 1986". The summary of the chronicle was as follows: "The tragedies greatly impacted NASA's plans and the confidence of the American people".

A few days later, on February 4, El Comercio published an article with this headline: "The telephone, a giant advance", signed by the scientific popularizer

Tomás Unger. The text reviewed the history and operation of "a momentous invention, which allowed the entire world to be connected".

In this section, we have not found a large number of news items. The hypothesis raised is only partially proven. Both in the pre-pandemic editions and during the pandemic, El Comercio published texts that deal with human progress, although with small differences, as can be seen in headlines such as "Research does not give immunity" or "Disasters that marked NASA".

3.2 *Have There Been Changes in the Treatment of Scientism?*

The second research question proposed is: Have there been changes in the treatment of scientism by El Comercio? The hypothesis is that, despite the pandemic, there is still great confidence in science, and this is reflected in the journalistic texts published by the newspaper, before the pandemic and a year after its beginning.

In the first block of editions analyzed, previous to the COVID-19 pandemic, El Comercio published, on January 23, 2020, a short notice in the Sciences section titled: "Experts discover a potential method to cure osteoarthritis". On that same page, a broader story appeared with this headline: "At full speed without polluting". It was an article about Formula E racing cars that do not use fuel, as they are completely electric.

On January 28, 2020, in its Sciences section, El Comercio published a short notice with the pretitle "Achievement" and this headline: "Artificially obtained heart muscle transplanted". It was a story about a group of specialists from the University of Osaka (Japan).

On February 11, 2020, El Comercio published a short news item titled "The new coronavirus could cause more than 3,000 deaths". The text stated the following: "Through mathematical models, specialists from the Complutense University of Madrid have estimated that the new coronavirus could affect between 60,000 and 70,000 people and cause more than 3,000 deaths". According to this piece of news, the virus would spread to 47 countries. As can be seen, these specialists fell short in their estimates.

A year later, in the second block of editions analyzed, El Comercio continued to publish texts that showed great confidence in science. For example, on January 20, 2021, on the front page and in the Science section, the Lima newspaper published an interview with biologist Henri Bailón, with the headline "Llama nano antibodies have therapeutic potential". In the interview, Bailón pointed out that, "since August 2020, scientists from the National Institute of Health have been working on the identification of llama nano antibodies capable of neutralizing the new coronavirus".

In a short story published on January 22, 2021, El Comercio reported on the use of satellites to count the number of African elephants. Another short piece of news on the same page was titled "Experts design a jellyfish-inspired robot".

On January 24, 2021, El Comercio published a news item titled "Artificial intelligence is capable of learning on its own", with the subtitle: "Through various studies, a method was created that allows artificial intelligence to discover the best way to learn things by trial and error". The text reported on studies conducted at the University of California with driverless vehicles, domestic robots and other types of devices that could use artificial intelligence to "learn without needing a trainer".

On January 27, 2021, also in the Sciences section, El Comercio published a short news item titled: "Drug reduced the SARS-CoV-2 viral load by 99%". It reported about an antiviral produced by the Spanish company Pharmamar.

On January 30, 2021, the Lima newspaper published on the front page a reference to its Sunday magazine Somos, with the headline "#WithoutScienceNoFuture". It included an interview with a computer scientist, Ragi Burhum, for whom "the only way out of the pandemic is to pay attention to science".

El Comercio published another short news item, on February 9, 2021, titled "A satellite internet system is installed in Manu", a Peruvian national park. And two days later, the Peruvian newspaper published another short story, in the Science section, with the headline "Chinese spacecraft successfully enters orbit of Mars".

On February 12, 2021, El Comercio published in the Science section an article by scientific popularizer Tomás Unger, titled "Vaccines versus the pandemic". The subtitle of the article was: "The development of vaccines against COVID-19 has been comparable to the 'turn of the tide'. The end of the war has begun". The text noted that the vaccines developed "are not only proving effective against variants, but even more crucial is the fact that once effective, vaccines can be adapted to deal with new and future variants relatively quickly". The article ended with this sentence: "We have not won the war against COVID-19 yet, but the tide is already turning".

As can be seen, the hypothesis raised is confirmed, since the level of confidence in science remains high over the months. It could even be said that confidence in science has increased, as can be seen in sentences like "science is the only way out of the pandemic", and the consideration of science as what is allowing humanity to change the trend of the war against the new coronavirus.

3.3 *Have There Been Changes in the Treatment of Vulnerabilities?*

Finally, the third research question proposed is: Have there been changes in the treatment of vulnerabilities by El Comercio? The hypothesis is that, after a year of the COVID-19 pandemic, journalistic texts take more into account that we are vulnerable.

In the first block of editions analysed, prior to the pandemic, we found that El Comercio published, on January 21, 2020, a news item entitled "Mysterious virus in China", in the World section. One of the subtitles was: "President Xi urges authorities that the virus be absolutely stopped". These words were pronounced during his first speech on the new coronavirus. Given what happened later around the world with the pandemic, the Chinese president's statement could seem somewhat naive or even pretentious.

A few days later, on January 27, 2020, in a news item about the first restrictions imposed by the Chinese government to curb the spread of coronavirus, health officials from the Asian country affirmed that the new coronavirus "is not as powerful as the SARS virus (severe acute respiratory syndrome), origin of a lethal epidemic between 2002 and 2003, but more contagious".

On the next page that same day, El Comercio published an article by Elmer Huerta, presented as a public health specialist, with the headline "What we know about the new coronavirus". The subtitle was: "The first analysis suggests that we are facing an infectious agent of moderate contagiousness and low lethality". Huerta stated that "the modern method of Crispr gene editing (which was not available in previous epidemics) will speed up diagnostic tests, which will allow the instant identification of the virus".

On January 30, 2020, El Comercio published a page about coronavirus, when it was still a problem limited to China, where 99% of cases had been detected. The headline of the main story was: "We are not in panic", words spoken by a Peruvian student who lived in Wuhan, where the COVID-19 pandemic began. The student, named Christian Virrueta, stated that he did not feel in danger, was not in a panic, and didn't want to be rescued from the area. Regarding the Chinese political and health authorities, Virrueta believed that "we are talking about a government that faced another crisis of a respiratory disease, SARS. They know how to deal with the issue". At the bottom of the same page, the Lima newspaper included information on the global combat of other past epidemics: smallpox, SARS, Ebola and AIDS.

On February 5, 2020, El Comercio published a story in which the newspaper echoed a call from the World Health Organization for countries not to impose travel restrictions due to the coronavirus. "These kinds of restrictions only increase fear and stigma, and have little public health benefits". As you will recall, just over a month later, many countries established strict mandatory quarantines and closed their borders.

In contrast to the news of 2020, important changes are observed in the journalistic texts published in 2021. On January 18, 2021, almost a year after the start of the COVID-19 pandemic, El Comercio published on its front page and its National section a piece of news titled: "More than 1000 deaths from the virus have been reported so far in 2021". The subtitle said that the Ministry of Health registered more deaths in eighteen days in January than in the entire month of April 2020, when the pandemic began. The article began with these words: "The virus does not know about calendars, nor about good wishes. When the majority of Peruvians expected that this new year would bring with it better indicators regarding the COVID-19 pandemic, recent figures have shown a harsh reality: that 2020 is not over yet".

The following day, January 19, 2021, the Lima newspaper published another front page showing human vulnerability. The headline on the cover was: "Hospitalized for COVID-19 double in just one month". The cover captions were: "So far in 2021, 216 people a day have been hospitalized on average. This implies a higher rate than last April and May"; and "The Ministry of Health registers 1646 critical patients in ICU beds. The peak of 1553 of last August was surpassed. Occupancy of ICU beds reaches 91% in the country". The text of the news item stated that "desperate requests for beds in intensive care units (ICU) are becoming more and more frequent. Not only outside some hospitals, but also on social media".

The main topic of El Comercio on its cover of January 20, 2021 was again about the COVID-19 pandemic. The headline was: "Use of ICU beds exceeds records in 12 regions". The subtitles were: "In Tumbes, Ucayali and Lambayeque there are no more available. In Lima, Áncash, Arequipa, Cusco and Huánuco it exceeds 95% of the total"; and "Expert warns that several regions do not have intensive care physicians and 1500 are required to meet the demand".

Two days later, in a news item on January 22, 2021, El Comercio titled another news item about the pandemic with this headline: "More adolescents infected". Citing a statement from the Social Health Security of Peru, the newspaper published that the number of infections among adolescents aged 12 to 17 years increased by 59% compared to the previous week, while in young people and adults the infections increased by 45% and 43% respectively.

In its edition of January 23, 2021, El Comercio also reported on the large number of young people infected by COVID-19. The headline was: "The young population is now threatened". In the piece of news, the dean of the Physician's

Association of Peru, Miguel Palacios stated that the virus attacks people who were not infected in the first wave of the pandemic: "Young people were not infected and now it is the more sensitive group. The crowds at the end of the year take their toll on us".

On January 29, 2021, El Comercio published a short news item titled: "COVID-19 can be more lethal in pregnant women". The text reported on a study published in the American Journal of Obstetrics and Gynecology, according to which the mortality rate is significantly higher among pregnant women compared to the general population of a similar age.

On January 30, 2021, the Peruvian newspaper offered its readers an analysis of the pandemic, prepared by Elmer Huerta, one of its regular collaborators. The headline of the text was: "About variants, reinfections and resistances"; and the subtitle: "Recent studies indicate that the new variants detected in South Africa and Manaus could complicate the current strategies of the pandemic". As can be seen, the collaborator took a turn in his approach compared to 2020, when he downplayed the pandemic and spoke of "low lethality".

On February 4, 2021, El Comercio published a news item about the number of deaths from COVID-19 in Peru since the start of the pandemic. Citing the National Death Information System as a source, the number of deaths from the new coronavirus then rose to 91,320.

Two days later, on February 6, 2021, the newspaper reported that Peru was the country in Latin America with the most infected pregnant women. The article informed that, in the Andean country, more than 40,000 pregnant women tested positive for COVID-19 and 76 died. The "neglect of the first level of care was a key factor", said the subtitle.

Finally, on February 13, 2021, El Comercio published an interview with the director of the Center for the History of Emotions in Berlin, Ute Frevert. The headline of the interview was: "Our frustration will not convince the virus to leave the planet". Among other statements by Frevert, one of them was: "Humanity has travelled a long way to learn to live with uncertainty".

In this section, the hypothesis is also confirmed, since the journalistic texts published before the pandemic minimized the severity of COVID-19. But after a year of pandemic, El Comercio emphasized the high level of lethality of the virus, which affects all kinds of people, regardless of their age, gender or social status. In the news of January and February 2021, the vulnerability of human beings was clearly presented, due to a virus that was causing thousands of deaths and the saturation of the country's hospitals.

References

Berzins, M. (2013). *Wounded heroes: Vulnerability as a virtue in ancient Greek literature and philosophy*. Oxford.

Cardona, F. (2018). *Mitología griega*. Brontes.

Cardona, O.D. (2001, June 29–30). *La necesidad de repensar de manera holística los conceptos de vulnerabilidad y riesgo. Una crítica y una revisión necesaria para la gestión*. Presentation at International Work-Conference on Vulnerability in Disaster Theory and Practice. Wegeningen, Netherlands. https://www.desenredando.org/public/articulos/2001/repvuln/RepensarVulnerabilidadyRiesgo-1.0.0.pdf.

Castel, R. (1995). De la exclusión como estado a la vulnerabilidad como proceso. *Archipiélago, cuadernos de crítica y cultura*, (21), 27–36.

Cavalcante, T. & Sadi, P. (2017). Los conceptos de vulnerabilidad humana y la integridad individual para la bioética. *Revista Bioética, 25*(2), 311–319. http://dx.doi.org/10.1590/1983-80422017252191.

Commelin, P. (2017). *Mitología griega y romana: El gran clásico de la literatura mitológica ahora recuperado*. La Esfera de los Libros.

Diccionario de la Lengua Española (2020). "Vulnerabilidad". https://dle.rae.es/vulnerable.

Dickens, C. (1854). *Hard times*. Bradbury and Evans.

Feito, L. (2007). Vulnerabilidad. *Anales del Sistema Sanitario de Navarra, 30*(3), 7–22. https://scielo.isciii.es/pdf/asisna/v30s3/original1.pdf.

García, D. (2006). Prometeo: tradición y progreso. *Nova Tellus 24*(2), 77–109. https://doi.org/10.19130/iifl.nt.2006.24.2.178.

Gawande, A. (2015). *Being Mortal: Illness, Medicina and What Matters in the End*. Metropolitan Books.

Grimal, P. (1951). *Diccionario de mitología griega y romana*. Paidós.

Grimal, P. (1998). *La mitología griega*. Paidós.

Günter, T. & Heike, S. (2017). *Exploring Vulnerability. United States of America*. Vandenhoeck & Ruprecht.

Herodotus (2018). *The Histories of Herodotus. Translated by George Rawlinson*. Scribe Publishing.

Jaspers, K. (2012). *La fe filosófica*. Losada.

Jennings, H. (2004). *A handbook of Greek mythology*. Routledge.

Kowarick, L. (2009). *Viver em risco*. Editorial 34.

Luján, C. (2010). *De Prometeo a Lucifer: la represión del relativismo y el establecimiento del amor como criterio absoluto*. Universidad de Alicante. http://hdl.handle.net/10045/14151.

Mora, M. (2010). *El hombre antes y después del fuego de Prometeo: entre antropología y mitología*. Universidad de Alicante. http://hdl.handle.net/10045/14125.

Nagy, G. (1999). *The Best of the Achaeans: Concepts of the Hero in Archaic Greek Poetry.* The Johns Hopkins University Press. http://nrs.harvard.edu/urn-3:hul.ebook:CHS_NagyG.The_Best_of_the_Achaeans.1999.

Pallares, M. (2014). *Perspectiva filosófica-antropológica de la vulnerabilidad.* Presentation at VI Congreso Internacional de Investigación y Práctica Profesional en Psicología XXI Jornadas de Investigación Décimo Encuentro de Investigadores en Psicología del MERCOSUR. Facultad de Psicología – Universidad de Buenos Aires, Argentina. https://www.aacademica.org/000-035/95.pdf.

Real Academia Española (2019). *Diccionario de la lengua española* (23a ed.).

Riesco, M. (2014). Progreso: una idea controvertida en una sociedad paradójica. *Educación y futuro: revista de investigación aplicada y experiencias educativas,* (30), 15–38. https://dialnet.unirioja.es/servlet/articulo?codigo=4685041.

Rivas, R. (2008). Una relectura de la idea de progreso a partir de la ética del discurso. *Andamios, 4*(8), 61–97. http://www.scielo.org.mx/scielo.php?script=sci_arttext&pid=S1870-00632008000100003.

Rodríguez Castro, S. (2006). *Diccionario etimológico griego–latín del español.* Esfinge.

Segura, M. (2020, May 10). La falsa apariencia de un virus comunitario. *La Vanguardia.* https://www.lavanguardia.com/vida/20200510/481069679234/la-falsa-apariencia-de-un-virus-igualitario.html.

Torralba, F. (2010). Hacia una antropología de la vulnerabilidad. *Revista Forma, 2,* 25–32. https://www.upf.edu/documents/3928637/4017811/forma_vol02_04torralbafrancesc.pdf/e8b20040-3260-4d99-86f4-4d2f230c6325.

Varela, N. (2019). *Feminismo 4.0.* Ediciones Cátedra.

Zukerfeld, R. & Zonis, R. (2005). Psicoanálisis en el siglo XXI: el mito de Aquiles. Sobre ideales culturales y vulnerabilidad. *Docta, revista de psicoanálisis, 3*(2), 28–46. http://apcweb.com.ar/wp-content/uploads/2014/10/Docta02.pdf#page=30.

CHAPTER 7

Blogging National Identity

Hara Stratoudaki

1 Introduction

Blogs and blogging are the successors of online communities formed before the advent of World Wide Web. They were introduced during late 1990s and are considered as one of the technologies behind the participatory web (Web 2.0). They were thought of as a means for democratizing the media by promoting 'citizen journalism' (e.g., Farrell & Drezner 2008; Jones and Himelboim 2010; Wall 2005; Wallsten 2007). Blogs forge complex relations with conventional media: they reproduce mainstream media content, resorting to 'information curation practices' such as finding, selecting, remixing, and reposting content (Helmsley 2018); on the other hand, they provide content to mainstream media and participate in agenda setting (Hennessy & Martin 2006). After the initial excitement with the new medium, blogs were met with skepticism, especially when quite a few promoted far-right rhetoric, spread conspiracy theories and fake news.[1] Nevertheless, blogs express a wide spectrum of views, while subtle differences are discernible between blogs supporting the same political actors and ideologies.

Blogs are not alone in their function as 'citizen journalism.' Newer social media play a similar role: Twitter, as a microblogging platform, is closer to blogs, while Facebook and Instagram users sometimes behave like bloggers sharing content and presenting their own accounts about current affairs. Despite the fragmentation into several social media, blogs are not facing antagonism. Bloggers are active in social media, usually posting their content at least on Twitter and Facebook.

In this chapter we will examine the relation between the discourse of mainstream media content channeled into blogs and the discourse developed by bloggers in their original content. We will search for replication and originality in the ways blogs construct the nation and national identity during a period of 'hot' nationalism. Our case study will focus on the blog posts collected during

1 See for example Hawley (2017), Salazar (2018). For Greece, see Afouxenidis and Sioula-Georgoulea (2018), Kompatsiaris and Mylonas (2014), Siapera and Veikou (2016), Smyrnaios (2013).

the two-day parliamentary discussion of the 'Prespes Agreement' between Greece and Northern Macedonia.[2] Thus, in the first part we present some facts about Greek political blogs during the 2010s. Then, we turn to our case study. The presentation of the findings follows in the third part. The discussion will take a step backwards, to consider the implications about the relationship between blogs and mainstream media in mythmaking.

2 Blogs and 'Identity'

The term 'identity' suggests certainty, an immutable core of the self, ensuring continuity and coherence within a rapidly changing world. However, identity – and especially collective identities – may be just as fluid and multiple as the surrounding social world. So far, researchers have focused on the state-constructed, institutionally organized, and transmitted identity and understood it as a single, coherent product of hegemonic narrative, a single 'program' (cf. Smith 1991; Anderson 1983; Hobsbawm & Ranger 1983). They imply that, more or less, the 'narratives' of nationalism and 'national identity' are identical. Thus, they ignore that national identity is, after all, the identity of the members of the nation. In recent decades researchers turned to the ways in which the 'ordinary members of the nation' perceive their national identity (cf. Connor 1994; Hobsbawm 1992; Guibernau 2007). Scholars urge to listen to the discourse of the 'ordinary' members of the nation, instead of substituting it with the dominant political narrative (cf. Edensor 2002; Skey 2010, 2011, 2013; McCrone & Bechhofer 2015). It is now acceptable to approach national identity as plural, as a product of informal flows of narratives, symbols and myths thus activating, producing, and reproducing different versions of identity.

A combination of the top-down elite narratives and the bottom-up discourses would provide a glimpse into the dynamics of national identity. Since "news consumption is gradually but steadily shifting away from broadcasting and print media to digital sources and social networking sites" (Kalogeropoulos et al. 2021, 109), blogs – occupying an intermediate position between the grassroots discourse of social media and the official discourses articulated by the government, political parties and institutions such as education, and the

---

2 The "Final agreement for the settlement of the differences as described in United Nations Security Council resolutions 817 (1993) and 845 (1993), the termination of the Interim Accord of 1995, and the establishment of a strategic partnership between the Parties" was signed on 17 June 2018 at the Greek village of Psarades on Lake Prespa, a lake mutually shared by the Greek and Northern Macedonia.

media – are ideal for the study of mutual exchanges between the two in the construction of national identity. It is such constructions that may be understood as mythological, in the way Roland Barthes treats the term: as a communication system, "not defined by the object of its message, but by the way in which it utters this message" (Barthes 1972, 107). A point made by Barthes is of importance here: mythical or mythologizing discourse consists of "a material which has already been worked on" (Barthes 1972, 108), so that it is already familiar and 'natural' or commonsensical. We don't expect to find new myths in our corpus, but rather to find familiar naturalized mythical narratives.

3 Greek Political Blogs

Smyrnaios and Karatzogianni (2020, 290) detect the origins of the Greek blogosphere in 2006, "involving a modernist technophile elite, both from the left and from the center-right, that forms a liberal consensus opposed to the traditional conservatism of Greek society, and engages in political activism against corruption, in favour of secularism". Soon bloggers became involved in social (the 2007 wildfires) and political activism (the 2008 riots after a police shooting killing Alexandros Grigoropoulos), culminating in the anti-austerity movement in early 2010s (Smyrnaios and Karatzogianni 2020; Ferra 2016; Siapera and Veikou 2016). It was those bloggers that supported the Left government of SYRIZA paving its way to becoming the main Opposition party in 2012 and continued supporting it till the electoral victory in 2015 and the referendum of July 2015. But they were now second to other social media like Twitter and Facebook.

In the meanwhile, blogs became also indispensable part of far-right communication strategy (Afouxenidis & Georgoulea 2008; Kompatsiaris & Mylonas 2014; Smyrnaios 2013), long before its presence in Facebook was banned, even though several far-right blogs were reported and banned by blogging platforms (Siapera and Veikou 2016). In his 2013 research, Smyrnaios found numerous far-right blogs, interconnected through hyperlinks into a community, and minimally connected to the rest of the Greek blogosphere.

In the 2010s, hand in hand with the multilevel crisis, trust in legacy media drop abruptly, and was only recovering by the end of the decade. On the contrary, trust to the Internet and social networks were on the rise. Trust to the Internet was higher to that of any legacy medium. In fact, trust to the Internet and social network was in Greece higher than the EU average (EBU 2021). Kalogeropoulos et al. (2021) found that Greeks do not trust the truthfulness and integrity of legacy media news and depend upon online sources (blogs and social media) which they consider as independent, authentic, and empowering in their personal truth-seeking. Reuters Institute (2019) has found that "the online media market in Greece is highly fragmented, with new digital-born players making up half the list of most popular websites," while few legacy media have built up a loyal audience online. Two-thirds of Greeks use social media as a source of news, while 20% use them as their main source (Reuters Institute 2019, 88). Blogs play an important role in this ecosystem, in parallel with the development of "digital initiatives aiming to strengthen investigative and independent journalism in Greece" (Reuters Institute 2021, 82).

During the last decade several blogs became professional or semi-professional, the latter employing a group of people to post news and copy content from legacy media and blogs, along with their own content. Misleading titles aiming at attracting visitors became a way for securing revenue from advertisements, paving the way to irrelevant or even fake content. According to the Greek Web Directory (apn.gr/greece) there were more than 1,550 Greek news-related and more than 800 politics-related blogs and sites, as of November 2021. A few blogs were ranked even higher than legacy media according to Alexa scores, but most address a medium-sized or even a niche audience. Thus, they are close to what Helmsley (2018) calls middle-level gatekeepers: They may influence political and journalistic elites, connect blogs of higher and lower status bringing them to the attention of mainstream media, and facilitating the flow of information within the social network. They engage in information curation practices, channeling information from mainstream media, along with their original content. Therefore, studying the content of such blogs vis-a-vis legacy media content is crucial in understanding the flow of ideas, information, and misinformation, virality of fake news, as well as the flow of ideology and myths in society.

4 The Case-Study

In early 2019, a political event summed up the year-long diplomatic and political controversy regarding the agreement on the name of the Former Yugoslav Republic of Macedonia. The discussion in the Hellenic Parliament for the ratification of the so called Prespa Agreement in January 24 and 25, following a heated controversy in the media, was met with rallies in Athens and other major cities supported by the opposition parties, and led to the collapse of the coalition government. Coming after a decade of deep unbridgeable divisions in the body politic between pro-and anti-austerity, then pro-and anti-EU. Though political parties and leaders were made to take a realistic U-turn when moving from opposition to government, the divide between supporters and adversaries of the Agreement was unsurmountable.

As part of a broader survey on national identity as presented in social media discourse, we collected data from Twitter (Stratoudaki & Skarpelos 2021), Facebook and blogs during 24th and 25th of January, 2019, querying for 'Macedonia,' 'Prespes' and 'Skopje.'[3] Our query found 6,747 articles published in 660 blogs. The number of texts is indicative of the importance given to this topic. Some blogs published even more than 100 posts within 48 hours.

Our analysis moved in two directions:

- Several posts were reproducing pieces from legacy media, or from other blogs. Such a reproduction is a means to overcome the need for information, as well as for resources not available to a blogger. For example, lengthy speeches by eminent politicians were transcribed in detail by legacy media websites, and then reproduced by blogs. Tracing such practices, we are able to map the flow of narratives and myths, and their diffusion among the blogs audiences. This flow should be understood as a blogs-media ecosystem, visualized as a network, and have its dynamics understood as the influence of the most cited nodes upon the blogs.
- On the other hand, blogs produce their own content. Narrative and myths may differ from those found at the previous case. Content analysis allows for comparing between reproduced and original content and understanding the degree of independent myth-making practices by the blogs.

A word of caution is necessary: blogs are not prone to announce their sources. Thus, they tend to confuse their audience about reproducing content from legacy media. In several cases, identical content mentioned different sources in different blogs thus obscuring to some degree the possibility to locate the original source. We also found cases where identical content was attributed differently by different blogs, or even not attributed by some of them. We decided that attribution is a crucial gesture of recognizing the relationship with a legacy media, therefore only existing attributions were considered.

5 The Blogs-Media Ecosystem

The relationship between blogs and legacy media has been under scrutiny since early 2000s. Though most blogs' readership is limited compared to media

3 Data collection was made by the PaloPro platform (https://palopro.io), for Web & Social Media Analytics. The PaloPro platform is a product of PaloServices (http://www.paloservices.com).

websites, in critical cases when legacy media limit themselves to reproducing the views of the government, blogs are more likely to give voice to those opposing its policies. In some cases, blogs' insistence on issues deemed as minor by the media eventually brought them on the agenda.

Smyrnaios (2013) and Siapera & Veikou (2016) attempted to capture the network of websites and blogs related to the Far Right in Greece. The range of the political spectrum was significantly limited, in both cases, while the links between websites and blogs might go back in time. In this chapter we broaden the range to include the whole of the political spectrum, thus producing a snapshot of the relationship between the two. A systematic elaboration of corresponding 'snapshots' could possibly document with greater certainty the ideological and political symbiosis or divergence between blogs and legacy media.

To achieve this 'snapshot' we resorted to the acknowledgement or attribution of sources in the posts. One should keep in mind, though, that not all posts acknowledged their sources, while different blogs might attribute identical texts to different sources. It looks as if the 'copy-paste industry' is much more extensive and has probably infected even legacy media as well. As a rule of thumb, we chose to confine our mapping to posts explicitly acknowledging their source.

Legacy media seem to have a significant role in shaping blogs' content, as well as their rhetoric. Several well-known legacy and digital media are included in our data. The top ten include print media, the Athens News Agency – Macedonian Press Agency, as well as online news websites. They play a crucial role in the online news ecosystem, since they form the nuclei of groups of blogs which reproduce their discourse and multiply their impact. The network of attribution is presented in Figure 7.1. Fourteen major groups (communities) of blogs and media were calculated (Blondel et al. 2008). The central position of one or a few legacy or online media within large groups is indicating the influence of their ideological and political position, as well as of the news they publish. At the same time, some smaller groups appear as rather polyphonic, lacking a single influential medium at their center.

Computational analysis allows for identifying the characteristic discourse of each group. Group A's discourse revolved around news about civilian attacks to the homes of pro-aggreement MPs, as well as around the words "cede" and "give in". Group B was gathering alt-right and conspiracy theory media and blogs, and its discourse was about "betrayal" and "traitors," while using the name "Skopje" to denote the State of Northern Macedonia. The far and extreme right Group C used words related to "humiliation," and mentioned consistently

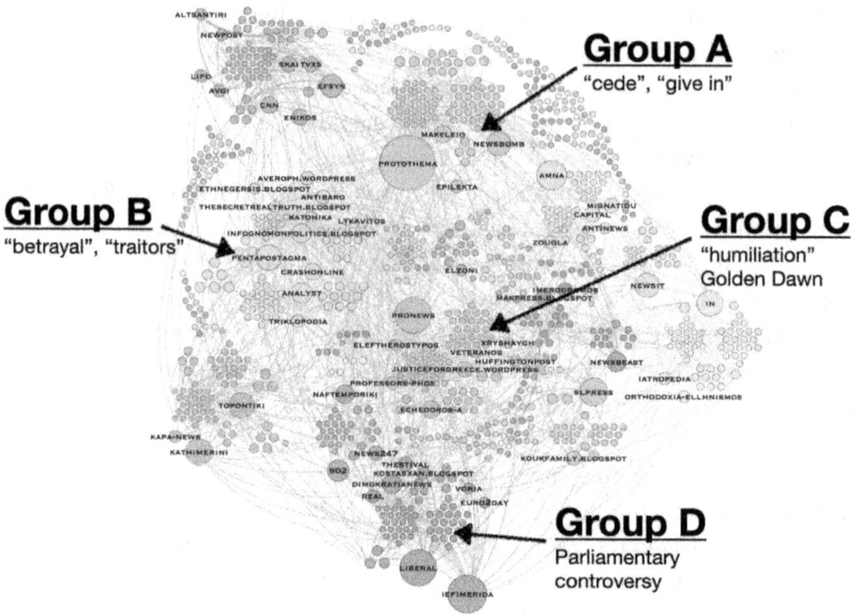

FIGURE 7.1 The blogs-media ecosystem
SOURCE: STRATOUDAKI 2020, 698

Golden Dawn party and its leaders. Finally, blogs in Group D emphasized the controversy within the Parliament, sometimes resorting to insulting phrases.

The remaining groups were not characterized by some distinctive words or theme. They acknowledged copying from sources with divergent political affiliations or promoting a reasonably neutral discourse.

6 The 'Prolific' Blogs

Within this broad image, one may categorize blogs in several ways. Here we will categorize them based on the number of posts uploaded during the screening period. This categorization reveals extreme differences: a handful of blogs published the largest volume, while most published only a small number of posts related to the Agreement. Ten blogs posted more than 100 (and up to 186) posts each, producing approximately 1/5th of the corpus. Along with a few more, they systematically copied content from legacy media (thus reproducing public discourses about identity), provided their own content (articulating a peculiar discourse about identity), and emphasized civic mobilization to call their audience to the rallies. At the other end, 75% of blogs were limited to posting 1–10 posts, usually presenting the ideas of the blogger, though in some cases they also reproduced texts from other blogs or legacy media (cf. Stratoudaki 2020).

In this chapter we will focus on the first category: the 'prolific' blogs. Our corpus consists of the 1,457 posts published by the fifteen more prolific blogs. Approximately one out of ten posts (11,2%) reproduced content from legacy media. The rest offered either original content or content copied from blogs and websites. The questions we are going to answer is:

RQ1: To what extend do content originating from legacy media is shaping the discourse of original content in the blogs examined?
RQ2: Which are the similarities or differences in the narratives about the nation and national self between the two kinds of content?
RQ3: Are blogs confined to repeating the narratives and discourse of legacy media? Or they offer their readership enriched or even original narratives?
RQ4: And finally, based on our previous research, how does the content of 'prolific' compare to that of the 'lesser' blogs?

To answer RQ1–3, we conducted content analysis coupled with natural language processing. We used topic modeling to identify common themes in our corpus. We applied Latent Dirichlet Allocation (LDA), which treats each text as a combination of topics, and each topic as a combination of words. Thus, more than one topic may be found in each post (Silge and Robinson 2017). The posts cover a wide part of the political spectrum, from the far right to the left party which was in government at that time. Most are opposed to the Agreement, while fewer (usually aligned with the rhetoric of Golden Dawn and alt-right conspiracy theories) are opposing to both the government and the opposition parties. Only a few were clearly supporting the government and the Agreement.

7 The Legacy Media

Legacy media present diversified narratives about events, leading to different explanatory devices. A central question of this chapter is concerned with the diffusion of such narratives to blog posts, and therefore their impact to the blogs' audiences. Or, to put it differently, the diffusion of media 'mythologies' to a wider audience through their reproduction, *verbatim* or not, by the blogs.

A close examination of the blogposts in our corpus that acknowledge legacy media as their source revealed that in some cases such attribution is a mask for presenting narratives irrelevant or even opposite to the source's content. Thus, blogs seem to attempt to provide extra credibility to their content and present their usually extreme discourse as mainstream.

Beyond that, usually blogs replicated news content, usually adding a title guiding their audience to a certain 'reading' of the text. Further examination has shown that the attributed to legacy media texts fall into the following categories:

1. Full reproduction or highlights of the speeches delivered by political leaders and MPs, statements, or excerpts of interviews in the media.
2. News about events and reactions throughout Greece.
3. Short commentary
4. Lengthy texts, usually incorporating a piece of information from a legacy medium, followed by an extended commentary by the blogger.

Despite the last category, the vocabulary used in the posts attributed to legacy media is for the most part decent, avoiding extremes.

8 The Blogs

The discourse of posts presented as original or attributed to another blog as their source is strikingly different.

1. Politics is the category with one third (33.9%) of the posts. In this category fell posts presenting and analyzing current affairs. It should be noted that the days before the parliamentary hearing and voting, some MPs had been leaving the party they were elected with, leading two parties to fall from their status. Thus, current affairs were an important aspect of politics during data collection. As expected, this category emphasizes the internal political scene, though sometimes posts combine such analysis with references to geopolitics and international relations. Texts fall into one out of two distinct groups: on the one hand there are texts transcribing the discourse of political and other eminent personalities in a neutral manner, while on the other hand texts mostly comment on events and announcements, tweets, speeches, adopting a personal point of view, which could be considered as populist.

   The words used in the second group of texts is especially interesting. They used words with strong cognitive and emotional appeal to identity as being at stake within the nation. They point to a deep divide within the national corpus, a schism in national identity. To narrate it they contrast 'patriots' to 'traitors,' 'heroes' to 'vilains.' They even provide a list with the names of the MPs who voted for the Agreement as evidence, and as a tool for remembrance: something between the Roman proscriptions and a reverse monument, a Pantheon of the 'traitors of the nation.' This way they personified their opponents setting the terrain for further mythologization, recurring to conspiracy theories and inventing 'evidence' of bribery and treason. Some texts are eager to describe this as a schism between the government and 'the people,' indicating that the nation minus the government is unanimous in its ideals. Others, usually in far right or alt right blogs, consider the political elites as conspiring against the nation, even those that voted against the Agreement.

2. Speeches delivered as well as tweets, commentary, and interviews by politicians. This category includes one out of four posts (24,7%). For the most part texts were polemic in style, as the controversy between politicians, MPs and political parties escalated. Despite this style, though, deviations from a political correctness are liminal and their source was mainly far right or populist politicians. While offering a starting point for the mythologizing analyses found in the previous category, such points are hidden in a few words instead of providing a full-scale narrative.
3. Journalistic posts with reportage about violent events with mobs surrounding the homes of some MPs, or events related to the discussion at the Parliament like occupation of public buildings and schools, or rallies against the Agreement. This category includes one out of four posts (25,9%), as well. They present no interest from the point of view of this paper, though they document a situation of unrest, as well as the moral pressure upon the supporters of the Agreement.
4. Geopolitics is the last category with a strong presence in the blogs content, consisting of 15.3% of the blog posts. It includes references to reactions by the International Press as well as foreign personalities (Presidents and Prime Ministers, Ministers of Foreign Affairs, the NATO Secretary General, EU officials etc.), as well as analyses by well-known specialists. It also includes geopolitical 'analyses' by non-specialists and discussion regarding the possible outcomes of the Agreement upon international relations in the future.

The latter group is exemplar of what is usually called in literature as 'popular geopolitics,' i.e., popular explanations of geopolitics by non-experts. While in past decades popular geopolitics research "focused on the elite visions of media moguls, movie directors, and lower-level yet still relatively empowered media functionaries like writers and reporters," with the advent of social media research came closer to the perceptions of the public (Dittmer and Gray 2010, 1664). The fear of de-bordering and re-bordering, based upon the experience of such procedures in the Balkans during the 1990s, leading to the creation of the Former Yugoslav Republic of Macedonia as an independent State, is outspoken in these posts.

This issue is related to a discussion about markers of national identity, which are seen as 'given over' to Northern Macedonia: language, ethnicity, nationality/citizenship. They were the main markers being negotiated in the Agreement, and – as they became salient – were being re-elaborated both collectively and individually. However, to a large extent, these markers were treated as clear and complete markers, indisputable in terms of their ownership and disputed at the same time in the sense that it was considered possible for others to usurp and appropriate them. This could blur the boundary between national self and alterity, producing a problematic identity.

9 Discussion

A comparison between the two types of blog posts, and despite the possibility of hidden (i.e., undeclared) affinities, content from legacy media was used 'as is' only to provide a background for the opinions of the bloggers presented in other pieces. The media used do express in most part similar ideological and political affinities with the blogs. A few even host conspiratorial pieces. Though, the legacy media texts selected to be used and attributed in our corpus was rather neutral. Even original or derived from other blogs content was at first sight neutral in most part, and only the title indicated the 'preferred reading' of the blogger. Despite that, mythologizing narratives about identity, involve one fourth of the original content. There are two main narratives, with their variations.

10 The First Narrative: A Divided Nation

In 1990s, N. Diamantouros (1994) provided a blueprint for a renewed version of an old cleavage between a supposedly 'Hellenic' identity, based on Ancient Greece and compatible with Western European ideals and socio-political values; and a 'Romeic' one based on the Byzantine legacy and held alive during the centuries of Ottoman occupation by lay people, leaning towards backward oriental values. Diamantouros found that the distinction after the participation in EU and the end of Cold War became one between official and lay, or underdog identity, thus aligning the former with the modernization projects under way at that time and the latter with conservation or hostility against them. In so doing, he promoted the idea of a cleavage between a national and diasporic elite sharing western values and a modernizing vision, and an underdog plebiscite. Until the beginning of the economic, social, and political crisis of 2010s, this distinction was seen as justifiable. Even the 'identity wars' regarding the abolition of mentioning religious affiliation on identity cards in early 2000s, and the changes in accepted historical narratives in school textbooks a few years later, were seen under this light.

The crisis has proved, at least for those considered as 'underdog,' the failure of the modernizing project, leading to the contempt of 'official identity.' This contempt was far from one-dimensional: it had specific expressions in the whole spectrum of political affiliations. It was expressed in the anti-memoranda movement, the 'aganaktismenoi' (i.e., indignados) movement, and later during the 2015 ballot it took the form of pro-or anti-European (stay with Europe or Grexit) alignment. The cleavage has been fluid and unstable (Ferra 2016; Ferra 2020) as political parties came to power or lose the elections. The whole decade became a laboratory where identities were constantly negotiated, and for the most part upon such bipolar constructs.

We found a version of such an 'underdog' understanding of the cleavage in our corpus, narrated under a heavily mythologized style. It is, for the most part, to be found in the populist political analysis category of blog posts and goes as follows: 'There is a deep divide within the nation, between the political elite (or a part of it) and its followers on the one hand, and 'the people' on the other. The former is treacherous and because of its ideology or just because of greed is selling out Macedonia, its name, its history, its Greekness, while the latter cannot but stand against this selling out. A sort of civil war is close.'

11 The Second Narrative: Conspiracies

The second narrative, found in the popular geopolitics category, asserts that: "Dark forces beyond Greece have decided, according to their own interests, that Greece should sell off the name of Macedonia. Corrupt and prone to bribery puppet politicians are willing to do the dirty job, proceeding against the will of 'the people'". Such narratives have been around for decades, explaining the pitfalls of Greek history since at least the WWI. Alien forces are seen as giving orders and docile politicians following them, leading the nation to one defeat after the other. Despite all conspiracies, though, narratives assert that the nation has the power to withstand defeats and safeguard its dignity among nations.

Such a narrative has deep roots in myths of national selection, myths of a 'chosen nation' with a special historical role to fulfill. Smith (1991) has shown that such myths have been crucial in the survival and self-renewal of ethnies or nations. Chosenness 'explains' (without need of any proof) the reasons behind the international plots against the nation, as hatred and envy; and produces a positive, even heroic self-image, to deny pitfalls and defeats.

12 Comparing Discourses

The comparison between the discourse of legacy media (as reproduced in our corpus) and blogs respectively, as well as between 'prolific' and 'lesser' blogs is demanding. Here we can only scratch the surface, but it is worth trying and an incentive for future research.

The blogs under examination copied an extensive part of their posts from legacy media, while a major part of the rest of their content is similar to that of the latter. It is mostly consisting of posts with factual information, or reproduction of interviews and social media content. In this, the discourses of the two converge. The tone is neutral, and no myths are used. On the other hand, an extensive part of the blogs content (tantamount to 20%) is prone to mythologizing narratives. Thus, the answer to RQ1 is split into two: content originating from legacy media is shaping the discourse of original content, while blogs prefer to use their own discourse in utilizing current mythologies in their narratives (RQ2). While blogs rely on legacy media for information and news, though they copy lengthy texts, they also produce original narratives mostly as explanatory of the events. They even use other devices, like the titles, to transform the light under which the audience should decode the texts (RQ3).

To answer the last research question, we should present in a condensed manner the findings of our previous research (Stratoudaki 2020). 'Lesser' blogs are those posting ten or less texts during the timeframe of the research. They form the vast majority of the blogs of our corpus. Analysis has shown that they used four topics in dealing with the issue of the Agreement: Topic 1 involved a comparison between the heroic past (either the ancient glory of Macedonia under Alexander the Great, or the heroes and villains of the Balkan Wars) and the present as a period of defeat. Topic 2 presented speeches and analyses reproduced from more 'prolific' blogs. Texts in this topic were close to or even reproducing the texts of our corpus characterized as populist politics. They develop the idea of a cleavage within the nation, with the majority of 'the people' opposing an unnamed minority basically consisting of politicians and their followers. In the same topic are to be found some texts related to popular geopolitics. Topic 3 consisted of texts focusing on identity markers, namely ethnicity, national name, and language. Finally, topic 4 articulated an anti-governmental discourse. The main point of convergency between 'prolific' and 'lesser' blogs is to be found in topic 2 of the latter, where content of the former was channeled to the latter (RQ4).

13 Concluding Remarks

The discourses weaving national identity are multilevel. Though official discourses were considered as constructing a unique identity among the nationals, and the media were seen as instrumental in organizing and reproducing such discourses along with other institutions like education, it is nowadays accepted that this is partly true. Other discourses, semi-official, like those presented online in blogs, or private as presented by 'ordinary' members of the nation in social media or in their discussions are as valid.

During a period of 'hot' nationalism, when events make national sentiment salient, such semi-official and private discourses are pivotal in understanding the workings of identity. On the other hand, during such periods people, politicians and the media make use of existing national myths, instead of creating new ones. Audiences need familiar cognitive and conceptual schemes, to place actors and actions in familiar spots within the mythic narrative structure. Thus, the 'prolific' blogs used two familiar myths: the myth of Ephialtes the traitor, and the myth of international conspiracy plotting against a chosen nation.

The comparison between our corpus and the corpus of blog posts of the minor blogs (Stratoudaki 2020) reveals that they both present the two myths, as described so far. On the other hand, when they decide to copy content from legacy media, it is mostly factual pieces that they select.

To reconstruct the broader image, one should consider that during the two centuries since the Greek Revolution and the formation of the Greek state, several changes in citizenship law summarize the official perceptions about the markers that unequivocally and unambiguously determine the participation in the nation. These changes were in dialogue with territorial changes which brought about the need for integration of new populations in the national body. Nevertheless, the descent from Greek parents has always been central (see Vogli 2007, Mavromatis 2018, Christopoulos 2019). *Jus sanguinis* shaped to a large extent the collective conception of identity, hence Greek national identity was considered as ethnic. However, from 1990 onwards, with the mass influx of immigrants and expatriates from the former USSR and Albania, former certainties were questioned and re-processed. Timid steps towards a civic identity based on birthplace (jus soli), inclusive of immigrants or at least their children born in Greece. The transition remains incomplete, and the two perceptions of identity are simultaneously active. Thus, the meanings of identity involve some degree of uncertainty. However, people are reluctant to live with such uncertainty, being afraid that since they can't be sure of their own identity, *others* may always appropriate it.

The prolific blogs focused upon the idea that within the nation there is a fifth column, eager to accept such an appropriation. This is the main identity-related anxiety expressed while the name of Northern Macedonia was discussed in the Hellenic Parliament. This anxiety seems to have been going through the whole period of the crisis: an anxiety regarding a divide within the nation; a cleavage of national identity not between different understandings of identity markers, but between different visions about the nation and its future.

In the texts we have studied, the concern for identity is present between the lines. The debate rarely touches on *substantive identity issues*. The multi-layered construct of Greek national identity seems as if, after a decade deep in a economic, social, political and national crisis, is still confused. It is more of an *identity function* that jumps from one level to another, from national to political, to social class, to individual identity, and back again. Therefore, the use of myths as devices for explaining current events is crucial. While offering a simplified and distorted image, it is seductively convenient and easily accepted as commonsensical. And blogs play a crucial role in recycling such myths and offering explanations of current turbulences based upon them. They are bidirectional channels allowing the reproduction of legacy media content, as well as multiplying the voice and supporting the outreach of other blogs' content to audiences.

References

Anderson, B. (1983). *Imagined communities*. Verso. *New York*.

Afouxenidis, A., and Sioula-Georgoulea, I. (2018). Exploration of far-right websites: reason and aesthetics. In M. Spyridakis, I. Koutsoukou, and A. Marinopoulou (eds.), *Cyberspace Society* (pp 91–127). Athens, Sideris. [in Greek].

Barthes, R. (1972). *Mythologies*. New York, The Noonday Press.

Blondel, V. D., Guillaume, J. L., Lambiotte, R., & Lefebvre, E. (2008). Fast unfolding of communities in large networks. *Journal of statistical mechanics: theory and experiment, 2008*(10), P10008.

Christopoulos, D. (2019), *Who is a Greek citizen? Two centuries of citizenship*. 2nd edition. Athens, Vivliorama. [in Greek].

Connor, W. (1994). *Ethnonationalism. The Quest for Understanding.* Princeton University Press.

Diamandouros, N. (1994). *Cultural dualism and political change in postauthoritarian Greece.* Estudios/Working Papers (Centro de Estudios Avanzados en Ciencias Sociales), 1994/50.

Dittmer, J., & Gray, N. (2010). Popular geopolitics 2.0: Towards new methodologies of the everyday. *Geography Compass, 4*(11), 1664–1677.

EBU (European Broadcasting Union), (2021). *Trust in Media.* Report. Online https://www.ebu.ch/publications/research/login_only/report/trust-in-media (last visited 15-11-2021).

Edensor, T. (2002). *National identity, popular culture and everyday life.* Oxford & New York, Bloomsbury Publishing.

Farrell, H., & Drezner, D. W. (2008). The power and politics of blogs. *Public choice, 134*(1), 15–30.

Ferra, I. (2020). *Digital media and the Greek crisis: Cyberconflicts, discourses and networks.* Emerald Group Publishing.

Ferra, I. (2016). Understanding the Greek crisis and digital media: a cyberconflict approach. In A. Karatzogianni, D. Nguyen and E. Serafinelli *The Digital Transformation of the Public Sphere* (pp. 259–281). Palgrave Macmillan, London.

Guibernau, M. (2007). *The identity of nations.* Cambridge: Polity.

Hawley, G. (2017). *Making sense of the alt-right.* Columbia University Press.

Helmsley, J. (2018). The role of middle-level gatekeepers in the propagation and longevity of misinformation. In Brian G. Southwell, Emily A. Thorson, and Laura Sheble (eds.), *Misinformation and Mass Audiences*, Austin: University of Texas 263–273.

Hennessy, C., & Martin, P. (2006). Blogs, the mainstream media, and the war in Iraq. American Political Science Association.

Hobsbawm, E. J. (1992). *Nations and nationalism since 1780: Programme, myth, reality.* Cambridge university press.

Hobsbawm, E. J., & Ranger, T. (eds.) (1983), *The Invention of Tradition.* Cambridge and New York: Cambridge University Press.

Jones, J., & Himelboim, I. (2010). Just a guy in pajamas? Framing the blogs in mainstream US newspaper coverage (1999–2005). *New Media & Society, 12*(2), 271–288.

Kalogeropoulos, A., Rori, L., & Dimitrakopoulou, D. (2021). 'Social Media Help Me Distinguish between Truth and Lies': News Consumption in the Polarised and Low-trust Media Landscape of Greece. *South European Society and Politics, 26*(1), 109–132.

Kompatsiaris, P., & Mylonas, Y. (2014). The rise of Nazism and the web: Social media as platforms of racist discourses in the context of the Greek economic crisis. In *Social Media, Politics and the State* (pp. 121–142). Routledge.

McCrone, D. and Bechhofer, F. (2015). *Understanding National Identity*. Cambridge, Cambridge University Press.

Reuters Institute (2021). *Digital News Report 2021*. Online https://reutersinstitute.politics.ox.ac.uk/sites/default/files/2021-06/Digital_News_Report_2021_FINAL.pdf (last visited 15-11-2021).

Reuters Institute (2019). *Digital News Report 2019*. Online https://reutersinstitute.politics.ox.ac.uk/sites/default/files/2019-06/DNR_2019_FINAL_0.pdf (last visited 15-11-2021).

Salazar, P. J. (2018). The Alt-Right as a community of discourse. *Javnost-The Public*, *25*(1–2), 135–143.

Siapera, E., & Veikou, M. (2016). The Digital Golden Dawn: Emergence of a nationalist-racist digital mainstream. In A. Karatzogianni, D. Nguyen and E. Serafinelli (eds.), *The Digital Transformation of the Public Sphere* (pp. 35–59). Palgrave Macmillan, London.

Silge, J., & Robinson, D. (2017). *Text mining with R: A tidy approach*. O'Reilly Media, Inc.

Skey, M. (2010). 'A sense of where you belong in the world': National belonging, ontological security and the status of the ethnic majority in England. *Nations and Nationalism*, *16*(4), 715–733.

Skey, M. (2011). *National belonging and everyday life: The significance of nationhood in an uncertain world*. Palgrave Macmillan.

Skey, M. (2013). Why do nations matter? The struggle for belonging and security in an uncertain world. *The British journal of sociology*, *64*(1), 81–98.

Smith, A. D. (1991). *National Identity*. Penguin Books.

Smyrnaios, N. (2013), The Greek far right on the internet: a graph analysis. *Ephemeron* (online http://ephemeron.eu/879, last visit 15/1/2022).

Smyrnaios, N., & Karatzogianni, A. (2020). The Rise of SYRIZA in Greece 2009–2015: The Digital Battlefield. In *The Emerald Handbook of Digital Media in Greece*. Emerald Publishing Limited.

Stratoudaki, H. (2020). Markers of Greek National Identity: The discourse of the blogs. In S. Koniordos (ed.), *The Political Phenomenon in Transition: Challenges to Democracy, State and Society* (pp. 691–704). Korinth, University of Peloponnese. [in Greek].

Stratoudaki, H., & Skarpelos, Y. (2021). Markers of National Identity while exiting (?) from the Crisis. In N. Nagopoulos (ed.), *Social Sciences Today: Dilemas and Perspectives Beyond the Crisis* (pp. 246–257). Mytilene, University of the Aegean. [in Greek].

Vogli, E. (2007), *"Greeks the race": Citizenship and identity in the national state of the Greeks (1821–1844)*. Herakleion, Crete University Press.

Wall, M. (2005). 'Blogs of war' Weblogs as news. *Journalism*, *6*(2), 153–172.

Wallsten, K. (2007). Agenda setting and the blogosphere: An analysis of the relationship between mainstream media and political blogs. *Review of policy research*, *24*(6), 567–587.

CHAPTER 8

Contemporary Mythologies of Television's Fictional Institutions in the United States

Melina Meimaridis

1 Introduction

Many of us share certain notions of how the police conduct a criminal investigation. Officers collect evidence, search for suspects, and interrogate them. These notions, however imprecise they might be, are part of what we imagine are common practices of this institution. Instead of employing technical knowledge, laypeople can image the daily workings of institutions relying on a set of TV narratives that present fictionalized versions of these institutions. For example, Law & Order: SVU (NBC, 1999-) presents viewers with the role of law enforcement officers in investigating criminal cases. Similarly, a viewer of the medical drama Grey's Anatomy (ABC, 2005-) can imagine how an operating room works despite never having entered that space. In this sense, the knowledge we have about certain institutions is often mediated by fictional experiences. Fiction, therefore, can act in the construction of meaning and expectations that subjects have about institutions, their professionals, and their roles in everyday life.

Television scripted series have become a popular phenomenon around the world. These productions recurrently fictionalize social institutions. For example, the Brazilian medical drama *Sob Pressão* (Globo, 2017-), the Mexican police drama *El Equipo*,[1] the South Korean legal drama Law School,[2] among several others. This is especially true regarding television series in the United States since some of the most-watched shows are institutional series, i.e., narratives centered on the daily workings of institutions, as law enforcement officers in Blue Bloods,[3] healthcare professionals in The Good Doctor[4] and firefighters and paramedics in Station 19.[5]

1 Produced by the Mexican network Canal de las Estrellas in 2011.
2 Produced by the South Korean network JTBC in 2021.
3 Produced by the US network CBS since 2010.
4 Produced by the US network ABC since 2017.
5 Produced by the US network ABC since 2018.

Despite the popularity of television's fiction, scholars from the field of Communication and other social sciences tend to maintain a certain rigid distinction between fiction and reality. They view them as worlds separated by an impenetrable barrier. However, this strict separation of fiction and reality neglects how popular culture is able to disseminate and build knowledge about the world around us.[6] Here, I understand that this barrier is much more fragile and permeable than it might seem at first. Leading from a social constructivist framework,[7] fictional institutions are understood as fulfilling a sociological role. While real-world institutions have become more autonomous and operate in society beyond the knowledge of the lay individual,[8] fictional institutions frequently reveal "what these institutions are". In this process, TV series present a world of ordered meanings in which the fictional institution plays a role in maintaining social order. But how do they do this?

In this chapter, I contend that TV institutional series have qualities that allow them to disseminate myths about social institutions. In this process, they can fulfill a mediating role between viewers and real-world institutions. The choice to center my analysis on TV scripted shows from the United States is based on the fact that this cultural industry has had a dominant role in the global television flows for several decades.[9] Moreover, these TV programs have become reference models for other countries.[10] An example is the recent boom in medical dramas in South Korean productions, such as Doctor Stranger,[11] Life,[12] and Hospital Playlist.[13] This dominant role has increased in light of the growing

6 Daniel Furman J. III and Paul Musgrave, "Synthetic experiences: How popular culture matters for images of international relations," *International Studies Quarterly* 61, no. 3 (2017): 503–4.

7 Peter Ludwig Berger and Thomas Luckmann, *The social construction of reality: A treatise in the sociology of knowledge* (New York: Doubleday, 1966); Nick Couldry and Andreas Hepp, *The mediated construction of reality* (Cambridge: Polity Press, 2017).

8 Anthony Giddens, *The consequences of modernity* (Stanford: Stanford University Press, 1991): 21–35.

9 Silvio Waisbord, "McTV: Understanding the global popularity of television formats". *Television & New Media* 5, no. 4 (2004): 359–362.

10 Maria del Mar Grandío Pérez and Patricia Diego González, "La influencia de la sitcom americana en la producción de comedias televisivas en España. El caso de 'Friends' y '7 vidas'". *Ámbitos. Revista Internacional de Comunicación*, no.18 (2009): 83–97; Yaeri Kim, "The invention of the Mideu: redefining American television in South Korea". *Media, Culture & Society* 42, no. 1 (2020): 109–125.

11 Produced by the South Korean network SBS in 2014.

12 Produced by the South Korean network JTBC in 2018.

13 Produced by the South Korean network tvN from 2020 to 2021; Pişcărac, Diana, "Medical k-dramas: a cross-section of South Korea's global cultural industry". *Romanian Journal of Sociological Studies* 1 (2016): 43–45.

presence of U.S.-based streaming companies, such as Netflix and Disney+, in markets around the world. These companies have directly impacted local audiovisual industries investing in the production of original content, such as movies, reality shows, and scripted series.[14]

Despite approaching several institutional series, I will focus on the fictionalization of the medical institution in Grey's Anatomy (ABC, 2005-) and the police in Chicago P.D. (NBC, 2014-). Each drama reproduces a particular structure, defined with reference to values, techniques, and the social organization of the fictionalized institution. Although both dramas reinforce the hero myth, there are certain particularities. While Grey's Anatomy presents its fictional institution through the principle of medical professionalism and the dedication of healthcare professionals, Chicago P.D. positions citizens as potential adversaries and the police as heroes, highlighting the moral and legal dimension of the institution's role in society. In this sense, while Grey's Anatomy and other medical dramas foster the expectation that doctors and healthcare professionals are 'good', Chicago P.D. and other police procedurals allow cops and detectives to be 'bad' in the name of justice. Here my main argument is that, although there are differences in the fictionalization process of each institution, through the use of myths, both series contribute to unrealistic expectations towards real-world institutions, their members, and their roles in society.

2 Myths and Television Fiction

The need to tell stories, folkloric legends, and myths has existed since the most ancient societies. Initially, individuals sat around a fire and listened to stories told by elders. Yet, nowadays, television and other media spread myths about society in the U.S. and the country's social institutions. The Academic debate about myths and mythologies is extensive.[15] The relationship between television and myths has already been detailed in many works, with scholars proposing that TV and its cultural products are capable of disseminating myths.[16]

14 Ramon Lobato, *Netflix Nations* (New York: New York University Press, 2019).

15 Roland Barthes, *Mythologies*, trans. Andrew Leak (Valencia: Grant & Cutler, 1994); Mircea Eliade, *The myth of the eternal return, or, Cosmos and history* (New York: Harper & Brothers, 1959); Claude Lévi-Strauss, *Structural anthropology* (New York: Basic books, 1963): 206–231.

16 Douglas Kellner, "Television, mythology and ritual". *Praxis* 6 (1982): 133–154; Roger Silverstone, "*The television message as social object: a comparative study of the structure and content of television programmes in Britain,*" *LSE Theses Online*, 1980; Robert A. White, "Television as Myth and Ritual". *Communication Research Trends* 8, no. 1 (1987): 1–8.

Here, I do not intend to be exhaustive in my review of this discussion and will lead from the structuralist tradition of the subject. I will shed light on some of the most important aspects that will serve as a backdrop for the analysis of myths in institutional series.

According to Claude Lévi-Strauss "mythical thought always progresses from the awareness of oppositions toward their resolution".[17] For the anthropologist, myths are an anxiety-reducing mechanism that deals imaginatively with contradictions in a given culture. Every culture has a set of binary contradictions, such as selfishness and altruism, that need to be reconciled through logical reasoning. These oppositions are often abstract generalizations, such as good versus bad, humanity versus gods, or life versus death. Common sense is at the root of many of these binary contradictions. By revealing cultural insecurities, myths provide a way of living with these contradictions through metaphors and images that transform these abstract generalizations into concrete representations. While not resolving cultural insecurities, myths are responsible for providing an imaginative framework for individuals to reflect on them.

A rational perspective, in which myths are an expression of thought, permeates Lévi-Strauss's view of myths. Alternatively, Mircea Eliade approaches the subject from an emotional perspective.[18] In the author's view, myths are connected to the sacred and this enables them to provide answers to the pain, suffering, and, above all, the chaos that modern life has become. Although in different ways, Lévi-Strauss and Eliade both contend that mythical narratives have more symbolic messages and meanings. These, through repetition, are able to reduce uncertainty and ambiguity, offering answers to numerous sets of dilemmas and humanity's existential conflicts.

In addressing Eliade's view of myths, Silverstone draws attention to the fact that it "finds its justification both in the individual and the social. The former is relieved of his fear of chaos and the latter, society, whose institutions might be conceived of as serving a similar purpose, are supported and buttressed by it".[19] In this regard, Eliade proposes that institutions would have had their models "'revealed' at the beginning of time, that, consequently, they are regarded as having a superhuman and 'transcendental' origin".[20] So, it is possible to argue that myths play a role in the maintenance processes of these entities in society.

17 Lévi-Strauss, *Structural anthropology*, 224.

18 Eliade, *The myth*, 1–20.

19 Silverstone, *The television message*, 110.

20 Eliade, *The myth*, viii.

On the other hand, Roland Barthes investigates the role myths play in industrialized capitalist societies.[21] For Barthes, myths are a system of meaning that, through the ideological character of the images and stories presented, serve to camouflage the nature of various aspects of reality, providing them with a natural justification.[22] The author highlights the role the media have in this process. According to Barthes' view, through mythical speech contradictions are repressed rather than resolved, and a society's dominant values are idealized. The author warns us that the naturalization process makes myths almost invisible to us.[23] Barthes highlights the ideological dimension of myths. Here I emphasize that myths can make social institutions seem like something natural, masking the fact that individuals created these entities throughout history.

Considering repetition as an intrinsic quality of television in the U.S.[24] allows us to examine this medium's mythical dimension and its capacity to produce and propagate myths. Television, by structuring its content around narratives, both in fiction (i.e., series, soap operas…) and non-fiction programs (i.e., TV news) plays a role in reiterating myths within a given culture. These narratives rearrange conflicting situations and events in terms of a familiar problem. An example is sports broadcasts that build a narrative around conflict and resolution.

Television in the U.S. has been widely used to propagate myths regarding national culture in an attempt to unite the people behind the same ideal of the nation. McConnell identified this process in the justification for the country's involvement in the Vietnam war.[25] By triggering mythical speech, TV is able to transform elements of everyday life into mythologies, for example, "police cars and guns eliminate violence; the middle-class home becomes the locus of family happiness".[26] In this way, television not only disseminates myths but also produces and propagates ideologies.[27] Richard White argues that television, through its mythic dimension, is effective in sustaining "our belief and hope that, after all, there is some order and meaning in the world".[28] The medium highlights this ability by bringing together everyday life, the strange, and the

21 Barthes, *Mythologies*.

22 *Ibid.*, 21–30.

23 *Ibid.*, 46.

24 Derek Kompare, *Rerun nation: How repeats invented American television* (New York: Routledge, 2006): 1–18.

25 Frank McConnell, *Storytelling and mythmaking: images from film and literature* (Oxford: Oxford University Press, 1979):109.

26 Kellner, "Television, mythology," 142.

27 *Ibid.*, 152.

28 White, "Television as Myth," 2.

familiar in a repetitive structure that will reiterate dominant myths of a given society. For Douglas Kellner, this repetition will be responsible for providing the viewer with the feeling that everything is under control.[29]

To this end, television series define situations in vague terms, such as disputes between heroes and villains or, more abstractly, between good and evil. In this way, the narrative places characters against each other in an attempt to lead them to their conflicts' resolution. According to Silverstone, television mediates the dimension of common sense and that of specialized knowledge.[30] For this, mediating characters are needed who "represent a higher wisdom and a synthesis of values above the polar conflict".[31] They possess specialized knowledge and will mediate the two spheres between 'us' and 'them'. In television journalism, this occurs through invited specialists who explain the causes of conflicts and propose solutions for them. The most common mediators in scripted TV fiction are doctors, lawyers, and detectives, central figures in institutional series.

3 Television's Fictional Institutions

Popular dramas as The Good Wife (CBS, 2009–2016), Law & Order (NBC, 1990–2010), and Chicago Fire (NBC, 2012-) are institutional series, yet each focus on the daily workings of different entities, the judiciary, law enforcement, and the fire department, respectively. For Berger and Luckmann, institutions not only define how things are but also how they should be. In this sense, they establish patterns of behavior that guide certain spheres of social life.[32] Likewise, fictional institutions function as elements of predictability providing certain narrative rules for the viewer. They frame the narrative within certain limits and expectations, for example, from a legal drama a viewer would expect to see lawyers fighting for the rights of their clients or incorruptible prosecutors safeguarding citizens from criminals.

By presenting the institutions' routines, objectives, conflicts, and codes of conduct, these fictional entities remind us of the role real institutions play in everyday life. In fact, real-world institutions have already recognized the importance of fictional institutions. Some even interfere in their fictionalization process. Frequently, concrete institutions use the argument that their

---

29 Kellner, "Television, mythology," 149.

30 Silverstone, *"The television message," 8.*

31 White, "Television as Myth," 3.

32 Berger and Luckmann, *The social construction of reality*, 63–109.

participation and/or interference in television is to guarantee that representations are "accurate" and to ensure that these productions reassemble the "reality" professionals face. Institutions from the U.S. as the American Medical Association,[33] the Central Intelligence Agency, the Air Force, the Secret Service, the Department of Defense[34] have acted directly in the fictionalization process of their institutions. Many of these entities even have dedicated sectors to deal with the entertainment industry.

Of course, this relationship between fictional and real-world institutions is controversial. In the case of the Pentagon's relationship and partnerships with Hollywood, David Robb noted that that cooperation between the studios and Phil Strub, the Pentagon's Special Assistant for Entertainment Media, allowed Strub to censor scripts that presented the army unfavorably in exchange for the use of helicopters, submarines and military tanks in audiovisual productions.[35] In this sense, the demand for precision and accuracy refers more to the favorable representation of the institution than necessarily to the 'reality' faced by its professionals. Police series are a good example in this regard. These productions tend to present homicides in greater proportion compared to the reality of U.S. cities.[36] Yet, these series feature extremely capable professionals who recurrently arrest criminals and solve cases. In their analysis of episodes from the 2003–2004 season of Law & Order: SVU, Britto et al. found that detectives and prosecutors had a 100% success rate in solving cases and arresting the suspect.[37] In contrast, this rate at the same time in the New York City Police Department was only 49%.

Therefore, the approximation of concrete institutions to television fiction goes beyond the demand for accurate representations. This interference reveals that real-world institutions recognize fiction as a space of authority and construction of knowledge. In this sense, by fictionalizing social institutions,

33 Joseph Turow, *Playing doctor: Television, storytelling, and medical power* (Ann Arbor: University of Michigan Press, 2010): 21–25.

34 Tricia Jenkins, *The CIA in Hollywood: how the agency shapes film and television* (Austin: University of Texas Press, 2016).

35 David. L. Robb, *Operation Hollywood: How the Pentagon shapes and censors the movies* (New York: Prometheus Books, 2004).

36 N. J. Brown, "A comparison of fictional television crime and crime index statistics". *Communication Research Reports* 18, no. 2 (2001): 192–9; Kathleen M. Donovan and Charles F. Klahm IV, "The role of entertainment media in perceptions of police use of force". *Criminal Justice and Behavior* 42, no. 12 (2015): 1261–6.

37 Sarah Britto, et al., "Does 'special' mean young, white and female? Deconstructing the meaning of 'special' in Law & Order: Special victims' unit". *Journal of Criminal Justice and Popular Culture* 14, no. 1 (2007): 39–57.

TV series become powerful systems of constructing meaning about real-world institutions. They also act as mechanisms that contribute to making institutions seem like something 'natural', as if they 'always existed', a capacity directly related to the nature of myths present in these productions.[38] Next, we need to consider which myths fictional institutions are disseminating in contemporary television fiction.

4 Myths and Fictional Institutions in the United States

The idea that TV scripted series can disseminate and/or reinforce myths is not new. Both Kellner and White use different television products in their analysis of the relationship between myths and television, especially regarding serial fiction.[39] Here, I understand that myths present an interesting solution to the narrative's need for conflict. Myths enable TV fiction to reorganize worrisome and distressing events in terms of a recognizable problem. In this process, they reflect on current uncertainties and fears in society. These productions translate social dilemmas and conflicts – many of which appear constantly in TV news – into mythical stories.

From a structuralist perspective, narratologists proposed that the dramatic narrative is built around a formula in which an initial state of stability is interrupted by a traumatic event, which ends the equilibrium, provisionally introducing a state of disorder and chaos that the characters will seek to resolve, restoring the equilibrium.[40] This structure is everywhere, in literature, film, and television, but it is particularly challenging in TV series since these productions need to keep the viewer's attention for long periods of time, demanding from the narrative a constant supply of chaos and disorder. Myths allow TV series to fulfill their need for dramatic tension through repetitive cycles of contradiction and resolution. Therefore, the potential to disseminate myths resides in these shows' narrative structure.

Television scripted fiction presents characters facing everyday controversies and dilemmas. These characters survive amid financial difficulties, seek better jobs, spend time with friends and family, suffer injustices and make mistakes, but most of the time they are able to overcome these issues. Whether it's after quitting a job (Grey's Anatomy, "Nothing Left to Cling To", 16×01), struggling

38 Barthes, *Mythologies*, 21–30.

39 Kellner, "Television, mythology," 134–43; White, "Television as Myth," 4–6.

40 Tzvetan Todorov and Arnold Weinstein, "Structural Analysis of Narrative". *NOVEL: A Forum on Fiction* 3, no. 1 (1969): 75–6.

with financial difficulties (Chicago Fire, "Sixty Days") or even dealing with the death of a loved one (Chicago PD "Start Digging", 3×23), TV series through myths drive conflicts to a well-defined resolution. For Hal Himmelstein, through resolutions, these shows would provide "a sense of order superimposed on the chaos of daily life".[41] Kellner emphasizes, however, that these solutions will be pseudo-resolutions or simplistic resolutions that "magically harmonize conflicting phenomena".[42]

This same logic organizes the everyday lives of doctors, police officers, firefighters, and lawyers in institutional series. This happens because fictional institutions supply the narrative with conflicts and/or controversies and guide them to simple resolutions. An extraordinary situation, for example, a crime, disrupts the order of everyday life and the main characters must intervene to restore it. For this, they identify the culprits, arrest and prevent them from threatening society again. From the detectives' point of view solving crimes is not an exceptional situation, but their daily livelihood, just as for doctors who treat sick people or firefighters who put out fires, these situations are part of their everyday routines. At the same time, these imbalances are necessary to maintain the institution's place in society. For example, a hospital's reason to exist is to fight death and heal sick and wounded people. In medical dramas, death is not the result of the action of a villain; it is the villain in and of itself. To fulfill this important role in the narrative, fictional institutions organize these conflicts through the use of myths.

Currently, institutional series in the U.S. disseminate and reinforce several myths. Here, I have chosen to focus on how they frame complex issues in terms of 'good' versus 'bad'. The political satire Parks and Recreation[43] is a good example in this regard. The comedy focuses on the lives of public officials in the department of parks and recreation in the fictional town of Pawnee, Indiana. In the episode, "Soda Tax" (5×02), Leslie Knope (Amy Poehler), a newly elected city councilor, has to face a set of obstacles when trying to pass a local tax on soft drinks. By taxing local restaurants, Leslie believes that the residents of Pawnee would cut back on sugar and, thus, improve the public's health. Yet, Leslie faces great resistance from the restaurants, who threaten not only to fire employees to make up for the decrease in their profits but also to remove her from the city council. The narrative then personifies the dispute between good and bad. Leslie is the good city councilor, taking care of the residents of

41 Hal Himmelstein, *Television myth and the American mind* (Westport: Praeger Publishers, 1994): 114.

42 Kellner, "Television, mythology," 136.

43 Produced by the US network NBC from 2009 to 2015.

Pawnee, while Kathryn Pinewood (Mary Faber), is the greedy representative of the restaurant association. This dispute, however, turns out to be more complex when Leslie asks residents if they even want the tax, finding ambiguity in their answers.

Throughout the series, Leslie frequently takes a stand against greedy local corporations. This is especially true in regards to the Sweetums candy factory, accused of polluting the city's air ("Camping", 3×08) and deceiving consumers with unhealthy products ("Sweetums", 2×15). The notion of 'what's best for the population' is widely debated in the series with each character having their own subjective view of the priorities and duties of public servants ("Are you better off", 5×22). In this sense, Parks and Recreation recurrently presents political issues through mythical lenses.

This dualistic structure tends to reduce complex structural problems in real-world institutions. These narratives often represent problems as individual issues which are exceptions to the norm. The myth of 'a few bad apples' is commonly used for this purpose. According to Anita Lam, this myth suggests that "there is an individual cause for an act of corruption rather than an organizational cause".[44] Through this myth, only a few members of the institution are corrupt (the so-called bad apples), while the fictional institution as a whole still works and has internal mechanisms to control and stop corruption. The bad apple myth is present in several contemporary institutional series such as Chicago Fire ("What I Saw", 7×15) and Chicago PD ("Hit Me", 3×13), for example. These narratives present acts of police corruption in binary and common terms, mainly reducing them to the clash between a good cop and a bad one. In this process, these productions engage in Barthes' view of myths. They camouflage the institution's responsibility for the problem, as well as the crisis that currently affects the police institution in the United States.[45]

Other institutional series also employ the mythology of "good" versus "bad" applying them to professional problems. For example, doctors versus death, firemen against an arsonist, and policemen versus criminals. The solution to these disputes, however, are usually temporary. In Law & Order: SVU, for example, in spite of the weekly success the detectives and prosecutors obtain, every new episode starts with a new criminal investigation. Next, I will examine how

---

44 Anita Lam, "Making 'Bad Apples' on The Bridge," in *Law and Justice on the Small Screen*, ed. Peter Robson and Jessica Silbey, (Oregon: Hart Publishing, 2012): 63–4.

45 Brigitta Hudácskó, "The Case of the Two Gregsons" in *Victorian Detectives in Contemporary Culture: Beyond Sherlock Holmes*, ed. Lucyna Krawczyk-Żywko, (Cham: Springer, 2017): 57–76.

Grey's Anatomy and Chicago P.D. use myths to construct meaning about the medical and the police institutions, respectively.

5 The Good Doctors of Grey's Anatomy

The medical drama Grey's Anatomy premiered on ABC in 2005. Created by Shonda Rhimes, the drama initially followed the life of doctor Meredith Grey (Ellen Pompeo) and other interns in the surgical program at Seattle Grace Hospital. Through the years, these characters have completed their internship, residency and become attending physicians at the hospital teaching new generations of surgeons. The drama presents the difficulties health professionals face in reconciling their personal and professional life and the ethical struggles surgeons face on a daily basis.

Television fiction centered on the medical institution usually reproduces a simple formula structured around the efforts of healthcare workers to save lives. The medical fictional institution offers countless narrative opportunities around different: 1) work environments (hospital, clinic, military base); 2) medical specialties (interns and residents, surgeons, military doctors, psychiatrists); 3) diseases and procedures. Furthermore, these productions can focus on the work of an experienced physician (Ben Casey)[46], or nurse (HawthoRNe).[47] They can also follow an entire team of healthcare professionals in a hospital (ER)[48] or expose the doctor-patient relationship (House M.D.).[49] Although there are variations in the formula, the main antagonists of these professionals remain constant: accidents, illnesses, and especially death.

Given the mythical nature of the dispute between doctors and death, medical dramas present these professionals as modern-day heroes. Doctors save patients through their scientific knowledge and their selfless work. The 'doctor-hero' stereotype has been established for several decades in television in the U.S. Initially, it centered on the figure of a paternal white male who was professional, brave, intelligent, and helpful.[50] These doctors were invulnerable,

46 Produced by the US network ABC from 1961 to 1966.

47 Produced by the US network TNT from 2009 to 2011.

48 Produced by the US network NBC from 1994 to 2009.

49 Produced by the US network Fox from 2004 to 2012.

50 David Lynn Painter, Alison Kubala, and Sarah Parsloe, "Playing doctor on TV: physician portrayals and interactions on medical drama, comedy, and reality shows," *Atlantic Journal of Communication* 28, no. 5 (2020): 322.

incorruptible, and with a life of dedication to others.[51] This representation, however, became unsustainable given the crises that the real medical institution has faced in the United States.[52] In the 1970s, the representation of health professionals began to be more humanized,[53] and in the 1980s these narratives started to present greater ambiguity in the medical profession.[54]

In spite of these changes, the basic formula remains the same: these narratives present doctors as heroes who save their patients' lives through their medical knowledge, access to innovative technologies, and their dedication in popular productions as Grey's Anatomy and The Good Doctor. To reiterate this formula, these TV shows present the ideal of professionalism as the internal organizing force of the hospital environment. Moral dilemmas frequently highlight the physician's professionalism, who sets aside his/her subjectivities and prejudices to save lives. This professionalism reassures viewers about the institution's trustworthiness.

The incorporation of the ideal of professionalism into this formula relates to demands and the interference of real-world medical institutions. For a long time, the American Medical Association (AMA, hereafter) required TV shows to represent physicians favorably. Many productions encouraged the AMA to review the scripts for each episode to ensure "medical and professional authenticity".[55] The association managed to exert great pressure against certain productions and their sponsors, encumbering TV shows that were contrary to the institution's interference and/or guidance.[56] Although this interference has decreased, other agents have begun to influence medical institutional series, such as the Hollywood Health & Society (HH&S, hereafter).[57]

---

51 M. Holoweiko, "Here's looking at: doctor-patient relations. Good news the pedestal is gone," *Medical economics* 75, no. 20 (1998): 54–6.

52 Jason Jacobs, *Body trauma TV: the new hospital dramas* (London: British Film Institute, 2003).

53 Holoweiko, *Here's looking at*, 54–6.

54 Turow, *Playing Doctor*.

55 Rebecca Feasey, *Masculinity and popular television* (Edinburgh: Edinburgh University Press, 2008): 70.

56 Turow, *Playing Doctor*, 88–94.

57 Established in 2001, HH&S is part of the Norman Lear Center (a research center belonging to the Department of Communication and Journalism at the University of Southern California). According to the institution's website, the organization "provides the entertainment industry with accurate and up-to-date information for storylines on health, safety and security". Thus, there is a mutualistic relationship between the organization and the audiovisual industry. While HH&S provides legitimate and accurate content, the industry disseminates scientific content to viewers. For more information, see: https://hollywoodhealthandsociety.org/ Accessed on July 20, 2021.

It is through the codes of professionalism that Grey's Anatomy reassures its viewers about the competence of healthcare workers. For this, the series emphasizes the importance of physicians being up to date with the latest scientific advances ("Raindrops Keep Falling on My Head", 2×01; "Love of My Life", 16×19). The drama also presents doctors as creative professionals who strive to save lives using all available knowledge and implementing innovative techniques ("Give Peace a Chance", 6×07; "Add It Up", 15×18). Professionalism is also triggered in the narrative through its association with rationality. In this sense, the series frequently reiterates that a 'good doctor' is one who separates his/her work from their personal emotions and subjectivities ("Owner of a Lonely Heart", 2×11; "An Honest Mistake", 5×16).

Yet, this does not mean that fictional doctors and other healthcare professionals never break rules or norms. Although the production presents professionals who follow the rules, there are frequent disputes between the hospital's ethical norms and doctor's subjectivities ("It's a Long Way Back", 7×19; "It's Alright, Ma (I'm Only Bleeding)", 12×19; "What I Did for Love", 15×23). While medical professionals strive to fight death the line between "saving a life" and "following protocols" sometimes becomes blurred. For example, when a doctor wants to help a patient, but to do so the professional must violate ethical norms ("Deterioration of the Fight or Flight Response," 2×26; "The Me Nobody Knows", 12×06; "What I Did for Love", 15×23). The narrative rarely questions these actions and equates these violations as a last resort by a dedicated doctor to save their patients. This mythical construction normalizes conduct violations as a way for doctors to save lives. This framing, however, is only possible because Grey's Anatomy and other medical institutional series construct doctors as heroes, who dedicate their time and even sacrifice their careers for their patients ("Jump into the Fog", 15×25; "My Shot", 16×08).

To reinforce the professionalism ideal, the medical fictional institution presents a strong institutional regulation. Healthcare professionals are recurrently ordered and instructed to follow ethical rules and up-hold hospital protocols in order to avoid mistakes and, more importantly, lawsuits. The narrative personifies this regulation through the presence of the hospital administrator. This character is responsible for overseeing the hospital staff, mediating conflicts, and avoiding lawsuits. The bureaucratic conflicts serve to dramatize the tension between medical ethics and the more mundane interests of hospital administration (Grey's Anatomy, "Everybody's Crying Mercy", 10×03; "One Day Like This", 14×17). This administrative hierarchy, however, is less strengthened than the militarized hierarchy present in the fictional police institution.

The organizing force of the professionalism ideal and the strong regulation allows the medical fictional institution to rarely present cases of medical errors. In 536 episodes of four popular medical dramas, Katherine Foss identified only 52 medical errors, most of which were due to the healthcare professional's irresponsibility.[58] According to Foss, when presenting medical errors, these dramas emphasized the burden of responsibility carried by healthcare professionals.[59] In Grey's Anatomy, I identified that when a physician misdiagnoses a patient, commits a medical error, or acts unethically, he/she may be: a) reprimanded ("Much too Much", 2×10; "Reunited", 16×04); b) suspended ("Crash Into Me [Part 2]", 4×10; "Throwing it all Away", 10×15; "None of Your Business", 13×12); c) fired ("Invasion", 6×05; "I saw what I saw", 6×06; "Everything I Try to Do, Nothing Seems to Turn Out Right", 10×23; "Judgment Day", 14×20); d) sued ("Sorry Seems to Be the Hardest Word", 10×09; "Help Me Through the Night", 16×10); e) investigated and have their medical license revoked ("My Shot", 16×08).

Foss's study indicates two different ways to present the issue of medical errors. In some cases, they are incompetent healthcare professionals. These characters "only appeared in the storylines about their incompetent behavior and were immediately dismissed".[60] Medical institutional series present incompetent or negligent characters as negative examples for other physicians. They are also used to emphasize the institution's authority, which quickly dismisses them from their positions, thus protecting patients. Added to this, these characters also serve to highlight the quality of other competent professionals represented.

In Grey's Anatomy, this construction is observable in the episode "The Self-Destruct Button" (1×07) in which the intern George O'Malley (T. R. Knight) suspects an anesthesiologist, Dr. Taylor (Larry Cahn), is performing surgeries inebriated. Initially, Dr. Derek Shepard (Patrick Dempsey) reprimands George for accusing a superior attending physician. Yet, Derek finds out that the anesthesiologist was in fact drinking before surgeries when Taylor falls asleep during a procedure. Dr. Shepard takes him off the case and apologies to George, taking responsibility for the incident. Dr. Taylor only appears in this episode, his violation – drinking during work – is presented as a risk to his patients and to the hospital's reputation.

On the other hand, when a competent professional makes a mistake, the narrative will construct this error as a learning experience that will result in a

58 Katherine A. Foss, "'When we make mistakes, people die!': Constructions of responsibility for medical errors in televised medical dramas, 1994–2007," *Communication Quarterly* 59, no. 4 (2011): 490.

59 *Ibid.*, 489.

60 *Ibid.*, 496.

better professional.[61] This construction is present in the episodes "Much Too Much" (2×10); "Stand by Me" (5×18); "Head Over High Heels" (15×22) and "What I Did for Love" (15×23). So, although Grey's Anatomy can present doctors making mistakes, the drama suggests that these actions are uncommon and will ultimately improve the quality of care, contributing to making doctors more considerate, caring, and responsible. Again, this serves to foster the hero myth associated with these healthcare professionals.

However, the ideal of professionalism cultivates the expectation that doctors will be exemplary regardless of circumstances. This is problematic, to say the least, as it disregards the prejudices and individual dilemmas that interfere with the performance of healthcare professionals in the hospital environment. In Grey's Anatomy doctors sometimes show bias when they blame patients for not searching for medical attention in a timely manner ("If Tomorrow Never Comes", 1×06; "How Insensitive", 6×21). At times, these professionals even reiterate a conservative and moralistic bias when treating prison inmates ("Wish You Were Here", 5×11; "Sympathy for the Devil", 5×12) or criminals ("Disarm", 7×11). This bias separates individuals between those who are worthy of medical care and those who are not. Nevertheless, the narrative mostly presents doctors that strive to save their patients' lives and who are encouraged to overcome their personal biases.

6 The Bad Cops of Chicago P.D.

The police drama Chicago P.D. premiered in 2014 on NBC. The series, created by Dick Wolf and Matt Olmstead, follows detectives from the elite Intelligence Unit of the Chicago Police Department's 21st District and their uniformed officers. The Unit's detectives are responsible for solving major crimes involving drug trafficking, murders, and the city's organized crime. Otherwise, the uniformed officers deal with minor offenses and infractions, conducting patrols and responding to other emergency calls.

Fictional series about law enforcement are one of the most popular formats in television. Although these productions vary from one another, they reproduce a common formula: the institution's members are responsible for maintaining order. They also reiterate a fundamental perspective: the police are protagonists in the fight against crime. According to Jason Mittell, police institutional series reproduce binary oppositions such as "law versus crime"

61 *Ibid.*

and "order versus chaos".[62] These oppositions serve to reinforce a certain worldview and feed specific national myths. The first opposition will order the meaning of the second, since the law restricts the potential of "order versus chaos" to a certain set of conventions and, more importantly, to the field of human action. Television police procedurals traditionally return to the status quo by the end of the episode. In this process, fictional law enforcement institutions reiterate security and prioritizes the victories and efforts of the police, to the detriment of the communities being policed.

This return to the status quo and the constant threat to order makes stories about crime "always, in a variety of ways, both reassuring and unnerving".[63] Richard Sparks considers institutional police series as tales of morality that society reproduces to reassure itself.[64] By reproducing the same formula these productions are able to meet a desire to see punishment imposed on a certain group of society. Drawing on the work of Emile Durkheim, Sparks proposes that the complexity of institutional justice processes led individuals to seek to satisfy their "punitive passions in the comforting simplicity of stories".[65] In this way, institutional police series tend to villainize the criminal, who deserves punishment,[66] and construct the police officer/detective as a hero. This narrative, then, is centered on a criminal action and an action of retribution by the institution (i.e., punishment).[67] The attraction of this apparently simple formula "is its ritual affirmation of the potency of law and order".[68]

Institutional police series reveal the moral and legal dimension of this institution's role in society, by presenting the citizen as a potential adversary and the police officer as a hero. By framing the narrative around adversaries, the capacity to reinforce a conservative discourse becomes distinct. These narratives frequently define criminals as being *a priori* 'evil' and justify the police's action against them. Yet, because of the mythical nature of this conflict, these

---

62 Jason Mittell, *Television and genre: From cop shows to cartoons* (London: Routledge, 2004): 146.

63 Richard Sparks, "Inspector Morse'" in *British Television Drama in the 1980s*, ed. George William Brandt, (Cambridge: Cambridge University Press, 1993): 87.

64 Richard Sparks, *Television and the drama of crime: Moral tales and the place of crime in public life* (Maidenhead: Open University Press, 1992).

65 Emile Durkheim, *The Division of Labor in Society* (New York: Free Press, 1964); Sparks. "'Inspector Morse'," 87.

66 David Marc, *Demographic vistas: Television in American culture* (Pennsylvania: University of Pennsylvania Press, 1996): 103.

67 Arthur A. Raney and Bryant Jennings, "Moral judgment and crime drama: An integrated theory of enjoyment". *Journal of communication* 52, no. 2 (2002): 404.

68 Marc, *Demographic vistas*, 69.

narratives end camouflaging social and economic dimensions of criminality. In this way, crime and poverty are explained through moral, not sociological terms.[69]

Because conservatism is the organizing force of the fictional police institution, police officers and detectives can break institutional and ethical rules to operate as agents of "moral justice" in dramas as *Kojak*[70] and *Hill Street Blues* (NBC, 1981–1987).[71] Here, the dimension of morality takes precedence over legality. Through a utilitarian logic, law enforcement officers use coercive force to prevent some kind of threat and end up abusing their authority. In other words, by representing criminals in a villainous way, these TV series feature police officers who break the rules to (apparently) prevent a 'greater evil' and reinforce the conservative mentality of 'us versus them'. In many cases, these series justify police misconduct by presenting these actions as acceptable and even necessary in the 'name of justice'. By framing these violations as acts of heroism, police institutional series normalize the dirtiest aspects of the profession.

The report "Normalizing Injustice" by Color of Change, published in January 2020, reveals that one of the greatest conventions of police series in the twenty-first century is law enforcement officers breaking institutional rules and protocols.[72] Popular TV shows as NCIS[73] and Criminal Minds (CBS, 2005–2020) often frame protocol violations as the means to achieve certain ends, specifically the criminal's arrest. Although these violations might foster disputes between the fictional police institution (interested in arresting criminals) and the fictional legal institution (interested in guaranteeing citizens' rights and due process), there is tacit tolerance for police officers to break rules in dramas, as Blue Bloods ("Excessive Force", 5×04) and Chicago P.D. ("Justice", 3×21). This is a moral, not a legal, prerogative in violating the law to restore the status quo. Of course, law enforcement officers can be suspended or lose their jobs in these narratives, but the reiteration of these violations is often followed by little or no consequences, according to the Normalizing Injustice report. This hypocrisy is fueled by the maxim the means justify the ends.

---

69 David Buxton, *From the Avengers to Miami Vice: form and ideology in television series* (Manchester University Press, 1990): 150.

70 Produced by the US network CBS from 1973 to 1978.

71 Sue Turnbull, *TV Crime Drama* (Edinburgh: Edinburgh University Press, 2014).

72 To access the report: https://hollywood.colorofchange.org//wp-content/uploads/2020/02/Normalizing-Injustice_Complete-Report-2.pdf Accessed on July 20, 2021.

73 Produced by the US network CBS since 2003.

While examining Chicago P.D., I identified the drama continues to reproduce the consolidated formula from other police dramas. A group of law enforcement officers strive every week to safeguard the city and its citizens by maintaining the status quo through the forces of law and order. The production reproduces a conservative bias that opposes the police, representatives of the order, with the criminals, who are recurrently vilified by the officers, often described as 'bad guys' or even associated with the notion of malignancy ("Now Is Always Temporary", 1×04; "A Little Devil Complex", 2×13). This action, again, reinforces the conservative 'us versus them' mentality. In this process, Chicago P.D. reduces the complex reality of a city the size of Chicago to mythical binary oppositions that call into question order versus chaos, law versus crime, and, above all, good versus bad. Thus, the drama presents the police as the institution responsible for regulating crime in Chicago.

Through conduct violations and abuse of power, Chicago P.D.'s narrative materializes the show's conservative bias. The production presents illegal conduct by police officers and detectives not as an exception but as the rule. At times, the narrative frames these violations as necessary to achieve justice. Take the kidnapping of Diego Dawson (Zach Garcia) as an example ("Stepping Stone", 1×01). Diego is the young son of Detective Antonio Dawson (Jon Seda), who is taken and used as a bargaining chip in exchange for the cartel leader Pulpo (Arturo Del Puerto). After his child is kidnaped, we see Antonio struggling to find his son while following internal protocols of the Chicago police ("Wrong Side of the Bars", 1×02). During the episode, Sergeant Voight (Jason Beghe) encourages Antonio to break the rules to find his son. In exchange for information, Antonio tortures a member of the cartel. This is just one of the multiple times the show presents police brutality. This abusive form of interrogation and other conduct violations employed by Voight and the Unit's members are often portrayed as effective. Overall, this construction minimizes the issue of police brutality and promotes misunderstandings about the institution's real purpose in society.

Several episodes show characters violating police procedures, mainly through brutality, to solve cases. Frequently, interrogations are aggressive ("Army of One", 4×22; "Snitch", 5×04), Voight and Olinsky even use black sites – places where they can torture suspects without the knowledge of the institution ("Stepping Stone", 1×01; "Start Digging", 3×23). However, even within the precinct suspects can be kept in a "cage," accessed only by the Unit's members. In the cage, suspects are denied their rights and tortured until they share the information needed to solve the week's case ("Wrong Side of the Bars", 1×02; "Emotional Proximity", 4×16).

This construction, however, is not without criticism. The drama presents struggles among the detectives in trusting Voight's questionable methods ("All Cylinders Firing", 4×03; "Informant", 7×07). Yet, in large part, Chicago P.D. presents the police breaching the line between 'following protocols' and 'stopping a criminal'. The drama does present some consequences for questionable actions, like when these professionals are suspended ("Reform", 5×01; "New Normal" 6×01). Nevertheless, they are later reincorporated to the Unit or even have their actions explained. In this sense, the production not only justifies but normalizes police misconduct and brutality by presenting them as necessary to obtain justice ("Wrong Side of the Bars" 1×02; "Army of One", 4×22; "Sisterhood", 5×15).

Interestingly, Chicago P.D.'s tagline is "break the rules, not the law". In practical terms, this is sophistry, but it is an important distinction that would separate the police (Good) from the criminals (Bad) they face every week. In this sense, the fictional police institution in Chicago P.D. reiterates that law enforcement officers, in order to do their jobs, have to violate this institution's norms. For Voight, there is a difference between being a dirty cop who hurts innocent people and doing whatever is necessary to stop criminals. Voight contends that "like it or not, you and all your self-righteous friends in the Ivory Tower, you need people like me out on the streets, doing the things regular cops are unwilling to do, going the extra mile to make sure the truly evil, the truly dangerous, go away. I thin the herd for the greater good" ("Homecoming", 5×23). This line of dialogue allows us to infer that Chicago P.D. reproduces a tough-on-crime vision of law and order.

While presenting the police officers and detectives favorably, Chicago P.D. constructs a negative view of the department's internal affairs and the state prosecutor's office. The drama presents these institutions as bureaucratic obstacles to police work, with their members being more concerned with following protocols and the political consequences of their actions than preventing criminals from threatening society. This construction is problematic considering recent criticisms of the real-world law enforcement institutions in the U.S., mainly toward police brutality against racial minorities. According to Donavan & Klahm, the construction that the ends justify the means in TV fiction can lead the viewer to justify police misconduct.[74] Eschholz et al., go even further stating that viewers might even believe "this is how policing is and 'should' be done".[75]

74 Donovan and Klahm, "The role of entertainment," 1266.

75 Sarah Eschholz, Matthew Mallard, and Stacey Flynn, "Images of prime time justice: a content analysis of 'NYPD Blue' and 'Law & Order'". *Journal of criminal justice and popular culture* 10, no. 3 (2004): 173.

Given Chicago P.D.'s conservative alignment, the manner in which it triggers the hero myth is different than in Grey's Anatomy. Voight is not presented as an idealized hero, virtuous, and the moral symbol for justice. But he is the hero that a violent city like Chicago would need. A tough cop who seeks justice at any cost and prevents chaos from taking over the city and the police institution itself. Nevertheless, Chicago P.D. also fosters the myth of the virtuous hero. Detectives Dawson, Lindsey (Sophia Bush), and Halstead (Jesse Lee Soffer) frequently question Voights tactics. Along with the uniformed officers' Burgess (Marina Squerciati) and Atwater (Laroyce Hawkins), these detectives are framed as dedicated civil servants who strive to help victims ("Ride Along", 6×04, "Tender Age", 8×03) and risk their lives to stop criminals ("Life is Fluid", 3×01; "Absolution", 7×09). They are also caring professionals who even assist individuals who have resorted to delinquency out of desperation ("Now Is Always Temporary", 1×04; "Thirty Balloons", 1×05). Voight himself has his most redeemable qualities highlighted when he sacrifices his wellbeing to protect the city of Chicago and its people ("Shouldn't Have Been Alone", 2×10; "Actual Physical Violence", 3×03).

7 Conclusions

Television fictional series approach existential dilemmas by reiterating social, economic, and cultural myths. Yet, they also present viewers with mythical constructions of social institutions. In this process, these programs can reinforce the importance of these organizations in everyday life. Here, the main objective was to explore these constructions in reference to law enforcement and medical institutions. Both Grey's Anatomy and Chicago P.D. foster the hero myth by presenting protagonists who strive to keep crime, injustice, diseases, and even death at bay. Both TV dramas contextualize the role of these institutions and their members in society, by presenting their objectives and the rules they follow. In this sense, television institutional series can play a significant sociological role in bringing viewers and real-world institutions closer by revealing their internal routines, organization, and hierarchies. In the narrative, these fictional institutions fulfill the role of watchdogs being responsible for maintaining and restoring order.

The fictionalized medical institution in Grey's Anatomy presents the hospital as the locus of medical expertise, science, and professionalism, associating these discursive constructions with the real-world institution. Alternatively, Chicago P.D. constructs the police and detectives as being courageous and, although they violate protocols, they do so to safeguard the population. Thus, while the fictional police institution has characters that can break the rules, the medical fictional institution has a higher degree of internal regulation that inhibits misconduct. The institutions' internal regulation will play different roles in each production. While the more bureaucratic regulation of health professionals refers to a concern with the professional's career and the hospital's reputation, the strong regulation of the police institution becomes an obstacle to police work.

Considering the significant role of the United States' audiovisual industry in global television flows, it becomes essential for scholars to investigate the fictionalization of U.S. institutions. These TV series travel around the world presenting the organization of the country's institutions and their importance in maintaining order. By fostering certain mythical constructions, these television series can shape the way viewers understand and relate to real-world institutions. While highlighting the strength of U.S. institutions in the country and for audiences around the world, institutional series become powerful mechanisms for the construction of knowledge and meaning in contemporary society.

References

Barthes, Roland. *Mythologies*. Translated by Andrew Leak. Valencia: Grant & Cutler, 1994.

Berger, Peter Ludwig, and Thomas Luckmann. *The social construction of reality: A treatise in the sociology of knowledge*. New York: Doubleday, 1966.

Britto, Sarah, Tycy Hughes, Kurt Saltzman, and Colin Stroh. "Does 'special' mean young, white and female? Deconstructing the meaning of 'special' in Law & Order: Special victims unit". *Journal of Criminal Justice and Popular Culture* 14, no. 1 (2007): 39–57.

Brown, N. J. "A comparison of fictional television crime and crime index statistics". Communication Research Reports 18, no. 2 (2001): 192–199.

Buxton, David. *From the Avengers to Miami Vice: form and ideology in television series*. Manchester University Press, 1990.

Couldry, Nick, and Andreas Hepp. *The mediated construction of reality*. Cambridge: Polity Press, 2017.

Daniel III, J. Furman, and Paul Musgrave. "Synthetic experiences: How popular culture matters for images of international relations". *International Studies Quarterly* 61, no. 3 (2017): 503–516.

Donovan, Kathleen M., and Charles F. Klahm IV. "The role of entertainment media in perceptions of police use of force". *Criminal Justice and Behavior* 42, no. 12 (2015): 1261–1281.

Durkheim, Emile. *The Division of Labor in Society*. New York: Free Press, 1964.

Eliade, Mircea. *The myth of the eternal return, or, Cosmos and history*. New York: Harper & Brothers, 1959.

Eschholz, Sarah, Matthew Mallard, and Stacey Flynn. "Images of prime time justice: a content analysis of 'NYPD Blue' and 'Law & Order'". *Journal of criminal justice and popular culture* 10, no. 3 (2004): 161–180.

Feasey, Rebecca. *Masculinity and popular television*. Edinburgh: Edinburgh University Press, 2008.

Foss, Katherine A. "'When we make mistakes, people die!': Constructions of responsibility for medical errors in televised medical dramas, 1994–2007". *Communication Quarterly* 59, no. 4 (2011): 484–506.

Giddens, Anthony. *The consequences of modernity*. Stanford: Stanford University Press, 1991.

Grandío, Maria del Mar and Patricia Diego González. La influencia de la sitcom americana en la producción de comedias televisivas en España. El caso de 'Friends' y '7 vidas'", *Ámbitos. Revista Internacional de Comunicación*, no.18 (2009): 83–97.

Himmelstein, Hal. *Television myth and the American mind*. Praeger Publishers, 1994.

Holoweiko, M. "Here's looking at: doctor-patient relations. Good news – the pedestal is gone". *Medical economics* 75, no. 20 (1998): 54–6.

Hudácskó, Brigitta. "The Case of the Two Gregsons". *Victorian Detectives in Contemporary Culture: Beyond Sherlock Holmes*, edited by Lucyna Krawczyk-Żywko, 57–76. Cham: Springer, 2017.

Jacobs, Jason. *Body trauma TV: the new hospital* dramas. London: British Film Institute, 2003.

Jenkins, Tricia. *The CIA in Hollywood: how the agency shapes film and television*. Austin: University of Texas Press, 2016.

Kellner, Douglas. "Television, mythology and ritual". *Praxis* 6 (1982): 133–155.

Kim, Yaeri. "The invention of the Mideu: redefining American television in South Korea". *Media, Culture & Society* 42, no. 1 (2020): 109–125.

Kompare, Derek. *Rerun nation: How repeats invented American television*. New York: Routledge, 2006.

Lam, Anita. "Making 'Bad Apples' on The Bridge: A Production Study of the Making of a Police Drama". In *Law and Justice on the Small Screen*, edited by Peter Robson and Jessica Silbey, 63–86. Oregon: Hart Publishing, 2012.

Lévi-Strauss, Claude. *Structural anthropology*. New York: Basic books, 1963.

Lobato, Ramon. *Netflix Nations*. New York: New York University Press, 2019.

Marc, David. *Demographic vistas: Television in American culture*. Pennsylvania: Universityof Pennsylvania Press, 1996.

McConnell, Frank. *Storytelling and mythmaking: images from film and literature*. Oxford: Oxford University Press, 1979.

Mittell, Jason. *Television and genre: From cop shows to cartoons*. London: Routledge, (2004).

Painter, David Lynn, Alison Kubala, and Sarah Parsloe. "Playing doctor on TV: physician portrayals and interactions on medical drama, comedy, and reality shows". *Atlantic Journal of Communication* 28, no. 5 (2020): 322–336.

Pişcărac, Diana. "Medical k-dramas: a cross-section of South Korea's global cultural industry". *Romanian Journal of Sociological Studies* 1 (2016): 43–60.

Raney, Arthur A., and Jennings Bryant. "Moral judgment and crime drama: An integrated theory of enjoyment". Journal of communication 52, no. 2 (2002): 402–415.

Robb, David L. *Operation Hollywood: How the Pentagon shapes and censors the movies*. New York: Prometheus Books, 2004.

Silverstone, Roger. *The television message as social object: a comparative study of the structure and content of television programmes in Britain*. PhD thesis. *LSE Theses Online*, 1980, http://etheses.lse.ac.uk/139/ Accessed on June 20, 2021.

Sparks, Richard. *Television and the drama of crime: Moral tales and the place of crime in public life*. Maidenhead: Open University Press, 1992.

Sparks, Richard. "Inspector Morse: 'The Last Enemy'". *BritishTelevision Drama in the 1980s*, edited by George William Brandt, 86–102. Cambridge: Cambridge University Press, 1993.

Todorov, Tzvetan, and Arnold Weinstein. "Structural Analysis of Narrative". *NOVEL: A Forum on Fiction* 3, no. 1 (1969): 70–76. Accessed June 9, 2021. DOI:10.2307/1345003.

Turnbull, Sue. *TV Crime Drama*. Edinburgh: Edinburgh University Press, 2014.

Turow, Joseph. *Playing doctor: Television, storytelling, and medical power*. University of Michigan Press, 2010.

Waisbord, Silvio. "McTV: Understanding the global popularity of television formats". *Television & New Media* 5, no. 4 (2004): 359–383.

White, Robert A. "Television as Myth and Ritual". *Communication Research Trends* 8, no. 1 (1987): 1–8.

CHAPTER 9

Mexican Drug Dealers in TV Series

Symbols of New Heroism or the Adulation of Bandits?

Omar Cerrillo Garnica

–A mí me gustan los corridos porque son los hechos reales de nuestro pueblo.

–Sí, a mí también me gustan porque en ellos se canta la pura verdad.

–Pues ponlos pues.

–Órale, ahí va.[1]

Los Tigres del Norte. "Jefe de Jefes" (Intro)

1 Introduction

A common media product since the origins of cinema and television has been when policemen chase thieves. There are many movies about bank robberies; westerns where the sheriff has a deadly duel with the most wanted criminal; or science fiction plays with gifted characters fighting each other to stop one side that wants to have control of the world.

In Mexico, the most visible criminal activity are drug dealers. There are European youtubers that speak about the most famous things in this country: lovely beaches, tacos, tequila and narcos. This tremendous fame comes from outstanding stories about carrying thousands of tons of drugs such as cocaine, marihuana or heroine across the USA-Mexico border, as well as stories about mass shootings in their confrontations against policemen; in addition, their capacity to move billions of dollars in tax havens for money laundering.

1 I like *corridos* because they are the real facts about our people / Yes, I like them too because they sing the whole truth / Let's play them / Ok, let's go. [Translation by the author].

This text is about how "the capos" commanding these operations become media pop products, specifically in TV shows. First of all, we are going to make a brief history of this illegal activity through the country until the more violent era in this 21st Century. After that, we are going to provide a theoretical frame to analyze media content about narcos, recurring to authors like Carl Jung, Mircea Eliade, Joseph Campbell and Patxi Lanceros, in which we can establish the mythical construction of drug-mafia leaders in mass media in Mexico and Latin America. Then, we are going to compare the official biographies of two famous capos: Miguel Ángel Félix Gallardo, leader of the Guadalajara Cartel in 1980s; and Joaquín Guzmán Loera *El Chapo*, leader of the Sinaloa Cartel in 1990s, 2000s and the beginning of 2010s. Both are main characters in two famous TV shows distributed by Netflix in Latin America and other parts of the world.

With this information, we will identify certain symbols that help to create a mythical image of these outlaws and later we expose the possible consequences of creating such kind of mythologies. This work aims to create a basis for a better understanding of drug culture in Mexico and Latin America.

2 Drug Trafficking in Mexico: From Underground Business to Pop Media Culture

Since Pre-Hispanic times, cultures from the Meso-American region have had a deep knowledge about psychotropic plants, like peyote, marihuana, ololiuhqui seeds, hallucinogenic mushrooms, to say the most common (Carod-Artal, 2015). All of them were part of ceremonial rituals where the shaman used plants to connect with gods, spirits and soul entities.[2] They weren't for common people's use, so the idea of "drugs" wasn't at use in these societies.

The modern concept of drugs started with the Opium Wars between China and United Kingdom in the 19th Century, whose consequence was the signing of The Hague International Opium Convention in 1912. Since then, other drugs have been added to the prohibition policy, such as hashish, marihuana, cocaine and others. The United States has become the nation that leads all efforts on

2 In the Nahua tradition, there are three soul entities that define each being: *tonalli, teyolía* e *ihiyotl*, each with different attributes that allowed the individual to live, consolidate as a human being and, at the same time, be part of the cosmos. *Tonalli* and *ihiyotl* were attributed with the power of growth and physical development of children, while *teyolía* was related to cognitive faculties, understanding and communication and social skills (Díaz-Barriga, 2014).

drugs prohibitionism around the world. That roll was sealed when President Richard Nixon declared "the war on drugs" in 1973 (Escohotado, 1998).

Mexico has its own road to prohibitionism. In 19th Century, some laws banned the use of certain drugs in the popular medical drugstores known as *boticas*. At that time, some Chinese immigrants arrived at the Pacific coast of Mexico, especially the states of Sinaloa and Sonora, where they settled and started to raise some exogamic plants, such as poppy, the plant from which opium is extracted. The constant wars in which United States were involved, created an increasing demand of morphine and other opium-based drugs, so Mexican farmers learned from Chinese to raise this plant in order to have a better income by selling these drugs to the United States.

When Nixon declared his war, Mexican farmers were already organized in small groups who were able to trade marihuana and opium to the United States in limited quantities. Even this situation, Nixon Administration implemented in Mexico an anti-drugs campaign called *Operación Cóndor*, which forced marihuana and poppy producers to create a better organization. In the late 1970s, some former police officers like Miguel Ángel Félix Gallardo or Juan José Esparragoza became drug dealers and started to develop a huge business from this cultivation, substituting peasants from the direction of the criminal groups. They noticed the need to bribe Mexican police and army, and also the American ones in order to increase the amounts of drugs to be moved across the border. They became businessmen and created a formal organization, where not just farmers, carriers and gunmen were needed. Other professions, such as lawyers or accountants were needed to manage the business. These capos became very powerful people who worked in the shadows in order to keep this enormous illegal commerce.

The bigger the business and power, the less these lords could hide themselves. First was the gossip, but later some more structured narratives started to witness their greatness, power and money. Some songwriters created "*corridos*," a popular format for musical chronicles that emerged during colonial times. In this kind of songs, music is just a basic support for verses in a narrative way, pretty similar to epic Medieval odes. These songs became strongly popular during Mexican Revolution, singing the adventures and missions of revolutionary leaders as Pancho Villa, Felipe Ángeles or Emiliano Zapata. Through songs, these characters became admired all along the country even if their campaigns were limited to certain regions. There are also *corridos* about thieves and bandits from the end of the 19th Century and the beginning of the 20th (Frajoza, 2019), like Heraclio Bernal, Joaquín Murrieta and Jesús

Malverde, a relevant figure in narco culture.[3] Songs helped to create an image of "good thieves", stealing from the rich and aiding the poor.

With time, the thievery songs converted into drug traffickers' ones. In 1930, "El Pablote", a song about a thief who was bragging about his income in a morphine sale while drinking in a cantina, was published. This was the first time that drugs were part of lyrics in a *corrido*. This relationship, drugs and *corridos*, became very popular in the 1970s. Chalino Sánchez and Paulino Vargas became important writers for some "norteña" musicians that were interested in these new songs. *Los Tigres del Norte*, a very popular group who sings odes to drug lords, has come to be the most important band in this genre. Hits like "Contrabando y Traición", "La Banda del Carro Rojo" or "Jefe de Jefes" became highly popular in the southern United States and all Mexico.

In a short time, this musical phenomenon demanded a visual complement. Some songs became the main plot for low-budget action movies; sometimes musicians themselves appeared as side characters in these films. Bigger media companies payed attention to this new cultural issue. In 1984, Televisa, a strong TV and media holding, created Fonovisa, a side record company that signed popular folklore musicians, some related to this drug trafficking chronicles, for instance *Los Tigres del Norte*. With the support of the major Mexican media company, this musical genre became very popular. Movies and songs in a TV broadcast corporation had a very obvious consequence: these groups developed their first videoclips. They began in the late 1980s and gained quality and popularity through years to come. In 1997, *Los Tigres del Norte* filmed "Jefe de Jefes" in Alcatraz Prison in California. This videoclip become a big success in Mexican and American television; hence, Televisa decided to evolve this business and in the late 1990s created the music channel called Bandamax with only folk music genres, many of them, with strong narrations about drug dealers and drug trafficking operations. It wasn't a hidden business anymore; it was a popular cultural market and big companies were in.

In the 21st Century, the war on drugs was not American but Mexican. The big organizations from the 1980s were divided in smaller but more violent groups controlling certain regions in the country and fighting against the other organizations to catch new territories. In 2006, President Felipe Calderón

---

3 There's not much information about Jesús Malverde's life, but there is about his death. He was hanged from a branch of a mesquite tree on May 3rd, 1909, because his compadre betrayed him. It is said that his body wasn't buried, and people threw stones at the body. Through time, Malverde was mystified and became a saint for burglars and drug dealers in Sinaloa, so much that a chapel was built in his honor. (González, in Frajoza, 2019).

decided to fight against drug cartels all around the country, putting federal police and the Army on the streets in many places in the country. This mobilization gained very weak results. Contrary to defeating criminal organizations, violence increased and everyday there were corpses all around the country, all related with this war. With more violent events, more stories were narrated through *narcocorridos*. The musical genre became more explicit, into what was known as *movimiento alterado,*[4] in which violent scenes are crystal clear on the lyrics. New artists emerged, such as Gerardo Ortíz, *El Komander* or the group *Buknas de Culiacán*. Videoclips were also as rude as the music, showing luxurious cars and big guns on the images.

Moreover, other cultural commodities were added to this new genre. The Spanish writer Arturo Pérez-Reverte published in 2002 his book "La Reina del Sur",[5] based in the story of Sandra Ávila Beltrán, the first woman that became a great drug dealer in Mexican cartels. *Los Tigres del Norte* composed a song inspired by this book which became their new hit in the new century. The videoclip was filmed in Pamplona, Spain, the main location of the book. Nine years later, the American-Latino broadcasting corporation Telemundo aired the series based in this book with more than 60 chapters; a second season was announced in 2017. A new fact: narcoculture became transmedia (Orduña, 2020).

Following "La Reina del Sur", other TV shows produced by different corporations reached high popularity. There were American shows –"Weeds", "Breaking Bad"–, Colombian shows –"Pablo Escobar: El Señor del Mal", "El Cartel de los Sapos"– and Mexican ones –"Señorita Pólvora", "El Chapo", "El Señor de los Cielos". Later, drug dealers' stories arrived to streaming systems, becoming a new TV genre for all the continent. With these new products, drug trafficking culture became certain kind of aspirational model for youngsters who lacked opportunities to have a better life. These narratives constructed a new antihero model that follows certain patterns to create the archetype of a powerful businessman surrounded by women, sport cars, jewels and personalized guns. Villains for some ones, heroes for other ones, there's a character charged with many ornaments that allow a mystifying process on it.

4 Altered Movement. Obviously, "altered" makes reference to the psychic state of mind, drugged.

5 The Queen of South.

3 Creating the Archetype

An obvious question we can find through this brief chronicle of the origins of narcoculture is how a criminal image can be represented as a hero in media. We need to follow certain theoretical ideas to understand the shift in this figure.

One of the basic readings about building characters is found in Carl Jung's theory of archetypes, a concept related to archaic ideas formed through symbols that are used to represent the world and humanity generally found in myths, legends and what Jung called "the secret doctrine" (1970: 11). Jung establishes that collective unconsciousness is formed through these models that have survived through time, creating as many stories as possible.

Jung's general theory defined twelve general models for creating characters in epic stories based in certain values, attitudes, aims and weaknesses each model has. The most relevant archetypes for this article are "the outlaw" and "the hero". Let's analyze each one. First, the outlaw is the natural rebel, the one that needs to break the rules in order to reach power. He aims to destroy the order that isn't working. In a very dark version, an outlaw becomes a criminal. On the other hand, the hero wants to prove himself as a courageous, strong person, able to fight as many battles as possible to protect the people he loves. In a dark version, a hero is arrogant and selfish, thinking about his own pursuit. Both archetypes will be relevant for the further analysis of the fictionalized versions of drug capos in TV series.

In addition, Mircea Eliade (2001) describes the way a hero aims for immortality through achievements that show him the way to be out of the common world and reach the mythical one. Music and poetry are crucial in this task since their testimony is the essence for reaching the eternal life of gods. The mortal being may die in the task, but he can survive through verses that generate a completely new story which is, literally, "out of this world". The story that is in the songs or poems is more powerful than the history, because through narrative, the hero and the events surrounding him got a deeper meaning that carries not just his own story, but all precedents that are similar and also empower him to his actions:

> This reduction of events to categories and of individuals to archetypes, carried out by the consciousness of the (…) popular sector almost to this day, completely agrees with archaic ontology. It could be said that popular memory restores the historical character of modern times into its significance as an image of an archetype and as a reproducer of archetypal actions, a significance of which the members of archaic societies have been and continue to be aware of.
>
> ELIADE, 2001: 32

The hero used to live in a historical timeline, but the passage to immortality lies always in a mythical timeline were events are more than facts and become a real thrill that transcends through time. This connection between a historical timeline and a mythical one is widely and wisely developed by Patxi Lanceros (1997). As we can see in Figure 9.1, the main contribution for this analytical frame built for this work is that the connection between these two timelines is only possible through the symbol. But it is more than just a connection between these two ways to watch events, it also allows us to connect past and future in the historical line as well as the ideas of origin and ending on the mythical side. Connecting past with origins, history with myths, is only possible through a feeling of yearning. In the other side, projecting an idea of future is only possible if we are aware of its apocalyptical approach, which can be reached through desire and craving. Both feelings, yearning and craving, are possible in the existence of symbols that can connect people with their rational and emotional way to watch back or forth in their own life.

In this sense, heroes and villains are constructed by symbols. They aren't common men that live just for spending time. They are expecting something more, so they push their luck in order to reach something higher and become immortals thanks to the stories that can be told about their past through the common life. These archetypes have survived ancient times and reached our era just because they have become symbols themselves.

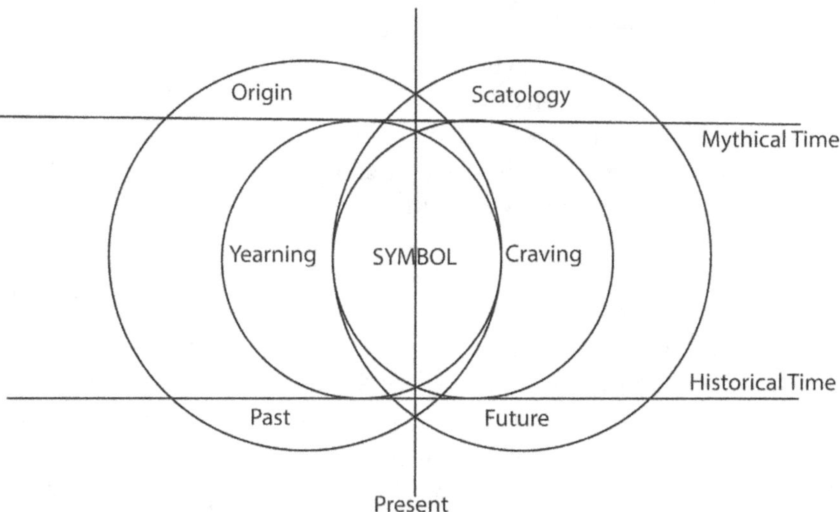

FIGURE 9.1 Patxi Lanceros' symbol as suture for mythical and historical timelines

Drug dealers behave like unsatisfied heroes who need more power and adventures to transform themselves. Joseph Campbell says about heroes:

> The hero, therefore, is the man or woman who has been able to fight and triumph over their personal and local historical limitations and has reached the general, valid and normal human forms. In this way visions, ideas, and inspirations emerge pristine from the primary sources of human life and thought (1972: 19).

Drug lords are generally humble people from small villages or towns, with common jobs like peasants, chauffeurs, policemen. They aspire for a better life, with cars, trucks and pretty women. They want to leave the town and know many other places in the country and in the world. They follow the "hero's journey", as described in twelve steps by Campbell (1972). They live in an ordinary world (1) where they feel uncomfortable; they receive a call to adventure (2); some of them hesitate to take it (3); but finally, they reach a prominent figure (4) that takes them through a threshold (5) for a new and unknown world; where the hero must find trials, allies and enemies (6); but there's a moment in which the trial makes the capo fall into an inmost cave (7); he must face a bigger task, an ordeal (8); after that, he receives a reward (9) that allows him to turn back home (10); with a feeling to be a new one, a resurrected one (11); thanks to the elixir (12) that makes him a better version of himself.

Drug capos want to transcend common life and become something more than just humans, achieving goals of opulence, power, pursuit, scope in their criminal activities. They like to be part of songs or build great mausoleums to pursuit immortality. Their elixir is money and fame, and all this narcoculture helps them to create a story about them that is not really in History, but it would be the main story to transcend time and frontiers, creating what should become the mythical chronicle about the character.

4 Methodology

As we have seen in the previous pages, drug capos emerged in very peculiar situations created by strong narratives where music and images are a very important part for generating a popular story. But this does not necessary mean that these stories should be powerful TV shows exhibited by Netflix and other worldwide broadcasting companies. The questions here are: How can these thieves be transformed into popular TV characters? What are the most important symbols surrounding narcoculture that allows it to become pop culture? Do TV series and folkloric songs help to create a mythical image of drug kingpins?

This work aims to identify drug dealers inside TV series as archetypes and symbols. For that purpose, we need to not only identify historical framing inside the plot, but also how mythical dimensions are narrated in order to build a bigger character inside the plot. For that purpose, two famous TV series were selected: *El Chapo,* which was created by Univision and later distributed by Netflix. This is a story about Joaquín Archivaldo Guzmán Loera, also known as El Chapo, the best-known Mexican drug dealer all around the world. The second one is *Narcos: Mexico* (Bernard, 2018), a Netflix production, which recreates the life of many Mexican capos in the 1980s and 1990s. The main character is Miguel Ángel Félix Gallardo, the first leader able to unify the small trafficking companies into a bigger and national organization. Both main characters are well recognized figures not only in Mexico, and both have *narcocorridos* composed about them, and both series became high rating shows.

A comparison between the capo's official story and the one provided by the series will be delivered; one for Miguel Ángel Félix Gallardo / Narcos: México; and another one for Joaquín Guzmán Loera / El Chapo. After these comparatives, we will find important symbols in TV series that correspond to the ones used in history and later build situations for an ideal past or an ideal future. With this information, both characters will be revised in a further analysis of information.

5 Joaquín Guzmán Loera, What We Know about Him

The most famous Mexican drug dealer, Joaquín Archivaldo Guzmán Loera, also known as El Chapo,[6] was born on April 4th, 1957 in a very poor town in Sinaloa called La Tuna, in the municipality of Badiraguato. He is a farmer's son who grew poppy and marihuana for small trafficking. Joaquín learned this activity from his own father as it was the easiest way to earn a living. He didn't finish elementary school; all his life has been dedicated to grow and later trade these illegal plants.

When he was young, he organized his first group of drug dealers that soon would be part of a wider organization commanded by Miguel Ángel Félix Gallardo, the first big lord of drug trafficking in Mexico. Later, he rose in the

6 Chapo is a diminutive for *chaparro,* that in certain areas of Mexico means "the short one", due to his short size: 1.68 cm.

organization, becoming a reliable man for the leaders Félix Gallardo, Rafael Caro Quintero and Ernesto Fonseca Carrillo "Don Neto". He was a truck driver and a gunman. When he gained positions inside the organization, he ordered the construction of underground tunnels to carry drugs inside them. These underpasses would become Chapo's signature for his criminal career.

In the late 1980s, the original leaders fell from grace. Caro Quintero and Don Neto were accused of torturing and killing a DEA agent, Enrique Camarena Salazar. Few years later, Félix Gallardo was also captured. Their national organization turned into local and smaller groups: the Tijuana Cartel, commanded by the Arellano Félix brothers; the Juárez Cartel, lead by Amado Carrillo Fuentes *El Señor de los Cielos*[7]; and El Chapo and his partner Héctor Palma *El Güero*[8] formed the Sinaloa Cartel. The division turned into disputes between Sinaloa's organization and the Tijuana Cartel, while the Juárez Cartel was specialized in carrying cocaine in planes. The fight between Sinaloa and Tijuana led to many bloody confrontations, like the murder of Héctor Palma's wife and children, a massive shooting at a beach night club in Puerto Vallarta, or the public massacre of a high Catholic figure, Juan Jesús Posadas Ocampo, a few minutes before he was to board a plane in Guadalajara.

The assassination of Cardinal Posadas led to Chapo's escape from Mexico as he was pointed out as one of the executors. He hid in Guatemala where he was arrested and later jailed in a maximum-security prison in Mexico in 1993. While Chapo was at jail, *El Señor de los Cielos* became the most powerful drug lord in the country all through the nineties. Despite being in prison, the Sinaloan was able to conduct his organization thanks to loyalty of some of his associates, like Ismael "Mayo" Zambada and Ignacio Coronel. Thanks to this entrepreneurial structure, Sinaloa was able to win the war against Tijuana even though El Chapo and El Güero were in jail. In 2002, when Ramón Arellano Félix was killed in Mazatlán Carnival, and his brother Benjamín was arrested in Puebla a few days later, the Tijuana Cartel was weakened, and Sinaloa became the biggest criminal organization in Mexico.

While his partners hit hard against their enemies, in 2001, El Chapo escaped from prison hiding in a laundry cart; he turned back into public leadership. With the defeat of Tijuana and the death of Carrillo Fuentes in 1997, Sinaloa called for a new national alliance under their control named *La Federación*. All the small groups agreed except for the Gulf Cartel, lead by Osiel Cárdenas

7 The Lord of the Skies, in English. Carrillo Fuentes got his nickname because of the method of transporting drugs, in the sky, through airplanes from Colombia to Mexico-Us border.

8 The Blondie, in English.

Guillén. With this denial, a new dispute, focused on the Eastern border cities that lead drugs into Texas, emerged. A nastier bloodbath covered the country. El Chapo's rivals recruited former military and navy officers into a merciless hitmen group called "Los Zetas", who then became so strong that they broke with the Gulf Cartel and became an independent organization. Juárez also left *La Federación* and became a new challenge. In this complicated situation, Chapo had another important challenge in Beltrán Leyva's Brothers, former partners in Sinaloa, who also left the bigger organization. They killed one of Chapo's son in a parking lot in a supermarket. All these situations brought the bloodiest years in the Narco wars in Mexico when thousands of people were killed every year.

Once again, Chapo was victorious in these battles. Zetas' leaders were captured, so was Vicente Carrillo Fuentes, the new leader of Juárez Cartel. Alfredo Beltrán Leyva was also seized, and his brother Arturo was murdered by Navy forces in Cuernavaca, a touristic place near Mexico City. Chapo was in control and he became more powerful and richer than ever. He was even mentioned by Forbes as one of the richest men in the world. But not all was right for the Sinaloa leader, because he was trapped one more time by Mexican authorities in 2014. However, one year later, Chapo Guzmán escaped a second time from prison by building a tunnel, one of his specialties. His fame increased with this new escape; but, at the same time, it was the beginning of the end. He was no more the most prominent figure in Sinaloa Cartel, because now "Mayo" Zambada was completely in control; even his own sons had increased their presence and power. Moreover, he accepted to give an interview to Hollywood star Sean Penn and the Mexican actress Kate del Castillo in 2015. This glimpsing made him vulnerable. A few months later, in 2016 Chapo was captured a third time. In this instance, he was extradited to the United States, where he was judged and sentenced to life imprisonment.

6 El Chapo, the TV Hero[9]

There are many media products about the most famous Mexican drug trafficker, but one of the most interesting is a TV series produced originally by Telemundo in 2017 and later distributed by Netflix in 2018 with three seasons available (Calderón, 2017). The cast has Mexican, Colombian, American and

9 Most information about Chapo's biography is found in Rodríguez Castañeda, R. (2015).

Venezuelan actors and actresses. Marco de la O plays El Chapo, Humberto Busto is Conrado Sol, Diego Vásquez is Ismael Zambrano, Rodrigo Abed plays El Señor de los Cielos, among many others.

Obviously, the main character is based on Joaquín Guzmán, following for the first season a complete hero's journey, like Campbell describes it. In the first chapter, Joaquín is just a gunman for the great capo, Miguel Ángel Félix Gallardo. Joaquín proposes his boss to build a tunnel to carry drugs through the USA-México Border. Félix Gallardo rejects his proposal, but Joaquín is stubborn and he decides to meet Pablo Escobar in Colombia to make an agreement directly with the Medellín Cartel to distribute their cocaine. Through many problems, Chapo completes this first task: he is no longer a gunman, now he is a leader inside the organization.

He tries to make allegiances, but he finds enemies instead: the Avendaño Brothers,[10] the ones that control Tijuana. Amado Carrillo becomes a mediator in this conflict and Chapo gets his allies in Heriberto Güero Palma,[11] Ismael Zambrano[12] and his loyal gunman Toño. There are some tasks that Chapo must face, but he isn't prepared for a shooting between his group and the Avendaño's, provoking the death of cardinal Posadas. He must run away from Mexico, but he is caught in El Salvador and sent to Mexico to prison. Our character meets his inmost cave in this moment.

There are new tasks to do in jail, like making new allies and confront his new enemies, the leader of guards and the director of jail. He has his ordeal going to *los acolchonados,*[13] the worst place in jail. In complete solitude, Chapo remembers his days as a farmer boy when he wanted to be something more. He admired the big boss Pedro Avilés and denied his drunk father. One day, he decided to take the boss's car, but he was caught and later examined by Avilés. He understood Chapo wanted to be part of his organization. So, Avilés gave him a task, his first shoot killing. Chapo went to meet his destiny: he killed that man on his own porch and became a member of Pedro Aviles's organization. As he crossed the first threshold, Avilés became his mentor and he entered his non-ordinary world.

---

10 Fictional name given to Arellano Félix's Brothers. Many other characters received fictional names but can be easily recognized in which one they're based on.

11 Fictional name to Héctor Luis Palma Salazar, "El Güero" (The Blondie).

12 Fictional name to Ismael Zambada "El Mayo".

13 Translated as "the padded room", a special cell where inmates are sent as a sever punishment. There's no light, no fresh air, just a small slit to enter food and water. Chapo spent months in this set.

This flash backwards lets the spectator understand the inner process in Chapo's ordeal. He resists as a real stoic, he comes out from the isolated cell more confident and powerful, able to negotiate his transfer into a softer jail. He wins this first round and fortifies his strength and power.

Season two means a new journey for this hero. Conrado Sol,[14] a government officer becomes his new mentor. *Don Sol* facilitates Chapo's transfer and further escape from prison, the moment when he crosses the threshold, now into the ordinary world, which will serve as scenario for a new underground world in this second round in narrative. Some partners are still on his side –Ismael Zambrano, Toño–, and there are new ones, like the Bernal Leyda's Brothers.[15] However, there are enemies too, there are some well-known –the Avendaño's Brothers– and later we will know new ones, as Golfo Cartel, *Los Emes*[16] and the new Juarez's leader and Amado's brother, *el Chente*.[17]

His new elixir becomes absolute power, so he calls every capo all around the country to a meeting to configure a bigger organization named *La Federación* under his leadership. Raciel Cárdenas,[18] leader of Golfo Cartel, rejects his proposition, so the war begins. Chapo calls his new ally, Conrado Sol to give him information about Raciel. Sol proceeds to catch him and extradite him to the United States. That enrages Raciel's brother, *Tony Tormenta*, who convinced *Chente* to make a common front against Chapo. *El Cano*,[19] leader of Los Emes, becomes mad about Raciel's detention, so he declares Emes as an independent cartel and fight against Chapo using extreme violence. Chente now becomes Cano's partner to fight the Sinaloan too.

Arturo Bernal Leyda, Chapo's ally, tries to negotiate with their enemies. He undertakes an agreement that makes him feel more powerful. Chapo doesn't recognize his achievement as Arturo wishes, and tension between both characters begin, to the point that Chapo offers Héctor Bernal Leyda's location to government leading into Arturo's departure from Chapo's federation.

With everyone against him, Chapo seems to be outnumbered. He declares clampdown in Culiacan to avoid his enemies, but in a moment of confusion, *El*

---

14 Conrado Sol doesn't make a direct reference to a single historic character. He is mainly based on Genaro García Luna, a prominent police leader that was captured in the United States accused to work for El Chapo. He is still under judgement in July 2021, the moment this text is written.

15 Fictional name given to Beltrán Leyva's Brothers.

16 Fictional name given to Los Zetas, a drug cartel.

17 Fictional name given to Vicente Carrillo Fuentes "El Viceroy", Amado Carrillo's brother and further leader of his organization.

18 Fictional name given to Ossiel Cárdenas Guillén, leader of Golfo Cartel.

19 Fictional name given to Antonio Lazcano "El Lazca", leader of Los Zetas.

Moreno,[20] one of Chapo's sons, is murdered by Chapo's gunmen. This becomes his new inmost cave. Chapo retires to one of his houses, getting away of all trouble. But he receives a call from Don Ismael, asking him to get back to business. This was his new elixir, a call to war. Chapo organizes his men and his government's allies to strike his enemies furiously. In this final operation, *El Chente* is caught and extradited, and *El Cano* needs to hide as a corpse so he can escape and erase his life as a drug dealer. Once again, Chapo is victorious and he is the most powerful *narco* in all the country.

In third season, Chapo is the most powerful drug dealer all around the world. Mayel,[21] Ismael's son, becomes his international operator closing deals in Russia and Malaysia, where they pretend to build a laboratory. DEA feels concerned for this business expansion, so they push Mexican government to capture Chapo. Conrado gives advice to Chapo and they agree to confiscate a big drug cargo to distract DEA from their demands, but it doesn't suffice them. A new strategy arises: to include Chapo in Forbes billionaire list, putting Conrado and president Alarcón[22] in a big alarm; but, in Chapo's side, it is a sign of his greatness. To commemorate this achievement, he orders to decorate his gun with gold and diamonds and a plate that says "El Billonario".

This is just the first DEA's move. They track Lora, Chapo's lawyer, and presses him to make Mayel return to Mexico, where they can seize him and take him to the United States. Don Ismael is worried about his son, but Chapo is confident they can continue with huge business.

Don Sol informs Chapo he's going to support Esteban Prieto[23] for president and with him on power, they can continue with their negotiations. Chapo helps in campaign but there is no difference: DEA still wants Chapo's head. He hides in the hills while his third wife is pregnant with twin girls. This situation stresses him, so when he sends them to Mazatlán, he decides to stay overnight with his family. That night, marines come into his house and seize him.

Chapo goes back to jail with severe observation: cameras everywhere, speech with guards forbidden, double-grid cell. He tries to bribe a guard to escape, but he receives more severe isolation rules. He is in a very desperate situation, but surprisingly, Conrado visits him and offers him help to escape. Conrado obtains jail architectural plans and gives them to Chapo's personnel in charge of the underpass construction.

---

20 Fictional name given to Edgar Guzmán López "El Negro", son of Chapo Guzmán.

21 Fictional name for Vicente Zambada Niebla "El Vicentillo".

22 Fictional name given to Felipe Calderón, former president of Mexico (2006–2012).

23 Fictional name given to Enrique Peña Nieto, former president of Mexico (2012–2018).

The moment comes and Chapo escapes again, becoming worldwide news. He notices that now things have changed outside. His son is disputing power with Dámaso, one of Chapo's most reliable men. He needs to go outside to reestablish order. While he was still in jail, he watches an interview of a famous actress saying good things about him. He gives instructions to his lawyer to arrange a meeting with Vanessa Espinoza for producing a film about his life. This meeting makes him vulnerable once again and finally he is seized a third time, being the last one, since this time, he is extradited to the United States.

7 Miguel Ángel Félix Gallardo, the First Big Kingpin[24]

When drug production in Mexico was still low scale, a young Miguel Ángel Félix Gallardo was a police officer and bodyguard for Sinaloa's governor Leopoldo Sánchez Celis. This policeman was born in Culiacán, Sinaloa in 1946 and started to work as a *madrina,*[25] a non-ethical position inside police corporations in Mexico. He became a closer friend to Sánchez Celis, a situation that allowed him to notice that collusion between criminals and politicians is a key point for success in illegal activities.

He left police and joined the first drug organization in Sinaloa at the end of 1970s, when it was still a local cartel lead by Pedro Avilés passing marihuana and opium to the United States. When Avilés was killed in 1978, Felix Gallardo commanded a new organization model including important figures in drug production and distribution, as Rafael Caro Quintero, Ernesto Fonseca Carrillo "Don Neto", Manuel Salcido Uzeta "El Cochiloco" and Juan José Esparragoza "El Azul". He noticed that a wider business would need other work style, so he decided to establish the cartel headquarters in Guadalajara, the second largest city in the country.

One of the most important decisions at that point of his criminal career was to make alliances with Colombian cartels, who were trafficking cocaine into the United States. He met Juan Ramón Matta Ballesteros, a Honduran criminal to make the connection. With this joint venture, Guadalajara Cartel increased in power, money, coverage and corruption. Félix Gallardo became the most powerful criminal in Mexico and, after Pablo Escobar's was killed, in all Latin

24 Most information about Miguel Ángel Félix Gallardo is found in Valdés Castellanos (2013).

25 This nickname is given in Mexico to police officers that are conduced to extorsions and torture in order to obtain information about suspects. Before 1988, there was no human rights institutions in Mexico that protected people from this kind of abuses.

America. He was the owner of luxurious hotels, night clubs and other businesses all around the country.

This increasing power was stopped when a DEA agent infiltrated the cartel. Enrique "Kiki" Camarena was exposed, then tortured and murdered. This situation made USA's government push into the Mexican one to capture the leaders of the organization. Caro Quintero was captured in Costa Rica and Don Neto in Puerto Vallarta in 1985. Félix Gallardo was skillful to avoid prison for a while, but he was finally arrested in 1989. Since then, he is still imprisoned in a maximum-security jail in Almoloya. The last criminal activity referred to him is that he ordered the division of the cartel and maybe the kidnapping and assassination of Güero Palma's family.

There are some confessions he wrote in diaries that one of his sons –he is said to have more than fifteen descendants– gave to a journalist.[26] In the diaries, he told the story of how some allies, like former police inspector Guillermo González Calderoni, betrayed him so he was vulnerable to be seized. From these stories, we also know that he lost all of his assets. He is getting blind and deaf caused by his age. He lost all power and influence, both in crime and in government organizations.

8 Félix in Narcos

In this narcoculture fever, Netflix aired in 2015 a series called *Narcos,*[27] starring the famous Brazilian actor Wagner Moura as the Colombian capo, Pablo Escobar; the American, Boyd Holbrook as DEA agent Steve Murphy; and the Chilean, Pedro Pascal as DEA agent Javier Peña. With big success, two more seasons were produced, a second one about Pablo Escobar in 2016, and a third one about the Cali Cartel, starring the Mexican Damián Alcázar, the Venezuelan Francisco Denis, the Argentinian Alberto Amman and the Portuguese Pêpê Rapazote, as the four commanders in this organization.

The big success of these series led into a Mexican setting. *Narcos: México* was aired in 2018 and assembled a cast with the Mexicans Diego Luna as Miguel Ángel Félix Gallardo, Tenoch Huerta as Rafael Caro Quintero, Joaquín Cosio as Ernesto Fonseca Carrillo; and the American Michael Peña as Enrique Camarena. The first season streamed in 2018 and a second one in 2020. There

26 The journalist Diego Osórno published *Memoria de un capo* from this information. We can't find the book, but we find some excerpts from it on a blog named *Nuestra Aparente Rendición* (2011).

27 In this series, names aren't fictionalized. Every character appears with his real name.

are rumors about a third one for 2021, but, as many other media productions, COVID-19 pandemics delayed the premiere.

The main story in first season is about Félix Gallardo and Kike Camarena. Each one of these main characters followed his own hero's path, however, we will pay attention to the Félix Gallardo's one as criminals are the main topic to this article. At the beginning of the story, Miguel is a police officer who arrives to Badiraguato's church in an army operation to catch drug smugglers. This is his ordinary world: he fakes to catch Caro Quintero and later hides him. Miguel visits the governor Sánchez Celis, who is his mentor. Then he goes to a narco reunion convoked by Pedro Avilés, where he expresses his intention to work drugs in a different way. Avilés sends him with Don Neto and Rafa to Guadalajara to negotiate with Naranjo's Brothers. He shoots his talker and becomes a defiant Sinaloan to the powerful people of Guadalajara. Some police officers take them with "El Azul", the leader of police officers that also negociate with Naranjo's Brothers. El Azul accepts to deal with Félix and shoots the other Naranjo. The threshold was crossed, and Miguel becomes the great narco, the leader of Guadalajara Cartel.

Don Neto and Rafa are clearly his partners, and later, Amado Carrillo joins the group. They have tasks to face, like dethrone Pedro Avilés, grow their own plants, convince local leaders to join into a bigger organization, among others. But the biggest enemy to face was, of course, Kiki Camarena and the DEA. The biggest task comes when he negotiates with Colombian leaders to expand his business into cocaine. His inmost cave comes when DEA finds and burns the enormous plant field where Caro grows his *sin semilla*.

The second threshold comes when Miguel negotiates with bigger figures inside the government. As a villain, there is no coming back home; he gets into a deeper circle inside the underworld. So, the final task to get into it, is to dismantle any evidence that accuses him of the kidnapping, torture and murder of Kiki Camarena, no matter his partners Rafa and Neto, who were caught by the police. He turns back with the rest of the group and reaffirms he is *El Jefe de Jefes* and he is still in command, now, of the group called *La Federación*.[28]

In the following season, there a new journey for our villain. As a sacred figure in drug trafficking, Miguel has a huge party, inviting all narcos, politicians and even leaders of Cali Cartel from Colombia to negotiate new agreements. Meanwhile, there are some fractures inside his organization that catch his attention, distracting him from a new menace of DEA.

There are other kind of menaces. It is time for elections and a strong opposition candidate is threatening the political system based on a unique party: PRI.

28 This name was really proposed by El Chapo when he tried to create a national organization.

Miguel helps PRI to win the elections with a cybernetic fraud, but this just extends his defeat; DEA is clearly on his back. He achieves to distract them a while putting focus on other narco leaders, like Pablo Acosta, his man on Juárez City, who's cornered by DEA and finally is shot dead.

Miguel tries to make a huge cocaine delivery to restate his relations with Cali, but he has no more support of his partners. Sinaloa and Tijuana are in an open conflict, while Juárez is collapsing with Acosta's fall. The situation pushed Miguel into betraying Cali, giving DEA information of a Colombian main warehouse in California. With this movement, he gains power a little bit, but he faces new and very powerful enemies. Finally, a lonely and desperate Miguel is caught by his former police snitch Guillermo González Calderoni. In a final scene in jail, Miguel predicts the future of drug-dealing capos in Mexico.

9 Capos, in between Historical and Mythical Life

Through the synopsis given, it can be said that drug capos follow a hero's journey when they are main characters in audiovisual narratives. But it must be said that there is no redemption in them. Both, Chapo and Miguel have a fatal ending in their series. No final elixir to become a better version of themselves. Nevertheless, just this small modification to the complete journey doesn't mean they are not portrayed as heroes, modifying their ordinary world to become someone different.

As we established in the first pages of this text, these characters correspond not just to heroes, but also to outlaws. Both archetypes are oriented to leave a mark on the world, to search for freedom and power, but with different approaches to rules. The hero wants to reestablish order while the outlaw, as the name says, does not want to be ruled. He must become the new ruler.

The interesting point in both series is how the outlaw is transformed into hero. In *El Chapo*, it is quite evident: he's the main character and the policeman, Conrado Sol, is a mentor and an ally in the story, not his nemesis. *Narcos: México* is more like the police-and-thieves Hollywoodesque story. DEA agents are the good guys. Kiki Camarena is a good friend and family man that gets into an underworld full of violence and danger. He has a hero's journey too, but he is not able to make the way back home. On the other side, Miguel finds in self-confidence his elixir to turn back and sit at the table with other narcos to make it crystal-clear, he is *el jefe de jefes*.

Another important element to speak about are symbols that appear on screen and allows the construction of the mythical figure of these characters. In *El Chapo*, when he was just a boy, the patron's car works as the first important symbol. He watches it with desire, he passes his hands softly, and, in the first opportunity, he asks to wash it just to take it out for a ride. Aviles's gunmen chase him and turn him back to the leader. All the car process becomes the meeting with the mentor and the pass of the threshold as we have seen few lines above. Cars and other vehicles are important symbols also in *Narcos: México*. The scene where Rafa buys his first mansion ends with a motorbike race inside the house. Miguel also uses a big elegant car to drive in Guadalajara. But not only fictional narcos, but the real ones also aim to have luxurious cars and trucks. The symbolic value of cars is power, not only in the TV series, but also in the historic events around drug trafficking in Mexico.

Religious symbols appear all along both series. In *Narcos: México* first scene, Rafa hides in a church from the Army, feeling it like a secure place. In *El Chapo*, the situation surrounding the cardinal's shooting is involved in the relationship between religion and politics. Arturo Bernal Leyda consults a clairvoyant to "know" if someone is betraying him. In his house in Cuernavaca, there is a figure of Jesús Malverde, the patron saint for narcos. This approach with religious and magical symbols helps to redeem a little bit their lives of crime. This is pictured on screen as it can be seen in ordinary life. Malverde's chapel is one of the most visited places in Culiacan. The religiousness surrounding crime incarnated in this non-official saint is a good example of how generosity can transform the outlaw in hero, by either mystify or mythologize him.

Music is another important symbol inside series. There are just a few parts in both shows where *narcocorridos* are shown; but that does not mean it is not important to narrate some scenes; for example, nightclubs and celebrations are accompanied with some precise music themes for a better narrative. There is just one scene where we can see a custom-made *corrido.* In El Chapo, when Joaquín is in jail for a second time, Quino[29] presents a band playing his song to Dámaso, becoming one of the tense moments between both characters. For a drug capo, ordering the arrangement of a song about himself is a notorious sign of power and greatness. It works like a medieval lord asking minstrel to sing praises for him.

A very important moment in *El Chapo* comes when he has been included in Forbes billionaire list. He chooses a new gun and order its decoration with gold and diamonds and a plate with the legend "The Billionaire". This gun is not a mere fictional detail, it exists in real life and its value is estimated to 2,000 USD. It is a common practice between Mexican narcos to decorate their guns with

29 Fictional name given to Iván Archivaldo Guzmán Salazar, Chapo's son.

plates of gold, silver and diamonds. Once again, it means wealth and power, but it also expresses their reckless spirit: they are the law.

There is a common story in Culiacán, Sinaloa of the day Chapo's son, known as El Negro, died. Guzmán bought every single red rose available in the city and later all of them were thrown from a plane in the sky while the coffin was passed across the streets. This situation is portrayed in the series, first, from the point of view of the florists running out of roses; then, with people in the procession and the petals and flowers falling on their heads. Through these dramatic filming, the spectator is able to mystify this moment where the hero meets his inmost cave.

A very interesting moment in *Narcos: México* comes at the beginning of Season 2. Miguel is giving a party for many people, celebrating his greatness. His partners have a very special gift for him: a tiger. In this case, it is a dramatized situation, because there was no evidence available of Félix Gallardo owning a tiger; but it is well known that drug dealers own savage pets. The Colombian Pablo Escobar built his own zoo, for example. But the point is not whether there was a tiger or not in Miguel's life; but it is on its symbolic value. He is as dangerous as this predator. In the scene, there is a story that tigers cannot kill their preys if they are watching the eye and, at the same time, a folkloric band is playing "The Eye of the Tiger". Yes, narcos are ferocious species, but they are betraying ones, stabbing each other in the back, never giving face to adversaries.

Through these symbols –cars, guns, religion, luxury– there is a possibility to transform the outlaw criminals into aspirational heroes. In this conversion, there is also a passage from past to future, from origins to scatology. He, who was originally a peasant with no further possibilities, can become, through a life of crime, into a billionaire, surrounded by women, people who obey them, a life in which all whims can be true. This path happened in both timelines, it is historical, real time when people like Chapo or Miguel transform their lives; but there is also a mythical time here, where all their adepts listening to their *corridos* and their popular stories, by watching news or TV series are desiring to take this path. Symbols unify history and story and helps to create a path of no return for anyone entering narcoculture.

10 Conclusions

As we can see through these pages, drug trafficking in Mexico is more than just an illegal activity. It is a lifestyle that has its consequent expressions in pop culture, transforming capos into special characters that assume a main roll in media but also in society.

It is important to state that we do not assume a determinist position. Just because capos are represented as heroes in redemption, that doesn't mean that media can create patterns in society. Our position is more into a circular model: society creates this kind of bandits and, when they become masters, they are able to promote their image through songs, books and TV series to become a model for youngsters. Drug dealers know that they are risking their lives all the time, that maybe they are not going to become a legend in this criminal world and, even so, their glorious days are always numbered. In this position, they need to reproduce the model, making their roll an aspirational one where young people with no opportunities in the legal and ethical world can become something more than just another poor man with no chance to make it.

Another important matter to say is that censorship has not shown any success. Governments can ban these TV shows, restrict books about capos and try to prohibit public exhibitions of narcocorridos; but there will always be a way to distribute and reproduce cultural products, even more so in digital era. A better way is to analyze this content in order to warn people about consuming it. For somebody, it is mere entertainment, but there is always a possibility to watch it from another position and become part of the solution, not part of the problem. We hope that with this article, we are generating a better understanding of narcoculture, their origins, their effects and also, how it is constructed to become a best seller.

References

Campbell, J. (1972). *El héroe de las mil caras. Psicoanálisis del mito*. México: Fondo de Cultura Económica. 241 pp.

Carod-Artal, F.J. (2015). Alucinógenos en las culturas precolombinas mesoamericanas. *Neurología*, 30 (1): 42–49.

Díaz-Barriga, A. (2014). Las entidades anímicas y su relación con el desarrollo de la niñez nahua prehispánica. *Alteridades*, 24 (47): 9–19.

Eliade, M. (2001). *El mito del eterno retorno*. Buenos Aires: Emecé. 112 pp.

Escohotado, A. (1998). *Historia general de las drogas*. Madrid: Alianza Editorial. 934 pp.

Frajoza, J. (2019). *Aromas de pólvora quemada. Música y cantos de bandidos*. México: Instituto Nacional de Antropología e Historia, Fonoteca Nacional. 345 pp.

Jung, C. G. (1970). *Arquetipos e incosciente colectivo*. Barcelona: Paidós. 182 pp.

Lanceros, P. (1997). *La herida trágica.* Barcelona: Anthropos.

Orduña, E. (2020) El narcotraficante, entre la literatura, el cine y la mitología popular. *Actio Nova. Revista de teoría de la literatura y literatura comparada,* 4: 397–426.

Rodríguez Castañeda, R. (2015). *El imperio del Chapo.* México: Booket, 344 pp.

Valdés Castellanos, G. (2013). *Historia del narcotráfico en México.* México: Aguilar, 483 pp.

TV *Shows*

Bernard, C.; Miro, D.; Newman, E.; Padilha, J. (2018–2020). *Narcos: México* [TV Series]. Gaumont International Television, Netflix.

Calderón, A.; Posada, D. (prod.) (2017–2018). *El Chapo* [TV Series]. Story House Entertainment, Dynamo Productions, Netflix.

CHAPTER 10

Mythic Representations of Heterosexual Relations in Popular Serials

Romantic Love against "Hyper Realistic" Porn

Christiana Constantopoulou

The art of narration is present in any society and essential for the meaning of social relationship; what makes "social link"[1] shows what is considered important for a community (indicating on what basis people are related with each other and what distinguishes them from "other" communities/ or societies). Roland Barthes[2] claimed that the narrative is one of the main categories of knowledge, used to understand and classify the world; in the sense that any discourse (even scientific) is first of all a narration. This statement is more or less accepted nowadays given that all discourses (political, ideological or cultural) take a storytelling form (Salmon, 2007). Walter Benjamin's essay,[3] has for many years been a point of reference about narrative and about the question why the various narrative forms play such an important part in our lives. Peter Brooks has analyzed narrative as a vital connection[4] arguing that literature constitutes a fundamental part of human existence; Christian Salmon[5] has explained (beginning from practices in the States) how the storytelling is omnipresent in managerial as well as in cultural environments; he approaches the storytelling as an art of telling stories and argues that it has invested collective imaginaries and has finally become a communication technique of governments (or other centers of economic power) being instrumentally used in

1 The French and German sociological bibliography consider this notion as the essence of any sociality.

2 Especially in his works *Mythologies* (1957) & *Poétique du récit* (1977).

3 Walter Benjamin (1936), *The Storyteller: Reflections on the Works of Nikolai Leskov* (also edited by Sam Dolbear, Esther Leslie and Sebastian Truskolaski, Verso, 2016).

4 P. Brooks' book (1994) entitled *Psychoanalysis and Storytelling* is a clear and exemplary demonstration of the ways in which the vital connections between psychoanalysis and literature can be articulated without reductive simplification. Following Freud's assumption that sexuality and narrative form are analogous; he proposes that literature constitutes a fundamental part of human existence.

5 Christian Salmon, 2007.

different spheres. This trend, tends to characterize the contemporary everyday life almost everywhere.

In order to "approach" any sociality, the art of storytelling is crucial especially when this art becomes so "massive" as the worldwide successful series; this kind of storytelling (very much appreciated by audiences) can reveal some emblematic representations of social ideas and beliefs such as the "romantic love". In fact, most of our cultural objects, all kinds of media products, advertisements, literature, films, artworks and songs but also photographs and self-made stories play with, refer to, the topic of romantic love as a dominant social myth worth being analyzed. How "love stories" deal with feminine heterosexual love? And what these representations interact with what E. Illouz (1997, 2021) has named "romantic utopia" (or "the end of love") in the frame of consumer capitalism, and with J. Baudrillard's (1981) statement that since the late 20th century, love is lived as pornography[6]? The attempt is difficult as modern societies seem to demystify the archetype of romantic love (whilst series showing more sex and less "love"[7] seem to attract more and more younger audiences).

1 From Popular Stories to Soap-Operas: Fantasies and Archetypes

Serials are one of the most favorite watching choices of ordinary (and not only) audiences. Going back to the late seventies and eighties and the worldwide success of *Dallas*[8] and *Dynasty*, *The Bold and the Beautiful*, *Baywatch*, or *Beverly Hills* we observe huge watching ratings all over the world especially as far as it concerns feminine audiences. One of the reasons of the huge popularity of this kind of productions (including soap operas but also comedy series such as "Married with Children" or "Friends") is that their stories turn around "everyday" problems (family or work adversities, love affairs and jealousies) even if the plot implies extraordinary situations (such as richness or fame for instance). At the same time they function as an escape into "dream",[9] in order to counterbalance the everyday banality (besides "escape" is not always synonymous to "alienation",

6 Forty years after J. Baudrillard's book on *Simulacres et Simulation*, "love as pornography" becomes an obvious reality, as it is an everyday use to upload videos (either of couples making love or gang rapes, not only in private parties, but even in schools or even in public places, often followed by blackmailing or degrading the victim).

7 As for instance the HBO series "Euphoria".

8 Even taking in mind Dayan and Katz's clarifications in 1985 as well as the Cultural Studies approaches.

9 In Woody Allen's sense in his film "The Purple Rose of Cairo" (1985).

because audiences have normally sufficient perception that it is "fiction" they watch); even if the flow of the story goes slowly or the next episodes are already "known", audiences continue to watch (watching is a pleasure of a dramatized experience and symbolic undertaking of roles, as it was the case with ancient theatre).[10] Symbolic representations of roles and relations are of extreme importance for the sociological research because they reflect prevailing beliefs and values of the collective imaginary expressing what Edgar Morin (1962) has named as "the spirit of the time". Popular shows turn around social roles (but even thoughts, desires and expectations) in a given environing cultural frame. In the fictional exaggeration of emblematic-crystallized-characters, (showing "good", "bad", "egoistic", "narcissistic" or "go-getter" behaviors), the heroes negotiate common problems and everyday dilemmas, where the imaginary but also several anthropological archetypes play a meaningful role.

Soap-operas were the avant-garde of the contemporary trend as far as it concerns cultural products as kind of everyday life narration (of the simple desires-overlooked by the "cultivated" culture). Initiated by the American cultural industries there has been an *"evaluative" turn* consisting in the mass representation of "common heroes" and in the highlighting of simple life happiness. The first extravagant stories concerning rich family lives (far away from the average viewer's conditions but always approaching romances and classic fairy tales) were followed by more down to earth scenarios. Houses, clothes and objects surrounding the central characters continue to be alluring and expensive, but they reflect the ongoing trend of the "culture of aesthetics"[11] which imposes for instance brands to the average citizen. The main concerns of the characters become less absolute, compared to the romantic handlings of older serials, the messages are more elaborated whilst dreams (although more related to the real standards of nowadays life) remain impressive and absolutely attractive where everybody can recognize and appreciate one's own self in a procedure of self-cognition. In this frame, the famous "American way of life" becomes very familiar (in a world where the American dream was an inspiration for a big part of the periphery in the planet). So for a big part of the audiences, the patterns shown-off in soap-operas are familiar and able to respond to peoples' needs of identification and of symbolization of behaviors. During the last 30 years productions from Latin America, Japan, India, Turkey and Korea, mixing the classical storytelling features with modernity and dealing with contemporary challenges, also gain big audiences worldwide.

10 We also take into consideration here J. Duvignaud's findings (1970), that humans are exemplary dramatic beings.

11 Maffesoli M. (1979).

When it comes to deal with "woman" as a symbol, it is very interesting to go back to the theory of cinema: the feminine image in the movies is never the reproduction of reality, but belongs to the space of the significant imaginary. As quoted by Christian Metz (1975) the cinema is a technique of the imaginary in a double sense: in the sense revealed by Edgar Morin (1958) but also in the sense suggested by Jacques Lacan (1973) when in search for human consciousness. All the mechanisms of the feminine representation concern an image suggested by the male desire to see "her" as lover, erotic booty, violence receiver and object; this psychoanalytic aspect is completely verified in the case of soap operas; the classical narrative cinema is configured on this significant economy of phallus (N. Kolovos, 1989). This trend is also followed by most popular serials (whose public is mostly feminine: an item particularly important as far as it concerns our main question on fictional representations of heterosexual love nowadays). Of course, other kinds of love begin to acquire more and more importance in several plots, still the romantic version (inspired by heterosexual love) remains predominant in most popular stories (although the heterosexual relations are also represented as stripped from feelings, especially in very recent serials).

Love stories are always at the top of audiences' preferences. For this analysis two serials were chosen as very emblematic on heterosexual love, enduring popularity worldwide: *Sex and the City* (as representative of single women's lives at the end of the 20th century)[12] and *Desperate Housewives* (as representative of the "ordinary housewives' life" at the beginning of the century).[13] Certainly attitudes and ideas change (slowly), still the research for romance in love remains *a powerful archetype*.

2 Sex and the City: Reporting "Single Women's" Love Affairs

Unlike to the constraints imposed by puritanism and conservatism,[14] mass audiences (and of course feminine audiences) at the end of the 20th century appeared to have at last the liberty to freely (and publicly) refer to themes that were traditionally "taboo" in the civil society such as "sex" (and especially feminine sex).

12 The series started in 1998 and ended in 2004.

13 The series started in 2004 (immediately after the end of Sex and the City) and ended in 2012.

14 Michel Foucault (1976 & 1984) has extremely well analyzed these constraints and their meaning.

For many years, the theme of heterosexual love was covered by romantic stories (often in "to be continued" style in popular magazines or in Harlequin books) which focused especially into the romantic relation and in the dream, fulfilling the readers' and afterwards the viewers' desires about how "love" should be (according to the romantic archetype in heterosexual love relation, despite its continuous demythologization during the fifty last years). The ideology of free public reference to feminine sex is imprinted in what we can call "The Cosmopolitan Style". When Cosmopolitan[15] first started, women were taught to think about household chores and raising children, but afterwards *the question of sexuality became dominant* (thought as what will make women happiest because it's what makes them truly empowered). The question does not concern the answer if *Cosmopolitan* is responsible for this change, but the observation that it reflects a main trend and "reveals" feminine sexuality as something very important (at least as important as masculine sexuality) in everyday life. This style almost prepared the international public sphere to reconsider gender stereotypes and opened the way to deliberately refer to female sex as it is done in the very popular serial "Sex and the City".[16] Although the regulation of heterosexual relations is always important to any society, feminine sexuality being particularly oppressed during very long periods of time, the contemporary storytelling of this serial was to at last refer openly to it.

The story refers to four feminine contemporary characters around thirties who search for the ideal male. Apart the dreamful items of the "culture of aesthetics" (branded clothes and especially shoes, fairy places in the heart of Manhattan, which still makes dream a good number of people), the four[17]

---

15 *Cosmopolitan Magazine* has been around since 1886 so it has seen quite a great deal of change over that time. The evolution of *The Cosmopolitan Magazine* into what is known today as *Cosmo* shows just how dramatic that change has been. In its early days, *The Cosmopolitan* was billed as a woman's fashion magazine that included articles on the home, family, and cooking, but also included articles like "Some Examples of Recent Art" and "The Progress of Science". When *Cosmopolitan* first started, women were taught to think about household chores and raising children, and *now they are told that our sexuality is what will make us happiest because it's what makes us truly empowered women.* The question does not concern if *Cosmopolitan* is responsible for this change, the vital question has to deal with the trend the magazine "shows" as important in feminine everyday life.

16 *Sex and the City* is an American television series created by Darren Star for HBO. It is an adaptation of Candace Bushnell's 1997 book of the same name. The series placed fifth on Entertainment Weekly's "New TV Classics" list, and has been listed as one of the best television series of all time by Time in 2007 and TV Guide in 2013. For a full description of the show and its contents, see https://en.wikipedia.org/wiki/Sex_and_the_City.

17 It seems that this number is crucial, symbolizing the four elements making a whole (in social life as in nature).

friends delete the prejudice of women being unable to be friends among them, as men can. The series takes as granted the friendship among women. The patterns of characters represented belong to the (upper) middle class with many contacts to richness and intelligentsia and the protagonists are not very young (they belong to late thirties and early forties) which means that their first priority is not to be married. Career and not family has been apparently their first important goal so, they are economically independent and successful professionals (but in professions still very attractive to women, such as article writer, lawyer, gallery manager or public relations responsible). Because the economic factor comes rarely to interrupt their everyday life, their problems turn primarily around relational problems, which Carrie (the article writer) undertakes to analyze in her column named "Sex and the City".

Analyzing quickly the central characters, there must be mentioned that:

Carrie searches for the perfect relationship which will be characterized by mutual love. The man with whom she's in love (Mr. "Big") "plays games" with her promoting the value of independence against marriage (something which is quickly shaken down when he gets married to another woman)! In all the episodes he upsets her (going towards her only when he needs her even if this can ruin her personal life)[18] being her unreachable dream.

Although she tries to go on with her life (and in order to live the absolute love, abandons her career and follows another beloved boyfriend to Paris), this *life seems very dependent to the boyfriend's needs* (who, like Big does not seem willing to sacrifice anything for Carrie: the same story of a selfish lover is so repeated!). A part of the fairy tale which is deeply rooted in the western imaginary for some centuries and still remains as an archetype (in the representation of heterosexual love) is the final union of two initial lovers (Carrie and "Big"): Carrie's "big" love, returns in her life (as he realizes that he loves her too) and romanticism wins.

Charlotte, the most puritan and most romantic of the four friends, believes in marriage and would like to have a happy family with children. It seems that this is not so easy for a woman like her although she corresponds to the emblematic image of an appreciated female figure (she's very beautiful and sweet) but is also a successful gallery manager. After many adventures with men not so chivalrous as she wishes, she abandons her work in order to be married; but her marriage is unsuccessful: she finally finds her alter ego in the lawyer who undertakes her divorce. The contrast between him (not very good looking) and

18 This interesting characteristic of "female sacrifice" is very often mentioned in classical literature.

her is obvious, making clear that beauty is only demanded when women are concerned. Good sex becomes the beginning of a successful marriage which is celebrated only when Charlotte changes her faith (and from good Catholic becomes Jewish in order to be relevant to her husband's demands)!

Miranda works in a law office and is definitely the style of woman who is first of all interested in her career and successful work. She is interested in sex but is not disposed to romance. Among her numerous erotic adventures, is Steve, a bar tender. Their social difference is clear and Miranda only wants him for sex. She accidentally gets pregnant of him, decides to keep the baby, but finally realizes that she needs him (for everyday life reasons) and they get married. After that and in order to give priority to the family despite her personal needs, she moves in Brooklyn (away from her beloved Manhattan) following very often the quite conservative "moral behavior" suggested by her Latin-American catholic housekeeper (who seems to take her dead mother's place, also reviving older relational standards among genders).

Samantha is the one who surpasses the standard feminine behavioral model: very competent to her work as public relations' responsible, she is completely "liberated" as far as it concerns "sex"; being all the time among people she has very often the occasion to meet many men and have sex with them: she seems to have no taboos and she declares that she has no sentiments for her partners. The erotic initiative (which is a socially male privilege) is one of her characteristics. She does not mind if her partner is engaged or married, she is not interested in relation the only thing that seems to interest her is the sexual pleasure. If there's a change she wants to make, this is breast surgery, in order to become more attractive (according to the feminine beauty standards, and this could be interpreted as a man's desire; for this very reason, she does not escape female "alienation"). At the end, even for the sexually-directed Samantha romantic love becomes an issue (provided by her latest love affair who is very much in love with her); there too, prevails the search of the "other half" as romantic value.

These are four emblematic feminine models (crystallizing images of the contemporary woman, who can be economically independent and relationally not engaged, able to decide for her life and her everyday behavior). Marriage is not a primordial wish in order to achieve social fulfillment, as it was in the past (their age can prove that their priorities concern their occupational and personal integration). Nevertheless, even under these circumstances their status (not only their pleasure via sex affairs) seems always *dependent to the role of the "man of their life"* while this is not the reverse case in most of the times. Even today, females often have to follow male choice in the frame of a household. In the serial the female protagonists change their faith, their standards, their career conditions, their city or their neighborhood and their appearance instead of romantic love (often implying absolute dependence). At the end the recipe of romantic love is what is at issue of female integration (eventually as counterbalance of its lack in real life).[19]

This serial seems to associate the expression of female sexuality with the romantic disposition and shows that sex liberation does not resolve the multiplicity of feelings, where the research of stable relationships is a central issue as it is proved by relevant research.[20] Contemporary solitary females consider this fiction as reminding them their everyday life, revealing their love issues and touches their unconfessed dreams about a fairy tale prince.[21] Extremely related to this observation, is Jean-Claude Kaufmann's research (1999). Kaufmann reveals some of the mechanisms which push contemporary females to not get engaged in a durable relation in order to be "autonomous" although their psychical (and family) standards still consider relational romanticism as a central value. Nowadays, in opposition to what happened in the past, the "matching rules" seem not to exist as in the past, yet, as far as it concerns the feminine condition, they are very much dictated by the archetypal myth of the charming prince (and this can also be deduced by Carrie's statements in her articles-which include "best seller ideas"). In the frame of the construction of the personal identity of solitary females in France according to Kaufmann's research, a very important role is played by the imaginary figure of the fairy-tale prince (dreamed and sublimated) while this archetypal image is transformed in a lot of less shiny princes of the everyday life. The relational variations between dream and reality are multiple (containing demythologization, anxiety and fear specially for the time which passes quickly, sadness-given that reality is so different compared to the imaginary idealizations, to the dream of "the prince"). The contemporary female reality is influenced and structured with this deeply-rooted although not always clear archetype.

This struggle between the storytelling archetype and the social possibilities of its realization is nowadays decisive for this extremely important sector of human life and is very well imprinted in this serial. The protagonists prove that the contemporary fantasy still concerns romanticism when it comes to heterosexual love; feelings, hurt egoisms, projections, everyday insecurities and hopes for fulfillment define the dreams for life with a touch of dream (including beautiful bodies, nice clothes, alluring shops). As it was explained

19 We will return to this point later in the concluding remarks.

20 Christophe Marx (2005).

21 Interview (of a person named Marion) published in the magazine Psychologies, in April 2006.

by E. Morin (1962) the consumption society cannot provide everything: as risk and security cannot be combined in real life, mass culture removes adventure offering slippers, and provides in the imaginary what cannot be really consumed, rendering virtual a good part of consumers' lives. Idols live in our place, free and dominant consoling us for the life which we lack, giving at the same time an example to the research of happiness: this century's happiness seems to be interwoven with archetypes, fantasies and models of the past coexisting with consumption choices of fairy like clothes and shoes (they do not appear magically out of Cinderella godmother's stick but can be found and bought in the luxury shops instead: completing the part of consumer capitalism).

3 Desperate Housewives: Dealing with Current Myths about Family and Household Life

The reference to *Sex and the City* would be incomplete without the approach of an equally successful creation, *Desperate Housewives*[22] (referring to many aspects of the contemporary private life and relations). The title is revealing of the feelings and of the hypocrisy hidden behind everyday behaviors. This serial also concerns four emblematic feminine characters and their relation to "sex" and "crime" (as they seem often relied).[23] Our method here too, is content analysis of the plot of the 8 seasons starting from 2004 (immediately after the end of *Sex and the City*-besides, "Desperate Housewives" was also called "Sex and the City of the suburbs") and finishing in 2012. It is supposed to take place in the imaginary "Wisteria Lane" of the imaginary "Fairview, Eagle State"[24] and it narrates the "ordinary" life of neighbors as seen by their dead friend (who undertakes the role of the narrator but also of the one who explains each episode's "morality"). We observe the habitual family life with the hidden sides of the housewives: secrets, infidelities, crimes, and mysteries although well-masked come sometimes to the surface and "shake" the superficially calm

22 One of the most successful series in the world and the most successful in the world in 2007 (with six Emmy Awards and Two Golden Globes), with many adaptations worldwide.

23 It is said that Marc Cherry who created this series was inspired by the police report (quoting Andrea Yates, a housewife who killed her children).

24 The recipe of an imaginary place which can remind of any contemporary town is quite old: it was first used in Guilding Light (a series started at the radio in 1937, moved to TV in 1952 and continuing for many more years) supposed to happen in the imaginary Springfield. This recipe was followed by many soap-operas as for instance in *Plus belle la vie* (FR3 August 2004) supposed to happen in an imaginary Marseille's town, named Mistral.

neighborhood. Secret desires leading to battles between social puritanism and personal wishes-the most often unconfessed-and choices, which always look towards the behavior which was not chosen in real life (and thus remaining repulsed but not destroyed to the sphere of subconscious).

3.1 *Family and Violence*

The suburban house (a symbol of a comfortable daily life) is a continuity of the "road" and of the neighborhood (some kind of public sphere) while the back windows hide the most private aspects of daily routine. As H. Newcomb (1982) had noticed about Dallas and Dynasty, the characters often express the borders between the values of old western life and modernity. Each "myth" appears as a part of a broader system with changing values, where the story comments basic existential problems (about life and death, gender and friendly relations): this kind of comments were undertaken by the chorus in ancient Greek dramas.

Family life is for the housewife (especially for the housewife of the suburbs) the intersection of the public and private sphere, out and in the house, expressing the kind of "ordinary" conservative American life (imposing the politically correct behavior and defining at the same time the borders of what can be accepted and what not).

One of the series' characteristics is the housewives' "interruptive conditions". Tania Modleski (1982) explains how housewives having to affront multi-leveled challenges are in a status of continuous suspension, stopping one work to get involved to a moment's emergency; this status does not permit them to concentrate to one thing in the frame of their household (this is the kind of "interruption" of a flow by the advertisements; this is also followed by the series' plot: a sudden phone call, a sudden visitor, a disaster or a revelation, release her from her "regularity" going from one challenge to the other in a sudden way which foments the violence of characters because of the violent involvement of misdeeds -or "illegal acts"- realized in the past).

In this frame, dominant myths on feminine friendship, gender relations and identities are reproduced and crystalized through the social criticism of the "neighborhood". The "neighborhood" plays the primordial role of the "chorus" judging and "controlling" the behaviors classifying them to accepted or unaccepted according to a code of values; the "secret" (unconfessed) side of the private life is called "dirty laundry"[25] (something always attracting audiences' interest).

25 In fact, this was the (meaningful) title of the series' advertisements in order to attire the attention of the numerous "life style" emissions also based on gossiping and of the related audiences.

A basic issue of not accepted behavior is infidelity (but also jealousy) often related to criminal offense. Many themes on female behavior which were first represented in movie plays (Haskell 1999), such as sacrifice, pain and death, the necessity to choose between two lovers and adversity in order to gain a companion are presented in this serial too, offering multiple dramatic satisfaction due to the coexistence of some challenges which are rather frequent after all.

The female characters of the series, are neighbors and friends and represent (again) four archetypal characters: the conformist (Brie), the dynamic (Lynette), the romantic (Susan) and the narcissist (Gabriella). The story narrates the way in which these persons affront different problems and dramatic incidents (while their dead friend Mary Alice, undertakes the role of the storyteller and commentator). All the facts turn around the problem *"what must be done"* (*according to the social code*-the criticism of the neighborhood) and *what the characters desire to do* (according to their main behavioral wish-often based on jealousy, the desire for a friend's companion or the attraction for a another than the husband male, the anger, the thirst for revenge, hidden passions, battle to gain more prestige etc.). The desire is often distanced from the socially accepted sphere of actions and the result is *violence* (evident or latent, oral, moral, physical) but also *blackmail*.

The hermeneutic code also functions presenting the *expectation* as a basic condition of truth according to R. Barthes (1966); because expectation is also "disorder" (in the sense that it is associated to some "dreamed change") this kind of storytelling, also shows the results of the unaccepted action in order to bring the audience back to the "order". Because the family still constitutes (for the ordinary life of many females) a strong support, it is primordial in the plot. Stereotyped beliefs appear as "common sense" (the lonely woman is often considered as a "danger" for families or as mentally disturbed). This kind of beliefs are also more or less met when the plot represents other minorities (African Americans, homosexual or of revolted social behavior). Feminine (more than masculine) existence is often covered by a mask (which can be put on or not); censure always concerns it (and in this sense fictional creations imprint dominant views of the collective imaginary).

3.2 *Everyday Issues*

Unaccepted behaviors (such as addiction to alcohol or drugs) although are disguised most of the times, question the established morality and can often lead either to a crime or to a revelation of absurd institutional approach of some marginalized cases (ex.: the almost insane management of the psychiatric clinic where Brie went for detoxification from alcohol). Normally, the protagonists try to hide their "dirty laundry". When this becomes difficult there's always the possibility of confession to friends (who then become a helpful entourage-when a secret is shared with friends it becomes the team's secret facing social rules: it can eventually lead to change society's preconceptions).

The main characters of the story, belong to the upper middle class (while in the classical soap operas protagonists belong to the world of richness) with problems which are not only relational (very often economic disaster is narrated and in such cases the characters are obliged to sell houses, accept a not-satisfactory job etc.); this means that the narration also concerns more common people. Together with the increasing number of solitary female population (well expressed in the serial *Sex and the City*) the storytelling had to also express vital issues of the rest of female population, which concerns the women in engaged relation and marriage (who have in a sense found their "charming prince" and have married him) but who nevertheless seem to be particularly oppressed. The psychologist Maryse Vaillant[26] considers that the big worldwide success of this series is due to the fact that it expresses the oppression exercised on married women. The "housewives" collaborate to their unhappiness because they respond to the demands of the social conventions but at the same time this prudery "kills" them. These elements are met in real life in the behavior of many females who continue to reproduce the same stereotypes with their mothers or even their grand-mothers. Such a big deal of oppression in order to correspond to social demands depresses them and brings them obviously in battle with the social rules (this also explains the latent violence of all the characters): the most exasperating side of the housewives' lives is that they are in front of an impasse: destiny which was also followed by their dead friend Mary Alice (the story teller) who committed suicide because of an impasse and now "sees" her friends from "heaven" (with a "distanced" eye).

The neighborhood's microcosm focuses on an "ideal" female condition (because it includes marriage and family) and deals with central issues (such as marriage and maternity). Family relations (based on power and abuse of power, but also violence and seduction) together with habits and attitudes related to the family [related to the family habits and attitudes] are analyzed in a background of oppression of one's self because of social rules (including struggle for recognition, solutions to physical or social disasters, kinds of solidarity etc.); this is all about ordinary daily scenes which always contain the extraordinary factor (crime as it appears in police reports). The central characters try in a permanent way to hide what can be socially judged as improper,

26 In her appointment in the magazine *Psychologies* (Paris, April 2006).

which is nevertheless always there in order to show the conflict between social barriers and individual options. Survival is a continuous struggle between the common-sense obligations (which in this case represent the exploitation of females by patriarchy) and the confrontation with them.

Common sense places the institution of family on the top of values. Most people believe in it trying to follow what is given as its "requirements". In this frame the idea of divorce frightens as a painful and troublesome discontinuity of a relation (which is supposed to be based on romantic love) in other words its failure. The friendship can be of help but only secondarily (in the sense that it is thought that if some elements considered basic are destroyed in a couple, they are rarely remediated). In this frame homosexual families exist too (but are still given in the story as different from the "norm" and vulnerable).

3.3 *"Juicy" Delinquency*

The story presents common (but emblematic) characters of everyday life, who try to deal with "standard" challenges: the most important is that anything touching females (and in extension any minority) involves the continuous attention (censure) of the environment (the neighborhood) on the minority's behavior (the entourage is much more severe when judging minorities and continues to be even in contemporary societies). Social criticism contains a main factor of imposition of one "order" (power) on the conventions which must be followed. These conventions must also be followed by the contemporary actors in order to avoid marginalization of any kind (in order to avoid being judged as "strange", "little delinquent", "psychopath" or "criminal")! We can here also understand the differentiations when it comes to "lies" (such as "conventional" or "fake") used to obtain or conserve a decent place in a given environment.

The story tells that most of common people (of minority common people as the case here) when affronted with out of common questions or provocations (very often in the frame of love affairs but also when money is involved) always "lie". Jealousy, hatred, diverse obsessions or "bad past" (a particularly unpleasant baggage) or sometimes fate can contribute to "juicy" managements. Dark motives (which are not very much considered as important by most sociological analyses while journal reporters classify them under the label of "behavioral disorder") are projected as elements of everyday life and characterize the (very much loved by audiences) protagonists of this narration.

It is a kind of representation which contains dominant views (as far as it concerns "right" and "wrong" behaviors), showing at the same time that the battle between "psyche" and "society" concerns all kinds of contemporary characters (those who are considered "correct" and those who are not so much).

E. Goffman's analysis (1956) about role playing and presentation of self, helps us also understand why so much effort is wasted in order to make characters be considered "normal" according to social demands.

What is considered as "normality" in the contemporary private sphere (the neighborhood undertaking the role of "public sphere" which controls, reveals and judges), can be deduced by the content analysis of the episodes. Despite the context of the contemporary United States, the patterns presented tend to be valid in most contemporary societies. Roles, reactions and symbolisms can also represent the contemporary common human being (including the dimension of gossip which according to Charles Horton Cooley-1909-in the contemporary societies is achieved by media). This dimension of "gossiping" (looking in the lives of others) permits to live "by delegation" via others' lives; it is what we may call "eye cannibalism" around scandals or otherwise "juicy" stories. These stories are very much appreciated by popular audiences, and this is one of the reasons why this specific serial has had big success. At the same time this popularity confirms the necessity to further study the "dark side" of any society (translating impulses, archetypes, and complexes), namely the side which dialogues with the imaginary.

The kind of stories who "sale" the most (at least to the feminine audiences) are those which include the romantic aura of a love story. Nevertheless, the romantic love links are not the reflection of our reality, they are just the myth (which still inspires the human sexual behavior, especially females' behavior). Even if sexuality is presented as pornography (as observed by J. Baudrillard, 1981) the *archetypal myth of its romantic expression* continues to inspire behaviors (even mixed with latent impulses).

4 Negotiating Heterosexual Love: Symbols, Archetypes and Emotional Capitalism

Media reflect the preoccupations and concerns of ordinary people and at the same time they participate into the ongoing cultural, social and political transformations. Arjun Appadurai (1996) has analyzed how *imagination plays a special role in the contemporary world*, because it is the main component of a *new subjectivity*, where *mediascapes* are a constructing element. *Mediascapes*[27] refer to technologies producing or diffusing information (journals, magazines, television channels and cinematographic studios)[28] while the images created

27 Word made up by "media" and "landscape".
28 Social Media could be of course included.

by media are all the more accessible to all kinds of people in the sense that away from a direct experience people can "see" the actual complex reality but in an imaginary frame. If we attach these deductions to the mass culture effects described not only by Edgar Morin (1958) but also by Adorno and Horkheimer (1969), we can certainly assume *that media mythologies compose a landscape in which contemporary people think and treat their private life.* In this sense, contemporary life is also invented in the frame of shows (the popularity of a show is a strong indicator of its emblematic meaning in peoples' minds).

As far as it concerns the more popular themes in the contents of fictional shows, it is undoubtedly confirmed[29] that they are *love, desire, ambition and vengeance*. It seems that these parameters are vital and provoke much interest for the everyday life scene (as it would have been described by E. Goffman).

The word *love* (which interests particularly here) has been used synonymously with enjoyment, enthusiasm, attachment, affection, sexual attraction, care, concern, loyalty, devotion, etc. It is though important to distinguish that *romantic love* (also known as romance) has a more specific meaning, and refers to "*intense attraction that involves the idealization of the other, within an erotic context, with the expectation of enduring for some time into the future*. "Romantic love" is special because, it is in contrast to the relationship between mother or father and child, uniting two (or more) individuals who have a certain freedom when choosing each other; it is also in contrast to friendship, because the romantically involved individuals, do not only share a bond, based on mental but also of physical intimacy, but they also share [also] an erotic encounter between the romantically involved individuals which demands *a much stronger interpenetration between autonomous systems/entities*" (Seebach S.,Núñez-Mosteo F., 2014).

This issue is very permanent (in times and societies), very important and very complicated (as it is in the very heart of social bond and of social life). Our analysis, reveals at least 4 major dimensions which must be taken into consideration in order to understand this "constitutional" myth of modern societies, although it becomes all the more evident that the dominant "visualization" of everyday life, includes very much "sex" as pornography (a condition which is in fact far away from romance); these dimensions are: 1) the female oppression (even "latent") in the contemporary mythical narratives, 2) the rarity of alternative forms of erotic love in the current myths, 3) the archetypal guidance of heterosexual love expressions, 4) the need to "dream" in everyday life (dreams include fantasy very much influenced by current values but have

29 See for instance Öztürkmen A., (2018).

also the power to mentally overthrow the ongoing reality eventually leading to another).

4.1 *The Oppression of Females*

As Feminist Studies Have Revealed, the Image of Romantic Heterosexual Love Certainly Oppresses Females, Seen (and Censured) by Men's Eyes (and Needs), and This Dimension Has Two Facets.

As indicated above (on dominant heterosexual love myths for single and married women in the modern storytelling) *the image of romantic love corresponds exactly to the ideals included in capitalist ideology* which is dominant today (although in many variations and different expressions):"male supremacy" is inherent in liberal/ capitalist ideology, going together with work division and family structure. Even if modern societies try to face in a more equitable way the diverse gender inequalities, these inequalities still exist while in any case the family institution is based on traditional structures (so this permanent issue requests even today, social conformism as far as it concerns heterosexual "matching").

Eva Illouz (1997) has argued that our most romantic moments seem to be determined by the portrayal of love either in films or on TV. [in film and on TV. She unravels the mass of images that define the contemporary ideas of love and romance (romantic utopia), revealing that they match with the demands of consumer capitalism. The romantic utopia (as she calls it) lives in the collective imagination and is built on images that unite amorous and economic activities in the rituals of dating, lovemaking, and marriage. Since the early 1900s, advertisers have tied the purchase of beauty products, sports cars, diet drinks, and snack foods to success in love and happiness. Thus, every cliché of romance ("from an intimate dinner to a dozen red roses" as it is said in a characteristic way) is constructed by advertising and media images that preach *a popular ethos of consumption* in a way that material goods and happiness are available to all. The culture of capitalism has fostered an intensely emotional culture in the workplace, in the family, and in our own relationship to ourselves. E*conomic relations have become deeply emotional and in the same way close, intimate relationships have become increasingly defined by economic and political models of bargaining, exchange, and equity* (E. Illouz, 2006); it is a dual process by which emotional and economic relationships come to define and shape each other, which is named by the author "*emotional capitalism*" and is met everywhere (in women's magazines, in talk shows, or the Internet dating sites).

The contemporary private life is "*product-directed*" (lots of essays have been published on this issue since the writings of the Frankfurt School theoreticians), there's no doubt about that. The capitalist culture alienates popular classes providing "democratically" goods to possess and thus feel happy (good looking, satisfied, accepted). A very important part of private life is of course related to love (and the still dominant heterosexual love). So "romance" nowadays cannot be separated from consumption (and even conspicuous consumption as would have said Thorstein Veblen-1899): female existence is also "consumed" among other "products" (and female identity follows this "spirit of the time").

Another Characteristic of Contemporary Modernity Is the Role of "Virtualization" into Relations (the Virtualization of the Social Bond)

The public sphere has become saturated with the exposure of private life and the private life is very much "developed" on-screen and online. In the frame of thishis process by which relationships become less important (because based on the "image" or the imagined other) relations evaporate and are easily dissolved. Sociology has to explore how this virtualization, makes social bonds collapse and dissolve very quickly (in contrast with the dreamed "love forever"): sexual issues are one of the contexts in which hyper reality (one of the key concepts in Baudrillard's theory) has intensely penetrated, as well.

E. Illouz (2021) has remarked the role that capitalism plays in practices of non-choice where "unloving" is particularly striking. She explains that the unmaking of social bonds, is connected to contemporary capitalism which is characterized by practices of *non-commitment* and non-choice, practices that enable the quick withdrawal from a transaction and the quick realignment of prices and the breaking of loyalties. Unloving and non-choice have in turn a profound impact on society and economics as they explain why people may be having fewer children, increasingly living alone, and having less sex; and all this happens in a frame of proliferation of visual pleasures on making love (as pornography, in the sense of J. Baudrillard already mentioned). In this frame, it is not strange why female sexuality remains the main "show" (revenge porn, videos and violations of privacy-which were partly the cause of the movement "me too" – prove this).

4.2 *Rareness of Alternative Forms of Erotic Love in the Contemporary Dominant Myths*

Greek mythology (which reflected Ancient Greeks' beliefs about erotic love) expresses in many stories forms of (non-heterosexual) love and of diverse forms of "sex presence"; for instance, Aphroditus was an androgynous Aphrodite from Cyprus, which in later mythology became known as Hermaphroditus the son of Hermes and Aphrodite. Thamyris, the Thracian singer who developed love for Hyacinth is said to have been the first man to fall in love with another man. Greco-Roman mythology features male homosexuality in many of the constituent myths. In addition, there are instances of cross-dressing, and of androgyny which are nowadays grouped under the acronym LGBTQ+.

LGBTQ+ themes in mythology occur narratives that include stories of romantic affection or sexuality either between figures of the same sex or of divine actions that result in changes in gender, love with divinities (many mythologies ascribe homosexuality and gender fluidity in humans to the action of gods or of other supernatural interventions). The alleged presence of LGBTQ+ themes in mythologies has become the subject of intense study. The application of gender studies and queer theory to non-Western mythic tradition is less developed, but has grown since the end of the twentieth century. Mythologies of the world often include being gay, bisexual, or transgender as symbols for sacred or mythic experiences. Devdutt Pattanaik (2002) argues that myths "capture the collective unconsciousness of a people", and that this means that they reflect deep-rooted beliefs about variant sexualities that may be at odds with repressive morality.

In fact, this kind of repressive morality is deeply rooted in all the contemporary societies which are over a thousand years converted to monotheist biblical religions (as for instance Christianism and Islam); the monotheisms in general do not accept any other "truth" but the word of God (or of prophets). It is known that the biggest persecutions towards homosexual people was in the frame of monotheist cultures. Heterosexual love (because the only natural way leading to procreation) was the only accepted in the field of these religions and for many years sexuality could not be seen outside this frame. It is not strange that the only kind of love "admitted" during many centuries almost all over the world was the only mythicized in any fictional creation. The contemporary "romantic love" (monopolized by heterosexual love) in the frame of consumer capitalism contributes to the dissemination of mythical forms matching with this dominant "common sense" in modern societies; "common sense" corresponds to the dominant mentality and sustains the economic system (or structure) of these societies.

An alternative modern mythology about erotic love is of course necessary (in order to include forms of sexuality which are not accepted by the biblical preaching). It might be some (often gothic based) creations in literature and films which show different kinds of erotic love.[30] It might be a different contemporary imaginary based on less strict moral rules and more familiarity with the ongoing reality. It is certain that in many levels, the contemporary societies

30 As it is for instance the series *Game of Thrones* which attracted a record viewership on HBO and has a broad, active, and international fan base. Critics have praised the series for its acting, complex characters, story, scope, and production values, although its frequent use of nudity and violence (including sexual violence) has been subject to criticism.

go on based on old conceptions as far as it concerns the social ethics and the political justifications, which sustain at the same time the capitalist system. In front of the lack of different interpretations and ideas, old emblematic figures seem to be the only available as far as the contemporary audiences are concerned, in expectation of new mythologies.

4.3 *Heterosexual Love Archetype*

The Canadian Psychotherapist T. Hayen (2020) explains briefly the meaning of archetype (and of archetypal romance) as follows:

> An archetype is a pattern of behavior, or more accurately, a pattern of "being" much like an *instinct*. According to psychiatrist, Carl Jung, the archetypes have formed over eons of human existence (or could have been fully formed when humans first appeared) and govern much of our individual existence. The Greeks, Egyptians, and Romans "invented" their pantheon as a representation of some of the basic archetypes (that's why they had so many gods and goddesses). Some of the more common archetypes are King, Queen, Father, Mother, Lover, Warrior, etc. They typically are divided between "masculine" and "feminine" (although not always) which has little to do with gender, as any archetype can be constellated (activated) in any individual regardless of gender.
>
> One of the first things to understand about archetypes is they typically have a "nice" side and a "shadow" side. This is easy to visualize when you think of a King having the attributes of both a tyrant and a benevolent overseer of his subjects, or a warrior being both, at times, a protector and a murderer. Sometimes this shadow is mixed with the brighter side of things, and it is always best to "integrate" them when they are being conflictual within ourselves – i.e., it is best to love ourselves in our entirety, rather than ignore the darker elements of our psyche and push them deeper into solitude, or project them onto others!
>
> So, what is an "Archetypal Romance"? When looking at a partnered romantic couple, of any sort, there will be certain archetypal forces, both good and bad, at play. They will influence the couple, and will drive, largely, their behavior and their responses to the other's behavior. I believe if we see these forces clearly for what they actually are, rather than what the culture tells us, or what we inadequately rationalize in our effort to make sense of them (due to their typically unconscious influence), we will be able to form a better relationship with our partners.
>
> *With heterosexual couples it is rather easy to relate the symbols and images of the archetypes with gender.* Gendered males usually identify with the typical masculine archetypes such as the King, the Magician,

the Warrior, and certainly the Lover. Gendered females likewise – Queen, Aphrodite (Maiden), Mother (Matron), Crone, etc. (there is a myriad of female goddesses, thus archetypes, to choose here.)

In non-heterosexual love-partnerships the masculine and feminine archetypes are constellated the same way but may not be gender correlated. A masculine archetype also does not need to be matched with a feminine archetype. All that is needed to understand archetypes and their influence over you is to be aware of them and their power.

Basic instincts of "survival" always play a central role in peoples' consciousness. Even if the contemporary culture is very much virtualized (online relations, platforms of friendships and companionships, porn films, remote work and education etc.), human physicality (which is often forgotten when technology and science promise longer or healthier life) is always a fact (fact which often provokes multiple reactions towards and against "death" as a natural order). This physicality is always there (including the human need to be fed, and to "continue" into life by procreation). Whatever different figures human sexuality eventually takes, there's this basic instinct which cannot be overseen: the heterosexual love instinct. Modernity has enveloped it with the myth of romantic love. As archetype, it is difficult to be oppressed anyway (and this is independent from its different cultural mystifications) and stands as an *anthropological dimension* of social existence.

4.4 *"Escaping" into Dreams*

The imaginary (apart its functions of giving meaning to the "real world") also contains the part of unavoidable "reverie" (necessary in order to affront a difficult and/or oppressive social reality, but also important to imagine new realities and invent alternative ones). Reverie is essential in everyday life. In the first place because "dreams" are necessary as counterbalance of a fade reality, and in the second place because they are the only way to change society. Humans of all societies try to escape from reality, running and hiding from its claws, seeking redemption from it wandering around alternate realities in order to enter in the sweet realm of dreams where everything is possible, encountering short periods of bliss in dreams (having also as possibility to make dreams become real).

4.4.1 Psychologically the Dreams Are Necessary as Counterbalance of a Fade Reality

There is no wonder why most humans constantly seek through different ways to escape reality to enter the realm of dreams. Real life can be oppressing, limiting, boring and destructive, therefore we use different methods to escape from the tedious routines and from the daily reality (in order to release oneself and travel to the place where dreams dwell, that wonderful place where everything is possible).

How beautiful and magical is that place where people travel with their imagination where anything can happen! In that place, there is no sorrow, no pain, no fear, no judgment and no limitations. There is pure bliss, a complete state of ecstasy that makes touch the sky with one's own hands. A person can be whoever he/she wants and do whatever he/she wants, the options are endless, and the perk of having no boundaries is that makes one's mind fly freely in imagination.

The imagination allows humans to extend their minds beyond the boundaries of physical reality. Because the imagination has no limits and is strictly one's own, one can make it into an exciting or comforting place to escape to when the real world fails to please him/her or becomes too difficult to bear. The imagination, an internal landscape for our thoughts, is a limitless realm in which we can take elements from the physical world and morph them into whatever we please. When the real world fails to satisfy us or becomes too difficult for us to remain in, there is always the option to escape into the imagination and attain enjoyment, peace, and safety knowing it is immune from intruders and under one's individual control. It might be argued that escaping into the fantasy of imaginations can delude persons and prevent them from acknowledging what is really going on outside. Although having an awareness of the external world is important, it does not stand in opposition to one's imagination. In fact, imagination can be used as a tool to enhance reality, making it more interesting and appealing. Imaginative stories play upon external realities while also inspiring and exciting their readers, encouraging them to delve deeper into their hidden meanings and allowing them to make new discoveries beyond the facts. Thus, the imagination does not just depend on reality for truths, but reality depends on the imagination for truths as well.

4.4.2 Dreams Can Only Become True If They Are Created, First in Imagination and Second by Making Them Happen, with Ideas, Plans, Commitment and Faith

In this sense a "different thought" (or even perception) may somehow change any reality: this is why, many contemporary researchers, characterize *the pleasure of viewing romantic love stories as "resistance" to the surrounding condition of violence and exploitation in heterosexual love affairs*. Mary Ellen Brown (1987, 1994) thus argues that soap operas create and support a social network in which *talk* becomes a form of resistive pleasure. *Engagement with soap operas creates an opening for women to serve as wedges into the dominant culture.*

"Soap operas" (as well as romance novels and the woman's film of the 1930s and 1940s) have all been characterized in dominant discourse by their excesses – too much talk, too much emotion, too little action, overdressed, overwrought, too much romance, too many plots, too many characters, too simple, too little sex, too little social commentary, too ordinary. However, despite the universal disdain heaped upon them, each of these genres was, or is, immensely popular with women. The soap opera is unique among the three genres in that *it breaks with classical narrative form.* It refuses closure, contains non-hierarchical and multiple plots and characters, and features a point of view balanced between unproblematic perspectives on female cultural existence – competent women, 'sensitive' men – and the traditional problems of women living within patriarchy like social rules governing sexual conduct. The soaps generate gossip both inside and outside of the programs themselves. Such gossip is a form of feminine discourse in that it *acknowledges woman's position in the existing cultural system.* Because daytime soaps are 'cheap' productions, they have a look and feel that is different from realistic television drama, but they evidence an ordinariness that evokes the everyday. "*The serial form of the soap opera, while using patriarchal myths, structures them in such a way that audiences can use them for their own purposes.* By incorporating the potential for gossip inserted in the soaps, women can also use them to validate the value of a feminine culture which in masculine culture has been invalidated but not suppressed. Women continue to understand and acknowledge the differences, while at the same time understand the masculine conception as well. This position gives them a *source of power* and all that remains is for them to use it". (Brown 1987). In other terms, the dominant myth can also be put in question and be contested, and this is the minority's myth to contest the fade reality.

We remind Roland Barthes' conclusion (1957) that the narrative is one of the main categories of knowledge, used to understand and classify the world (in the sense that any discourse-even scientific-is first of all a "narration"). The art of storytelling is crucial especially when this art becomes so "massive" as the worldwide successful series with their emblematic representations of "romantic love" in the contemporary society. This kind of series ("talking" about love affairs and massively received by female audiences) narrate the contemporary romantic utopia (romantic love "forever" covered with fairy landscapes and luxury).

Who believes this kind of storytelling? This story telling describes on one hand the capitalistic exploitation of female sex, according to which a female should always "follow" male's choices (as it happens in the *Sex and the City*), or "hide" other options (as it happens in *Desperate Housewives*). This storytelling on the other hand narrates the myth (the utopia, as E. Illouz names it) of romantic love providing a "different reality" where males would be sensitive, loving and strong at the same time! Female audiences, know that this inspiring utopia in real life finally includes ordinary "fake princes" (as described by J.-Cl. Kaufmann, 1999) instead of the romantic prince narrated in the stories. Until new mythologies can include and describe all forms of love (as in other cultures, for instance ancient Greek, Roman or Indian), the romantic love myth is abundantly available in the contemporary societies; eventually helping to imagine new expressions of heterosexual love. Ideas change slowly: in this context societies have to imagine again connecting myths.

References and Bibliography

Appadurai, A. (1996), *Modernity at Large: Cultural Dimensions of Globalization*, MN: University of Minnesota Press, Minneapolis.

Bacon-Smith Camille (1994) *Enterprising Women, Television Fandom and the Creation of Popular Myth,* University of Pennsylvania Press, Philadelphia.

Barthes R. (1953), *Le degré zéro de l'écriture* Seuil, Paris.

Barthes R. (1957), *Mythologies* Seuil, Paris.

Barthes R. (1966), « Introduction à l'analyse structurale du récit », *Communications* 8, p. 1–27.

Barthes R. et al. (1977) *Poétique du récit*, Seuil, Paris.

Baudrillard J. (1981), *Simulacres et Simulation,* Galilée, Paris.

Beer G. (1970), *The romance*, Methuen, London.

Benjamin W. (1936) *The Storyteller: Reflections on the Works of Nikolai Leskov First printed in Orient und Okzident, 1936; rep. in Illuminations, trans. Harry Zohn; ed. & intro. Hannah Arendt* (NY: Harcourt Brace Jovanovich 1968), pp. 83–109.

Berger, John (1973), *Ways of seeing*, British Broadcasting Corporation *and* Penguin Books, London.

Brooks P. (1992), *Reading for the plot. Design and Intention in Narrative,* Harvard University Press.

Brooks P. (1994), *Psychoanalysis and Storytelling,* Blackwell, Oxford.

Brooks P. (2000), *Troubling confessions. Speaking Guilt in Law and Literature,* The University of Chicago Press.

Brown M.H., (1987), "The Politics of Soaps: Pleasure and Feminine Empowerment", Australian Journal of Cultural Studies, Vol. 4, no 2.

Brown M.H., (1994) *Soap Opera and Women's Talk: The Pleasure of Resistance* (Communication and Human Values), Sage, California.

Chollet Mona, (2021), *Réinventer l'amour* (*comment le patriarcat sabote les relations hétérosexuelles*), Zones, Paris.

Clanton Gordon, (1987) *Jealousy,* Lynn Smith, University Press of America, Baltimore.

Constantopoulou Ch. (2012), *Television a Virtual Coffee-House* (in Greek) Papazisis, Athens.

Constantopoulou Ch. (2021) *Symbols, archetypes and phobias* (in Greek), Papazisis, Athens.

Cooley Ch. Horton, (1909): *Human Nature and the Social Order,* Scribner's Sons, New York.

Cowan Jane K., (1990), *Dance and the body politic in northern Greece,* Princeton University Press, Princeton, N.J.

Duvignaud J., (1970), *Spectacle et société,* Denoël, Paris.

Foucault M. (1976), *L'histoire de la sexualité, la volonté de savoir,* Gallimard, Paris.

Foucault M. (1984), *L'histoire de la sexualité, 2. L'usage des plaisirs & 3. Le souci de soi,* Gallimard, Paris.

Gauntlet D., (2008), *Media, Gender and Identity: An introduction,* 2nd edition, Routledge, NY.

Gill R. (2010), *Gender and the Media,* Polity Press, Cambridge.

Goffman E., (1956), *The Presentation of Self in Everyday Life* Doubleday, New York.

Gunter Barry, Svennevig Michael (1987) *Behind and in Front of the Small Screen: Television's Involvement with Family Life,* London, John Libbey.

Haskell, Molly (1999), "The Woman's Film" in Sue Thornham (ed.), *Feminist Film Theory,* New York University Press, New York, (p. 20–30).

Haul Ryan, (2010), *Divine Madness: Archetypes of Romantic Love,* Routledge, London.

Hayen T. (2020), *The Archetypal Romance,* The Archetypal Romance | Todd Hayen, PhD, RP (toddhayentherapy.com)

Horkheimer M., Adorno Th., (1969), *Dialectic of Enlightenment,* Continuum, New York.

Illouz E. (1997), *Consuming the Romantic Utopia: Love and the Cultural Contradictions of Capitalism,* University of California Press, California.

Illouz E. (2006), *Cold Intimacies, the making of emotional capitalism,* Polity, Cambridge, Oxford, Boston.

Illouz E. (2021), *The end of love,* Polity, Cambridge, Oxford, Boston.

Katz E.- Liebes T. (1985), *Decoding Dallas Overseas* Media Values no 32, CML California.

Kaufmann J.Cl. (1999), *La femme seule et le prince charmant,* Nathan (Pocket), Paris.

Kolovos N. (1989), *Sociology of the Cinema* (in Greek), Aigokeros, Athens.

Lacan J. (1973), *Les quatre concepts fondamentaux de la Psychanalyse,* Seuil, Paris.

Larochelle, D.L., (2021), *The appropriations of a "guilty pleasure": the reception of Turkish soap operas by the Greek audiences,* PhD thesis (in French), Univ. Sorbonne Nouvelle, Paris.

Livingstone, Sonia (1998), *Making Sense of Television,* Routledge, London and New York.

Maffesoli M. (1979), *La conquête du présent* PUF, Paris.

Maffesoli M. (2008), *L'ombre de Dionysos, contribution à une sociologie de l'orgie,* (Éd. du CNRS, Paris.

Marx Ch. (2005), *Mais où est passée la libido* Eyrolles, Paris.

Metz Christian (1975), « Le signifiant imaginaire » in *Psychanalyse et Cinéma,* Communications, no thématique, p. 3–55.

Modleski, Tania (1982) *Loving with a Vengeance: Mass-Produced Fantasies for Women.* London: Methuen.

Modleski, Tania (ed. 1982), *Studies in Entertainment,* Indiana University Press, Bloomington.

Morin E. (1957), *Les stars* Le Seuil, Paris.

Morin E. (1958), *Le cinéma ou l'homme imaginaire* Minuit Paris.

Morin E. (1962), *L'esprit du temps, essai sur la culture de masse,* Grasset, Paris.

Morley, David (1986), *Family Television: cultural Power and Domestic Leisure,* Comedia, London.

Morley, David (1992), *Television audiences & Cultural Studies,* Routledge, London and New York.

Neale Steve, Krutnik Frank, (1990), *Popular Film and Television Comedy,* Routledge, London & New York.

Öztürkmen A., (2018), "Turkish Content": The Historical Rise of the Dizi Genre, "TV/ Series", 13, pp. 1–12, DOI: 10.4000/tvseries.2406.

Pattanaik D. (2002), *The Man Who Was A Woman and Other Queer Tales from Hindu Lore.* Harrington Park Press, New York.

Salmon Ch. (2007), Storytelling, la machine à fabriquer des histoires et à formater les esprits, La Découverte, Paris.

Salmon Ch. (2009), *Storytelling saison 1 : Chroniques du monde contemporain,* Les prairies ordinaires, Paris, .

Seebach S.,Núñez-Mosteo F., (2021), "Is Romantic Love a Linking Emotion?" Sociological Research Online, 21 (1) 14 <http://www.socresonline.org.uk/21/1/14.html>.

Silverstone Roger (1994), *Television and Everyday Life,* Routledge, London & New York.

Taylor, Ella (1989), *Prime Time Families: Television Culture in Postwar America,* University of California Press, Berkeley.

Thorstein Veblen, (1899), *The theory of Leisure Class,* MacMillan.

Thomas L.-V. (1979), *Civilisation et Divagations,* Payot, Paris.

Thomas L.-V. (1984), *Fantasmes au quotidien,* Méridiens, Paris.

Thomas L.-V. (1988), *Anthropologie des obsessions,* L'Harmattan, Paris.

Walter N. (2010), *Living Dolls, the return of Sexism,* Virago Press, London.

Weeks J., (1981), *Sex, Politics and Society,* Longman Group Ltd, London.

CHAPTER 11

Concluding Remarks

Consumer Storytelling in Advanced-Modern Societies

Christiana Constantopoulou

Humans have always loved stories (especially exciting, intriguing, and emotional explorations of people, places, and events). Journalism is rooted in good storytelling still, in recent years, *there has been an increasing interest in journalism storytelling* (as it is considered a good communication tool). Numerous scientific publications examine storytelling as a communication technique either in print media, radio, and television or in digital media. It is broadly recognized as a channel that can achieve both commercial and social goals, and that can also influence the audiences which use new information technologies; as social media grows in popularity, it has become the perfect platform to tell, hear, and share stories about online connections and communities.

Storytelling becomes a rather prevailing communication style particularly used by brand advertisement. Brands recognize the binding power of stories, and it should come as no surprise that more and more businesses are using social media to weave yarns and tell stories that hook and captivate their customers. Social storytelling can be described as taking information that is not that exciting and making it feel important, impassioned, and relevant.[1] As "marketing" has imposed its own reasoning all over the world (communication being related to consuming goods) the contemporary storytelling reflects current lifestyle in all "stories" (from those which explain what are "crimes" in everyday life, why universities should be privatized, how technology is our salvation against different threats such as Covid-19 or ageing etc., for instance). The media (mass or social) narrate in an "advertisement" style discourses, facts, fakes and dreams of the contemporary life; this "marketing style" is more or less followed in "fictional" products dictating what must be done or must be thought in everyday life, emblematically including the importance of

1 For example, we can take the idea of someone marketing a car that is pretty much the same kind of saloon car as the one that everyone else has driven for years. If it tells a story behind how the car is made, makes it feel real, exciting and somehow more compelling, there is much more "meat on the bone". Brands that tell stories and excite audiences in this way see a huge return on their investment, as customers start to feel involved, and more likely to buy.

brands (for clothing, loving or thinking how everyday goes and how relations should go).

Examples from different countries come to confirm that beside the frontiers, "marketing" based stories "narrate" the "reality" of the contemporary modernity (social representations about it, which is rather crucial as human beings understand their reality by emblematic symbols). It is even very indicative to remark that the meaning of the word "communication" is almost monopolized nowadays by advertisement; this monopolization shows again the "Spirit of the Time": modernity, minimizes the communicational process, into "utility messages" which serve to convince others (mostly in order to buy consuming goods).

Fairy tales, beginning with "once upon a time" narrated (and still narrate) the philosophy and the values of the society which creates them. For instance, ancient Greek myths narrated the origin and nature of the world, the lives and activities of deities, heroes, and mythological creatures, and the origins and significance of the ancient Greeks' own cult and ritual practices in order to signify their beliefs, rules and phobias. It so happened with many other known to us cultures such as Celtic, or Arabian Stories and Legends or popular sayings collected by Nasreddin HodjaTales of the Turkish Trickster. Societies need "storytelling" to summarize their philosophy/ ideology. Louis Vincent Thomas[2] has collected very funny traditional popular narratives of the Diola people of Western Africa, representative though of their thought, fantasies and social structure. All the non-Western Cultures had this kind of "narratives" imprinting their beliefs and values.[3]

In Western Culture the "narration" (narrative form of expressing thoughts and beliefs) was separated from "discourse" (which expressed "logos" and science) and it only became "storytelling" for children. Bruno Bettelheim[4] analyzes fairy tales in terms of Freudian psychoanalysis and is convinced that classical fairy tales (such as Cinderella or Snow White) are superior to contemporary children's literature precisely because of their elements of menace and cruelty, since they produce neither aggression nor fear, but help children to cope with these feelings. At this point, we should remind that cartoons (which do not always have the time to constitute a solid literary corpus) contain

2 Louis-Vincent Thomas (1982), *Et le lièvre vint… récits populaires diola,* L'Harmattan, Paris.

3 Anthropological Studies have classified as "myths" the other peoples' narrations about their world and everyday life.

4 Bruno Bettelheim, (1976), *The Uses of Enchantment: The Meaning and Importance of Fairy Tales* (1976) Thames and Hudson, London.

menace and cruelty (they were initially very much criticized because of that before becoming the rule of current children's entertainment stories).

It is only lately that social scientists have understood and admitted that narration is essential to describe a culture; communication studies have revealed the importance of storytelling in the contemporary life. The advertisement storytelling becomes the kind of narrative expressing central values of the societies of the so-called advanced modernity: it is all about consumption as had long ago analyzed Jean Baudrillard[5] for whom, consumption is the major feature of Western societies, the "global response which underpins our whole cultural system". It is not strange if every narration turns around consumption, nowadays.

The articles of this volume have shown that all cultural expressions (from broadcasting to serials) in many countries of the planet, in a direct or indirect way preach consumer goods in any sector of our life: from knowledge to relations and to representations or expressions, media narratives reflect the consumer storytelling structure of advanced-modern societies.

5 Jean Baudrillard, (1998) *The Consumer Society, Myths and Structure,* Sage, London (first Published in French *La société de consommation, Denoël, Paris 1970*).

Subject Index

Names Index